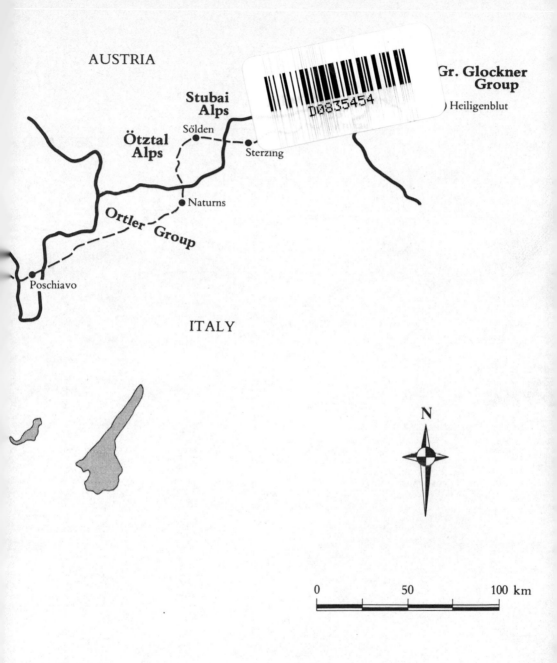

AUSTRIA

Stubai
Alps

Ötztal
Alps

Sölden

Sterzing

Gr. Glockner
Group

) Heiligenblut

Naturns

Ortler Group

Poschiavo

ITALY

N

0   50   100 km

HIGH LEVEL

The Alps from End to End

Daniel
Sept. 1983
from Pat.

HIGH LEVEL

The Alps from End to End

by

DAVID BRETT

LONDON
VICTOR GOLLANCZ LTD
1983

British Library Cataloguing in Publication Data
Brett, David
    High level: the Alps from end to end.
    1. Mountaineering   2. Alps
    I. Title
    796.5'22'0924   GV199.44.A/
ISBN 0-575-03202-2

Printed in Great Britain at
The Camelot Press Ltd, Southampton

What follows is an idiosyncratic account of a high-level traverse I was able to make from one end of the Alps to the other, taking in several summits and many high passes, in the summer of 1981. The last chapter is a short "guide" to the route. This may be regarded as a development of the old high-level route, or as an unusually long and arduous walk, or as "an aberrant, unknown sport, practised by those who are not quite all there". (For that reference, see *The Alpine Journal* 1981, p. 35).

Both the route and this written account of it I should like to dedicate to the good friends I have made in the mountains, to the shared memory of good times, bad times, and to some hair-raising times. But they may not wish to associate themselves with such an absurd enterprise, and so I will not name them. But I will name my son Matthew, who suggested the whole thing, who must take some of the blame, and whom I thought about continually.

> Hocus-pocus, porridge and gruel
> Don't make this route too long and cruel.
> Hocus-pocus, non compos mentis
> Back to the valley the good Lord send us.
> Old Rhyme

Contents

1. La Bérarde to Modane: breaking in   11
2. Modane to Courmayeur: good times   31
3. The Valais Alps: bad times   54
4. Lepontine and Adula: hard pounding   76
5. More hard pounding: Bernina and Ortler   101
6. Ötztal and Stubai: and better times   131
7. The best of times   157
    Appendix   191

List of Illustrations

(following page 86)

The author, with a heavy pack, crossing the Col de la Leisse on the sixth day.

At the Plan de Valfourche, with the peaks of the Ecrins massif behind.

Early morning; and crossing through the intricate passes of the Thabor range on the third day.

The Val de Leisse, and above the peaks of the Grande Casse and the Grande Motte. One of the few valleys that goes the way you want to go.

The Rutor peaks, and in the far background the Valais Alps with the Matterhorn on the far right.

Storm and much new snow on Mont Blanc.

The good track that I followed above the Val de Nendaz – behind, the peaks that I crossed in cloud the day before.

A break in the weather on the trek over to the Simplon Pass.

Camp 15, under the boulder at Täsch; with the smallest tent in the world, my home for 44 nights.

Monte Leone from Alpe Veglia; the most impressive peak of the Lepontine Alps.

Alpe Devero; a half-abandoned village restored for holiday cottages – just as with hill-farming villages everywhere.

The Ofenhorn, above the upper Vannino lake. I was able to climb this peak from the snowy saddle to the right – all except the last few metres!

On automatic: shivering in my shelter just below the summit of the Ofenhorn.

In the Lepontine Alps. The beautiful Nefelgiu col which I crossed on the twentieth day after climbing the Ofenhorn.

(following page 118)

The Adula, or Rheinwaldhorn; and below it, the infant Rhine. To the right of the main summit is the rocky eastern summit that I climbed over on my way from the Länta valley. A long hard day.

The green hills of Juf.

The Lagh de Cavloc, near Maloja, where I ate breakfast before trekking over the Muretto pass back into Italy.

Peaks to the south of the Val Viola – a fairly remote area, full of surprises. There are enough good mountains in the Alps for a few lifetimes.

The Cevedale glacier; my descent took the steep snow fully on the right of the glacier.

The soloist's friends: cairns discovered, as I descended into the Val Martello from the snowfields of the Cevedale. Ahead is the Cima Venezia, and other peaks. The 29th day.

The Windachscharte. An evil little pass in the Stubai Alps – but leading to marvellous territory.

Looking westward from the summit of the Gross Möseler. With first the Hochfeiler, and then the Stubai and then the Ötztal Alps beyond.

A pass in the Zillertal Alps; the Weisszint-scharte.

The fifth of the five Hornspitze peaks, from the Austrian side.

On the same day as the last photograph, looking into Austria. The peaks of the Turnerkamp and Gross Möseler from the fourth Hornspitze.

The Hinterer Maurerkees Kopf, from the Sulzbach glacier. This was the best and most exacting summit, which I reached up the long right-hand skyline.

Camp 41, and a view back over the Venediger group. In the centre is the Maurerkees Kopf and to its right the Krimmler pass, that I had crossed that morning.

The final morning. After the storm on the Grossglockner, I took a low walking pass, and came round, slowly and steadily, to Heiligenblut. One must not count on good weather.

My camp below the Gross Venediger; evening sunlight.

Maps

The Grand High-Level Route   *endpapers*

1. La Bérarde to Modane   13
2. Modane to Courmayer   33
3. The Valais Alps   55
4. Lepontine and Adula   77
5. Bernina and Ortler   103
6. Ötztal and Stubai   133
7. Zillertal Alps   159
8. Venediger/Glockner   169

HIGH LEVEL

The Alps from End to End

Chapter One

LA BÉRARDE TO MODANE: BREAKING IN

THE JOURNEY OF a thousand, or 600, miles begins with a single step.

Eleven in the morning on the 11th of July, at the road-head of La Bérarde. Two hotels, a bar, a small group of houses and barns and below the road, tents. Hot, bright and thundery; with the sun glaring through trails of mist: and above the houses long slopes of shrub, boulder and pine leading up (I knew but could not see) to big crags and bigger crags still, and finally to snow and ice. I sat in the shade and still did not know what to do: the Tyrolese Alps are a long way from La Bérarde. Much better to pitch my tent down by the river, put my feet up, eat well, and get off early in the morning. Or perhaps to have three days here, climbing some moderate peak, to get acclimatized and fit.

Incapable of decision, tense and nervous – was it only from lack of sleep? – I took a middle course of action. I went into the restaurant next to the bus stop and ordered an omelette, bread and a demi-carafe of rouge. Never make any decision on an empty stomach: if that was to be my rule for the next few weeks I should begin by obeying it now, at the start.

I ate as slowly as I could, as a condemned man eats his breakfast. My sack sat on the bench beside me, piled high with tent and rope and hung with my axe and other bits of metal: I did not like the look of it. And I did not like the look of the unnaturally bright sun or the enormous length and height of the hillsides that rose up like tidal waves from the very edge of the road. The air seemed thin and unsustaining and took the edge off my appetite – or was that nervousness. Could I admit to myself that I was nervous to begin: that I might, in truth, be scared stiff of committing myself to such a preposterous, even absurd activity. I ought to stop shillyshallying, pay up, set pack on back and GET TO WORK!

And that is just what I did.

(I know that this is going to be long, hard and painful; that I shall be bored, lonely, cold, wet, hot, thirsty and utterly fatigued for most of the next two months. There will also be times when I am thoroughly frightened, anxious and homesick. And even though I have been doing this sort of thing for years there is also a perfectly good chance that I won't get out of it alive. Not because of any intrinsic foolhardiness (I am painfully cautious most of the time), but because of the many rather than the severe and obvious sources of danger. I do not expect to die dramatically on a lonely mountain, but I know how many streams there will be to cross, how many broken tracks, how many little hidden crevices in rock or ice. It is the accumulation of danger or discomfort that oppresses, not the most extreme examples.)

My aim was the village of Heiligenblut at the foot of the highest Austrian peaks; I had that very clearly in mind. Several points I knew I had to reach in between – the town of Courmayeur, the resort of Zermatt, Airolo (a small town at the foot of the St. Gotthard pass), Maloja (a resort in the Engadine area of Switzerland), the village of Sölden in the Ötztal Alps, the Brenner Pass and finally Heiligenblut. My overall plan was to do for the Alps as a whole what the traditional "high-level" route does for the distance between Zermatt and Chamonix – take a very direct high-mountain line linking the major climbing centres. But in between those points I knew I would have to improvise according to weather, fatigue, terrain and all those unforeseen contingencies that make meticulous route-planning redundant. I had, of course, spent a very long time with maps, had several with me, and a notebook full of copied-down advice from numerous guides: but "friction" must be reckoned with. "Friction" is a key idea in the theory of warfare: friction, says Clausewitz, is the sum of uncontrollable contingencies, of natural agencies and human ineptitude that tend to the obstruction of the plan of battle. It was only realistic to expect a bit of friction.

The first friction, and the last, was weather. As midday approached large clouds supplanted the mists and began to threaten rain; there were rumbles and bangings and a glistening air about the spurs of granite.

The Dauphiné Alps are a complicated clump of mountains without any main direction to their ridges and ranges; the valleys are

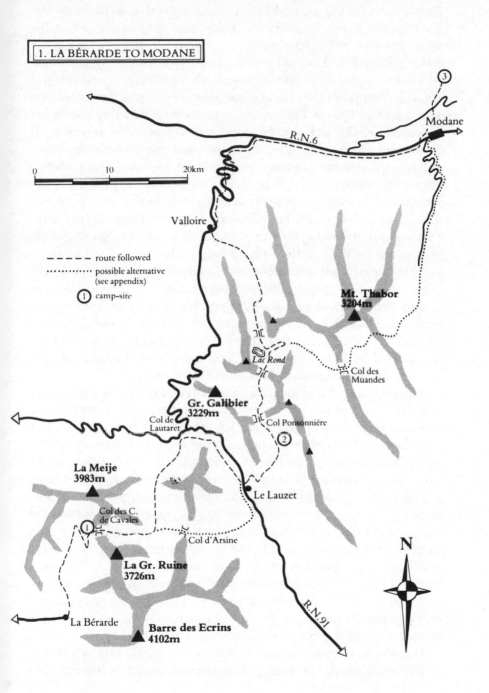

1. LA BÉRARDE TO MODANE

0   10   20km

route followed
possible alternative
(see appendix)
camp-site

Modane

R.N.6

Valloire

Mt. Thabor
3204m

Lac Rond

Col des
Muandes

Gr. Galibier
3229m

Col de
Lautaret

Col Ponsonniére

La Meije
3983m

Le Lauzet

Col des C.
de Cavales

Col d'Arsine

La Gr. Ruine
3726m

La Bérarde

Barre des Ecrins
4102m

R.N.91

N

deeply cut, making the peaks seem even larger than in fact they are. La Bérarde is in the midst of them and is a main centre for mountaineering, but because the slopes are steep and rocky it has not been developed as a ski resort: also, it is a desolate spot reached by a very narrow road. It feels remote, though it is only an hour and a half by bus from the city of Grenoble. There was almost no one about when I left the houses and scarcely anyone along the path I followed. Peaks and clouds were indistinguishably jumbled all above me, while the valley floor receded. One could see other valleys, other ridges coming into view as the convoluted terrain began to unfold itself. I was unable to prevent myself stopping frequently to survey the scene and identify peaks and spurs and glaciers that I had studied on the map. I was suffering sharply from that tremulous excitement that one gets when re-entering high mountains for the first time after a long period away from them.

This is partly astonishment, that everything is so much larger than you had imagined or remembered, and it is partly delight at simply being back in a place where you know you can exercise your skills, but it is also partly fear: and I must write honestly in this respect – I was distinctly frightened. I had a good estimation of how much hard work and danger the next two months might contain, and my lively imagination kept enlarging upon it.

The path zigged and the path zagged above or beside a vehement and deeply-cut stream whose colour – like dirty milk – showed it to be descending from an active glacier. Boulders were banging about in its bed and I was pleased when the path took me back to the right, away from the insidious clatter, and into dells and gullies full of wild flowers of many descriptions, but mostly harebells and large alpine daisies growing thickly amongst the clumps of rhododendrons. The dwarf rhododendrons of the Alps have a wonderful magenta flower, but make a mat of texture that is thicker than heather to walk through. The path was buttressed here and there with stones or timber and there was a notice to say that this was a national park. So many British mountain paths in the past twenty years have been eroded into ugly scars by the passing of many feet that I admired this care for the scenery; but, as I was to find out, the French have their ecological disasters as well.

But all the time what fully occupied my mind, except in those moments in which I looked up from the path ahead, was the need to set a deliberate and businesslike style. Not to waste energy, always to set each foot down carefully, always to get a steady pace. That was the way to calm my apprehension, to get my feet adjusted to the steepness of the slopes, my breath to the growing height and my shoulders to my sack.

The sack was quite small. I don't think it ever weighed more than 50 pounds. It was new and bright red: through the flap was pushed my lightweight tent – the smallest and lightest my money could buy: within the sack was all that I reckoned I would need. I had spent a long time thinking about this problem and had come up with a very neat arrangement of little packages, plastic bags, plastic boxes, pans and stove. I had also a 30 metre rope of 7 mm diameter nylon, a small collection of rock pegs and slings with carabiners, a hammer with curved pick, crampons and a short ice-axe. A long ice-axe would have been better, but I didn't have the money for one: besides which, I knew quite well the limitations of specialist equipment. What I had looked for in everything that I packed was: for how many purposes could it be used? I took nothing that couldn't be versatile. And then I had to find room for the food, so I had brought detachable pockets for the sack and into these I had packed some four days' provisions of a basic sort. I could hardly have taken less, yet as the weeks passed I found I was able to discard a number of items.

As for clothing, I had in the sack or wore just what one would normally take, with the addition of a smart pair of trousers and one decent shirt. I also had a change of footwear in the form of a pair of cheap "trainers" – that, I knew, would be important. And so, climbing steadily up above La Bérarde during the middle part of the day, I felt physically prepared, but morally unsettled.

The path continued.

The path continued until it reached an area of birch and scrub willow, set in a plain where two torrents met in a tangle of subsidiary streams. I passed several of these and emerged on a grassy level field, and there suddenly I had my first full view of the peaks I was to cross. Up a subsidiary valley, which contained great heaps of stony moraine, there was a view of an enormous mountain face emerging out of the clouds. The Barre des Ecrins is the largest, or at any rate the highest, peak of the Dauphiné Alps, and from most sides it is a hunched and lumpy pile; but from this angle, from the north-east, it presented a Gothic architecture, all finials, crockets, pinnacles and gargoyle-like excrescences. There was a tall subsidiary spire and any number of angulated buttresses. The general effect was not cathedral-like, because this mountainside seemed to be in quite low relief; rather it was more like the neo-Gothic of the House of Commons – a plethora of complicated ornamental shape stuck on to the surface of a solid mass – in this case a huge gable end of mountain form. But this great intricacy terminated in a pure dome of gleaming snow. This gave the impression of eccentricity. The architecture of mountains is always surprising, and nowhere more so than in the Dauphiné.

In England I had had the notion of climbing one of the subsidiary peaks of the Barre des Ecrins, for training purposes, and of crossing eastward directly under the flanks of the main peak. But here was my first piece of improvisation, in the face of uncertain weather and a clear case of timidity: I was to take the path northward and seek out the high but easier pass of the Col des Clots de Cavales. When the path divided at a bridge of planks over the right-hand torrent, I took the left-hand way which was marked with a painted arrow on the rocks "Ref. de Châtelleret".

I will undertake to explain the general rules under which I was working. Rules are essential to every game – they are its meaning. The first and main rule was to get from La Bérarde to Heiligenblut by myself, unsupported. This was modified by a secondary rule; that in the deepest valleys I could use transport. As a corollary of the first, I had to be carrying my own food and shelter; this in turn limited my scope of action since I did not want to undertake any technically difficult climbing with a heavy pack. Yet this self-sufficiency was also a source of freedom, which gave rise to the third general rule – always prefer a high-level line to a low-level line, technical difficulty being equal. Last but not least was the overriding imperative of safety. In taking this northward pass I was opting for an easier and safer route; but one still high enough to be considered mountaineering rather than walking.

So at three in the afternoon on the 11th of July I was walking up a broad and steadily rising glen, flanked by very steep slopes of grass, scree and slabby rocks, with glimpses now and then of the ends of ridges. Behind me was a view into the heart of the main groups of mountains, before me an expanding panorama of mountain walls.

The path was gentle, wandering across the turf or beside large boulders, skirting streams and pools and threading its way through little woods of birch or dwarf willow. It climbed only gently. Just to walk along it was a good enough reason to be there. If asked to explain any longer-term reason, any motive, and any plan-of-life involvement, I would have had to answer then that I had very little reason at all for what I was doing except that it was the first necessary bit of work. That if I was going to cross the Alps to Austria, I had to start up this valley.

The one sure mark of success in this wilderness of trash that constitutes our life today, is that you can get out of it. And I was *making tracks*.

Half-way along, the valley bent a little eastward and began to steepen. Here I encountered the first extensive snow-bed, that lay right across the valley floor. It seemed to be the remnants of a great winter avalanche, since it was full of boulders, roots, dirt and scraps of vegetation. But as the valley turned so it became clear that the snow-bed extended for a very long way and that I had reached the lower limits of the permanent snow. And this was at only 7,000 feet. This looked like the second bit of friction – and a serious piece of evidence. If the snow was lying very late and low this season it would mean much hard work: on the other hand, I reasoned (walking across its crumbled and insecure surface) it would also mean that glaciers and high-level areas might well be easier.

Now the sun was shining fiercely and the way was hard as the path traversed the snow or bands of scree. The thunder had receded, and there was an opening of views on to glacier slopes. Now I began to meet people descending, light-heartedly skipping without rucksacks while I toiled upwards. There was a family party, two couples, a group of scouts; all had been visiting the refuge which was, they told me, not very far ahead. I was not disposed to believe them, knowing how slowly one climbs, how quickly one descends. And as the sun was hot the snow was wet, and slipped and collapsed and subsided under my feet.

In this way I came into the upper part of the valley, which was broad once again and sloping steadily up before me, floored with a field of boulders within which I could see the refuge at about two miles' distance. Straight ahead, and it was difficult to tell how far away since there were no reliable guides to scale, was the peak of the

Meije, with an enormous precipice below it; and left and right more peaks. Up to the right I could see what appeared to be my pass – a nick in a much nicked skyline: up to the left a fine succession of snowy crests. Clouds drifted across or over the peaks, and the sunlight was intermittent; but my expected storm had not arrived. It was troubling some other valley, some other climber.

I arrived at the Refuge du Châtelleret around four in the afternoon. It turned out to be a sturdy cottage-like structure, two storeys high, abutting against an immense rock. Outside was a little terrace with benches on which a small group was sitting – they looked clean, colourful and relaxed as they drank their beer. Within, in what at first was almost darkness, there was the guardian and a group of four French climbers – dour types. I didn't want to be drawn into a conversation with anyone, so I sat in a corner. For a long time I was shy about the whole undertaking, and would tell no one what I was up to. Huts like this, at a low altitude, do a good trade in light meals, cold drinks and postcards: there is usually a number of walking parties on the terrace, laughing and joking. The mountaineering groups stay indoors, lie on their bunks, eat and say little or nothing. It was not certain to which of these classes I belonged. I bought a bowl of soup, and unpacked some of my own food to go with it; aware of being an object of curiosity. Though I did not realize it at the time, this was the first of many such experiences of social ambiguity. I came to dislike mountain huts for this very simple reason; I was marching to a different tune. But this time I put it down to my continuing tension.

It was a new feeling, and unsettling. There are many people like myself, not so much drop-out as fall-out. We tend to resolve the problem by taking up activities and belonging to special groups – little "counter-cultures" of our own. Here in this hut I should have felt as at home as a veteran in barracks; instead I felt miserably conspicuous and odd. It is easy to see why: I was equipped for climbing, yet carried a tent; I was pale and foreign, but clearly not on any holiday; and I was abnormally absorbed in my own movements like an actor about to step on to a stage.

It was not until I left the Refuge du Châtelleret that I felt my traverse had truly begun.

The path was now distinct but very narrow; it ran back down the valley side while climbing steadily. If that sounds obscure it is because here was a fine example of optical distortion. The path seemed to descend, but in fact rose. This is an effect that one often notices on a small scale – over about a hundred yards, for example – but on this occasion the path, visible for nearly a mile returning southward, appeared to lose about 200 feet whereas having got to the end of the visible section I found I was about 300 feet above the hut, and the stony plain at the bottom of the valley floor, up which I had walked gently, seemed very steep from here. This peculiar effect was due, I believe, to there being absolutely no genuinely horizontal arca anywhere in sight.

The way ahead was up: this is what I had come out to do. Steeply up, by grassy rocks and slabs where the path vanished to scratchings. Well above me, in a lurid evening sunlight, was the peak of La Grande Ruine – a shattered and jagged sight; to the left of that a complicated knot of ridges and gullies; to the left again a cone of pale grey granite, on my side of which, hidden, was the high pass of the Cavales. Behind me were more peaks, mostly hidden in tinted mist, and below that the shadowed gulf of the valley.

The path, in so far as it was a path, gave out at an area of rocks; a scrambling passage led round to the left, skirting the foot of a pinnacled ridge. This led on to a huge slope of scree and boulders, mixed with outcrops of rock; there was the sound of many waterfalls, large and small, and of water trickling through the rocks at my feet. Finding the path again, level for a few yards, I made it into my bed. All the tension I had been feeling had gone in the climb up from the hut; all the insecurity dropped away like a heavy sack at the day's end. This is what I had come out to do and this is what I did better than anything else. I slept in complete comfort.

How does one come to do something as solitary as this? How does one pick out such a task? I am talking to myself. Such a trek is an obscure, solitary and perhaps rather crazy thing to want to do . . .

Morning. Cold mist filtering a cold light.

I was brewing up my second cup of tea and lacing up my boots when, with a clatter, the four Frenchmen from the hut came over the rib just below me. Was this the way to the col, they asked. I replied that I damn well hoped so or I was wasting my time. They vanished into the mist, full of confidence. I had nothing like an adequate map for this section, and was using a 1:100,000 tourist sheet. But there was no other feasible pass for some miles, and the track, in so far as it could be traced, was an old one. It had even occurred to me that it might once have been a mule track, from the name of the pass. Cavales? surely that meant something to do with horses – as in cavalry? Well, if a horse could do it, then so could I.

Pack on back again, I set my course upward by the sounds of the party ahead. After a while I caught up with them as they ate a second breakfast on a rock, and we had a pleasant conversation. Two of them were coming my way, the other two would do a harder peak, and all four of them would rendezvous at some third point. The weather, they assured me, was going to be fine. As for me, I told them I was walking over to the Vanoise National Park, which was true.

After a short while I found myself on a slope of ice, and then in the throat of a steep couloir. I put on my crampons and got ready for serious work; axe in hand I started to work slowly up into the mist-filled cleft. There was a determined line of footsteps, some days old, so I assumed I was in the right place. Also, there was a can of sardines, open and rusting, to be seen. This had to be it: or if it was not, then I would look very silly. The pack seemed heavy, and I was gasping for air. Well, I thought, you've not been at 3,000 m for a couple of years, so what do you expect. Down below, the two Frenchmen were moving more easily than me, gaining slowly. Well, I was not in a race. The ice became glassy for a hundred feet or so, and I was scratching about rather inelegantly, looking for a way on to the rocks, when I spied an old rusty hawser descending out of the murk. I tiptoed over to it and somehow set foot on the rock. There is always some problem in getting off one material on to another, and here it was highly disagreeable, what with my panting, and scratching about, and the weight of the sack; and the hawser, when I seized it, was fearfully cold and unpleasant and didn't truly assist the ascent up to the ridge. I was groaning with cold and effort as I suddenly came out into brilliant sunlight, followed shortly by the others. I had done it; the first objective was achieved; and the way below was easy.

All behind was cloud, but all before bright blue skies and a view of rocky peaks and green valleys. The main peaks of the Dauphiné

Alps were hidden by the banks of mist, but before me was the way I had to go. After a cheerful goodbye and plenty of mutual well-wishing the Frenchmen set off to climb the steep rock pyramid to the north of the pass – the Pic Nord des Cavales; and I set off down the immense snow-slope, skiing on my heels for 2,000 feet and more.

By ten in the morning I was clean over the range and brewing up soup and sausages in a pleasant meadow called the Plan de Valfourche. This valley was even more beautiful than the one I had left, and the peaks around it were more varied and visible. The "plan" itself contained a fine pool and was the flattest neatest turf to be imagined. I spent two hours here, relaxing and sunning myself and trying a new way of packing the sack. No matter how well one plans, action always provides new imperatives: in this case, the position of the tent was causing annoyance, so I tried packing it into the sack and rearranging the rest accordingly. Later I became quite expert in packing the contents of the sack in just the order I would need them during the day.

Here at the Plan de Valfourche I made ready my headband, by putting a sling round the base of the sack and threading another through it in such a way that I could slip it over my forehead and take the strain of the sack like that. This is thought to be a hard thing to do, and if you use a headband you must expect people to ask ridiculous questions, to call you "Sherpa". But it is by far the best way to support any load of 40 or more pounds; and with a little ingenuity you can adjust it so that the weight is also taken partly on the shoulders. Properly fixed, the headband transfers the weight directly down the spine and requires no effort from the neck muscles except that of leaning against the band to keep it steady and in place.

The first objective having been achieved I began to sort myself out for the next one – the crossing of the Thabor peaks, which comprise an extensive area of low but complicated ridges and summits between the Dauphiné Alps and the Vanoise National Park. I hoped to achieve one or other of the tops of the range, but had no information about them whatsoever. Also, my map was not good for difficult route-finding.

People preoccupied with safety at all costs are probably shaking their heads over my lack of good maps; but there was a very practical reason. Weight. Everything I had was cut down to the minimum to avoid weight; I had even gone to the extent of cutting the labels off my clothing. The maps I had cut down into strips, and my notes I had photocopied and reduced. My safety resided in having plenty of supplies with me at all times, and good equipment: so organized, it hardly matters if one gets lost for a day or two. In fact, I was never lost once, in spite of a great deal of bad weather; though there were a few occasions when I did not know where I was. (The difference between the two is subtle, but categorical.)

The craft of navigation and way-finding requires both explicit skills and tacit understanding, of which the second is by far the most important. Sea navigation needs a considerable knowledge and mental dexterity but above all it needs what I shall call a kinetic imagination, or insight. I believe great navigators are able to sense as well as know that the movement of the ship in water and air is part of the whole moving force of air and water that comprises the ocean system. The boat itself, particularly if it has a wooden hull, is a system of immense complexity almost the equal of the living creatures within it; and this linked system, man and boat, is comprised within the linking systems of air and water. The best navigator senses this as a complex image that he feels almost as if it were a living thing within him. The extreme sensitivity of a well-found boat of whatever size to the twin mediums through which she cuts and by which she is driven is communicated to the helmsman through touch, balance and sound. This understanding cannot be described in a text, but it must be learnt: a vast imaginative capacity is being exercised in sea navigation and I call this capacity kinetic insight, because force and movement is its essence.

In contradistinction, way-finding in mountains (with or without maps) requires a plastic or sculptural insight. In mountains the navigator's imagination works upon structure, form and texture. Once again, there is a substantial body of knowledge that can be employed and can be obtained, but the prime requisite is the imaginative capacity to reproduce the topography as a mental image. This topography is not simply that which can be shown upon a map, but includes the textural topography of conditions underfoot and in the air, and the structural or geological grasp of form that enables us to foresee what the shape of the mountain will be on the other side, how the rocks will slope to give what terrain, how valleys will end in cut-offs or headwalls. One must have an inner grasp of the grain of the land just as a carpenter understands the grain of the wood. This is true both in the grand scale of the mountain range or in the minute scale of the next few inches of rock that you can't see round but must know how it will be shaped and whether it "runs to holds" or is "blank".

Mountain route-finding both in the grand and the minute requires this understanding which is further modified by the changing texture underfoot. Snow and ice are inscrutable substances; vegetation can be thick, sparse, helpful, hateful, slippery or adherent. You need to foresee. The keenest pleasure that mountain travel can give one is the realization that you made the right decision on the basis of your insight.

So now for more improvisation. In front, due east, was a group of steep peaks to be passed on the right or the left. I went round to the left or northern side along a traversing path which emerged quite suddenly beside the mountain road over the Col du Lautaret. I had in mind camping here, in order next day to climb a peak called the Grand Galibier, but when I looked at this peak I thought that discretion was the better part of enthusiasm. It was an immense heap of shale and crumbling slate, and so were all the ridges about it. (Anyone else might wish to go right, by way of the Col d'Arsine, and arrive at Le Lauzet to meet my route.)

At that point I had the good luck to fall into conversation with an elderly man who knew the district. He and his wife were eating a magnificent Gallic picnic; their activity this summer, he said, was to show his very aged mother the sights of the Alps. He indicated his little Citroën within which his very aged mother was sitting. We all drank a glass of wine together and it was wonderful how my French improved. We discussed how best to cross the Thabor peaks. After more wine and pâté and bread he had it all worked out on the basis of his own experience and another map on which the winter ski tours were marked. His advice turned out to be very good. On no account, he said, was I to miss these mountains, since they were extraordinary.

So, two hours later, I toiled up a narrow ravine above the hamlet of Le Lauzet, leaving the Dauphiné Alps wrapped round in another thunderous mist, and set off towards Thabor.

Here broad green valleys were interspersed with sudden lime-stone cliffs and turrets, or by orange red ribs of shale; there were lakes in deep hollows, small ravines, caves and luscious pastures. I found the path that had been described to me and set off north again, steadily climbing to a green shelf. Here I pitched my tent and ate an evening meal, watching the lightning flashes play about the broad hump-back of the Barre des Ecrins, and the thin veils of rain pass up the valleys. This, my first full day, had been very long and very successful.

Research, be it into the history of design theory or ways around the mountains, is a dour business. Pick and shovel work; you pick up the facts and you shovel them into your head. I researched my way from France to Austria in detail, and on starting out I had a lot of confidence in my chosen line. On the whole, that confidence held and I only made a few variations from the original plan, and all of those were forced on me by bad weather, by "friction".

My route was, of course, a compromise. I had no time to include the Maritime or Julian Alps; the Dolomites lay too far to the south and the Bernese Alps too far to the north, but between the all-inclusive and the feasible I struck what I believed to be a sound and logical line. In the course of research it became obvious that I was not the first. Since the days of Martin Conway there have been "end-to-enders" but most of them have been on skis, in the winter and spring. I read of three foreign and one British party who had done that. One hard man, in the 1930s, had skied from Salzburg to Nice by himself. But I did not find any acount of a solo trip of the sort I was planning. I wanted to make a line that would have some classic quality to it; one that others might want to follow because it was so elegant. Yet the ambition is obvious enough and I had to assume that something similar had been done before, and since I would not be the first, I had to make sure I did it in style, neatly and safely. Martin Conway, who had started off in the Maritime Alps one spring in the 1890s, had taken a friend, two guides and two porters, and they could all keep an eye on one another.

Perhaps, I thought to myself that night, I had started off too fast. I went through all the alternatives again, all the variations, all the possible points of supply over the next few stages. In this there was an obsessional aspect, because the activity of research sucks up all the spare mental energy: the myth of the absent-minded scholar is no myth, and in the weeks before setting off I had become a very narrow-minded man. There in that tent in the Thabor range, I felt myself screwing up the psychic pressure tighter and tighter.

It rained in the night and I was disturbed by peculiar rustling sounds that could not be traced but which I later discovered were polythene bags "unscrewing" themselves. Flashes of lightning kept me awake. Poking my head out of the tent flap at five in the morning I saw nothing but an opalescent mist, which did not clear until I was well on my way. From now on my mornings were almost invariable; a cup of strong, black, sweet coffee drunk whilst lying in my bag, followed by a handful of porridge oats or some dried fruit. Then I would get up quickly, pack my sack in the order I thought necessary, and be on my way before six; around ten I would eat again, substantially, and then again around four. If I was to do an "evening shift" – as I had done the night before, I would pause for longer at four, and eat better. I always stopped to camp while it was still light, and started as soon as it became possible to see.

The mountains of Thabor consist

> of quartz
> of lime
> of schists of iron red
> and shale, burnt purple
> > lapis
> > iridescent blue
> lakes without exit
> and green meadows

They also consisted of deep soft snowdrifts: there was no way I would climb the Grand Galibier from this side either. I could have done with skis over some sections.

Slowly the mist cleared and there were views into deep cwms that held milky-blue lakes. These were the sort of lakes from which one might expect a hand to appear, clasping a sword: it was mysterious, complicated and very varied terrain. Now and again I had glimpses of tall spires of rock, or more lakes (or was it the first one), and now and again a vista across the top of the mist towards

peaks I could not identify. By one lake, after the first pass, I saw
some tents and figures emerging from them: over the second pass
(which was very deep in snow) I found footprints no more than a
day old. Marmots whistled at me through the mist; choughs cawed
at me. The sun came out and the sun went in. Finally, around nine
in the morning, I came to an isthmus between two lakes where the
little path I had been following for most of the early morning,
joined a jeep track travelling east. This was the track I was to follow:
and I did take it for a mile or so to a point where I could hope for a
view of the main Thabor peak. But when I got there, nothing was
in sight but a rolling snow-field and a wall of blackening cloud: it
looked like the Grampians in February. That, I thought, was not
what I wanted at all; having already had a taste of the deep late
snow, and knowing how slow and heavy movement became in it, I
determined to take an avoiding action.

Retracing my steps I struck off north again over another snowy
saddle and descended into a broad valley called the Combe de
Plagnette, which ran slightly west of north. Here I found a
determined path leading down into some scrubby birch and alder
woods and past abandoned chalets, leading at length to the little
winter resort of Valloire.

A small incident happened as I walked along this path – I found a
little scattering of rubbish, a tin, pieces of paper and plastic and
orange peel. Not liking the sight of it, I bent down, took off my
sack (always ready for any excuse to do that) and pushed the litter
into a nearby marmot's burrow. And then I understood that those
who left the litter had done exactly the same thing, thinking
themselves to be tidy. The marmot, naturally enough, had thrown
the rubbish out of her hall. Since the marmots were to be my main
companions I thought that I should begin my journey in a more
considerate way: so I reached into the burrow, pulled out the
rubbish I had so inconsiderately replaced, and took it along with
me. Don't you worry, I said out loud, you won't find me messing
up your doorway. This little incident was to have serious repercus-
sions because it began my prolonged dialogue with these creatures,
that achieved an unusual level of fantasy in the last two weeks of my
Grand High-Level Route.

The walk down to Valloire was pleasant enough, with fine views
behind of the Thabor summits, but the resort itself seemed a strange

sort of place – several luxurious but apparently empty hotels, unused ski-lifts, cafés with bright awnings and no customers. I wished I had stayed up in the mountains – even though a fine rain was now falling and high up above the wind was tearing up the cloud sheet into shreds. I ate a hamburger from a stall and tried to figure out the best way down into the main Maurienne valley. It was still only two in the afternoon.

The biggest obstacles on the whole of the Grand High-Level Route were not mountains but valleys; the half-dozen great trenches into which one must descend and out of which one must, somehow, climb. The Maurienne is the not the biggest, but it is the most sudden – a 6,000 foot deep cleft whose forested flanks drop by cliff and gully down to a rushing river, a railway and a road, all three crammed into so narrow a space that the houses cling to the cliffs to keep out of the way and the factories burrow underground. To add to the confusion there are thick pipelines and water conduits and generating stations at every corner. The Maurienne valley is full of industry because, thanks to its depth and the immense quantity of water falling into it from streams and glaciers, it has abundant cheap electricity.

And there is absolutely nothing to do but to descend into it and climb right out again. If there had been a bus, I would have taken it; my rules permitted me. But there was no bus and so I set off walking down the road, looking for a track or a pathway that might be more pleasant. Rain fell, sluggishly.

And then came a stroke of luck: a passing car stopped unasked and its occupants offered me a lift to Modane. In retrospect I can see that I had several such strokes of luck and met an unusual number of helpful and friendly people. Toward the end of my traverse I began to be aware of this and wonder if there was any cause and I came to the conclusion, which I think was correct, that my demeanour (being different from that of the normal holiday-maker or hiker) attracted the interest of observant folk. I gave (and I imagine this) an impression of intentness and deliberation, and people who were curious wanted to find out why. I don't suppose they were especially conscious of this, any more than I was fully conscious as to why I felt ill at ease in the mountain huts. But the human creature is finely tuned to unorthodox behaviour.

The driver and his wife were making a tour of the region and today they were looking for clear skies and good weather, travelling into

Italy by the Mont Cenis pass. They set me down beside the station at Modane.

Most people just pass through this town; it is utterly without interest to the tourist except as a place to change money before crossing the frontier. I thought it had an entertaining humanity about it, scruffy, lively and much to be preferred to the chill commercialism of Valloire. The café I sat in turned out to be the meeting place of the local chapter of hell's angels who arrived, in exotic splendour, while I was ordering a "Stella". The sight was familiar – polished machinery bestridden by the followers of Genghis. They were instantly pursued by a patrol car out of which emerged two immaculate flics. An altercation followed. Would the leader of the pack care to accompany them? The leader – a blond tough with hair hanging in a pigtail down his back and a coat of greased rat-pelts – talked himself out of it with astonishing fluency. The gendarmerie shrugged their tailored shoulders and got back into the car as nonchalantly as possible; they left to howls of derision and many and complicated gestures. More roaring machines arrived till the street was full of them and their fumes. Such was Modane.

That evening I walked up through the steep pine-woods above the town and camped in a glade not far from some chalets. It was raining steadily.

The great art of this sort of travel lies in keeping comfortable, and a good deal of that lies in keeping dry. Really heavy rain is not the problem; the most insidious and unavoidable dampness is the sort that accumulates in overgown forests after a few days of downpour; the sort of dampness that is released at every move you make, that attaches itself to every surface or texture, that showers down upon you at every stir of every little branch. Your feet become damp as you walk up through the sopping grass, and slowly the damp creeps up your knees to your thighs, no matter what you are wearing. And the damp creeps in through the pockets and the neck of your waterproof and even seems to penetrate the skin on your face. The moment anything is exposed to air, it becomes damp; so you crawl damply into a damp sleeping bag: and the interior of the tent, be it never so impermeable, becomes sticky with condensation. And even the emergency matches, wrapped in plastic and kept in a watertight tin, will not strike. And the bit of bread you have saved becomes musty and the cheese loses its firmness. The air you draw in is a sort of cold steam that condenses in your lungs so that you cough like an old sheep. Two or more in a tent can at least keep each other warm, if not dry, but solitary bivouacs in such a drenching are an experience to avoid. I was to have three others before the journey was over; and this was the easiest.

The question of comfort is the central question; the question of danger is subsidiary to it, since most of the dangers of mountaineering are extreme cases of the ordinary, simple discomfort. Mountaineering, ocean sailing, exploration of any kind all involve periods of acute misery amounting at times to a threat to life (as in exposure, thirst, sleeplessness). The ability to put up with acute discomfort without the impairment of ability and judgement is one of the preconditions of achievement in these fields. The examples that immediately come to my mind are those of the early seamen-explorers; but other people will think of the crossings of deserts or jungles. Nearer to home and to our immediate period, the same concentrated power of endurance is found in certain sports such as single-handed ocean racing, and extreme climbing.

The willingness to accept extreme discomfort for altruistic or at least non-economic reasons, is enigmatic. To think of it in terms of individual psychology does not seem to me to be helpful – though I suppose some personal factor always helps to decide why one person rather than another is willing. It is better – I guess – to think of it in terms of culture. For my part I remember studying *King Lear* over twenty years ago and reading the storm scene with great attention. In this scene, Lear progressively sheds the built environment. Thrown out of the great hall of civilized life he finds shelter in a primitive hut (which perhaps is *the* original primitive hut); finding a madman in the hut he starts to tear off his clothes. "Unaccommodated man is no more but such a poor, bare, forked animal as thou art. Off, off you lendings." In his delirious way, Lear is reversing the story of the Garden of Eden, casting off what he calls "sophistication" and looking for an existence untrammelled by things and history. Such an enterprise, of course, is only possible to the very sophisticated and highly rational, who know what they do and are capable of making the distinction between knowing and doing.

If I follow my own reasoning correctly, this seems to suggest that the extreme sports are a form of practical existentialism, in which the participants shed as much of the comforts of material things and the reassurances of given ideas and definitions as they can, in order to apprehend some essence of life. Not "human nature", because that supposes a given definition, but human existence. One of Graham Greene's novels begins with the sentence "I feel discomfort, therefore I exist". One of Byron's letters says that "the whole object of life is sensation, to feel that we exist, even though in pain". Yet of course the sportsman does this in the bounds of a whole set of rules and expectations, often dependent upon the technology his intention denies.

Much of the appeal of the extreme sports, and of the gentler levels of them, such as this, may well lie in this realized ambivalence. Perhaps I wouldn't be doing this if I hadn't read *Lear* for my 'A' levels.

These are the sort of thoughts that come to one in the reading room of the Victoria and Albert Museum, where I am writing this, which is utterly devoted to things and history and not devoted at all to deliberate discomfort. Such thoughts never come to one whilst in the midst of the activity that gives them birth. Then all one can think of is some stratagem to keep the matches dry.*

---

* Footnote: when your matches are wet, sleep with them between your vest and your shirt. However, if you roll over on them, they may, possibly, ignite themselves. The thought of being in a sleeping bag, in your clothes, inside a small tent, with a flaming box of matches a vest's thickness from bare skin is unbearable. But the trick always works.

Chapter Two

MODANE TO COURMAYEUR: GOOD TIMES

WHAT WAS I doing there? While the traveller tries to get some sleep in his damp bag, and while the water sloshes off the pine-tree tops in drops as full as tea-cups – making a crack like a pistol shot when they hit the tent – the author ought to explain to the reader just how this all happens.

There is one good sporting question that everyone who cares for an active life will understand as they approach the middle stage of existence. What to do next?

I remember many years ago, at the height of a young man's most arrogant fitness, crossing the high and unfrequented Col de Talèfre between France and Italy in order to descend to Chamonix. Myself and companion had done eight major routes in twelve days, which for the Mont Blanc range was really going hard. Our plan was to "knock off" the summit of Les Courtes on the way over the range. Up early from the Couvercle hut (with the idea of being in Chamonix for lunch!) we were approaching the summit before dawn when we became aware that there was a figure in front of us. An old man. Well, he looked old to us, though perhaps he was in his middle fifties. We overtook him, of course, and self-indulgently passed him by scampering up much steeper ice. The ridge was followed easily, by snow and rock; at times we saw him, closely behind us; at other times he had vanished. At the end of the summit ridge, one makes an easy descent to the glacier, and as we clambered down we were amazed to find that he was overtaking us. At the glacier edge, a huge overhanging crevasse was barring the way. After casting about for an easier line we found none and had to jump it – safe enough but quite literally it was like jumping off the roof of a council semi. Where had the old guy gone to? He wasn't going to risk his old bones doing that, surely? We picked ourselves up, shook the snow out of our shirts and trousers and checked for any sprains; and then we saw him 50 yards away, carefully arranging an *abseil* point, and lowering himself slowly and neatly on to the safe lower lip of the rift.

He was back at the hut ten minutes before us. I have never forgotten that "old man".

The secret of his success was – to do everything very slowly and so demonstrate the truth of the story of the tortoise and the hare. He was, in effect, prolonging an active life in the mountains by choosing the rules by which he worked.

Some sports – the athletic kind – hardly permit of this; but mountain sports, sailing and some face-to-face competitive sports such as fencing can be prolonged into later life. Yet the question arises – how do you organize your pleasure?

For my part I found that most of my earlier climbing partners had grown into easier pastimes such as lunchtime drinking. I was doing some of that myself, but I wasn't yet committed to it. Others had betaken themselves to more exotic activities such as wind-surfing, parachute-jumping, scuba-diving and so forth. These I did not like because they needed too much equipment, because they were too smart, because they were too expensive. In the case of sky-diving, because they scared me out of my wits. Some others had taken up dinghy or even yacht sailing, and that (though I loved it) I could in no way afford.

To climb consistently and to climb well one needs regular partners with the same expectations and I didn't have any. Or, rather, those I had were moving to other parts of the country, having second marriages or first families, or becoming profession-ally ambitious. The pattern of their lives did not mesh with the pattern of mine which was slow, rather scruffy, stationary, anti-equipment, and without ambition.

I took up mountain running and found I could do it more than adequately: sometimes I did very long runs, over two days, crossing the tops of the Pennines or the Lakeland fells. In a mountain marathon I found myself not so far behind the best. But it was the solitary quality of such running that appealed to me, the self-reliance and the self-regulation. I began to think of that old man again . . .

There was also the restlessness we all feel in our fortieth year. Some men take up adultery, but I took up solo mountaineering; the one, of course, is not a substitute for the other but both may be a

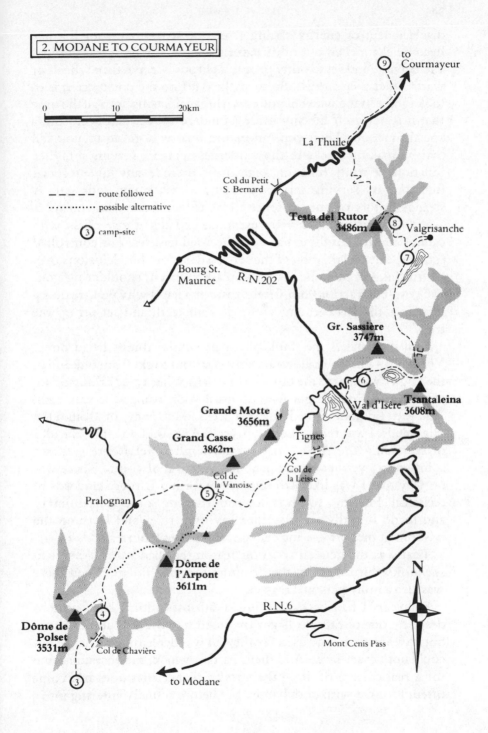

2. MODANE TO COURMAYEUR

0   10   20km

- – – – – route followed
- · · · · · · · · possible alternative

③ camp-site

to Courmayeur ⑨

La Thuile

Col du Petit
S. Bernard

Testa del Rutor
3486m ⑧ Valgrisanche

⑦

Bourg St.
Maurice   R.N.202

Gr. Sassière
3747m

⑥

Val d'Isère   **Tsantaleina**
3608m

Grande Motte
3656m

Grand Casse
3862m   Tignes

Col de
la Vanoise   Col de
la Leisse

Pralognan   ⑤

Dôme de
l'Arpont
3611m

R.N.6

N

Dôme de
Polset
3531m   ④

Col de Chavière

Mont Cenis Pass

③

to Modane

displacement of energy arising from the sense that your life has become channelled out of its natural course, forced through pipes and culverts and set to other people's purposes, set to turn wheels or water other men's grass. So to strike out into the unexpected is to look for the living water of your own life again, conscious all the time that it is not your life any more (if indeed it ever had been) but a social function. Then you rationalize this by arguing to yourself that by making tracks to the wilderness you are serving a higher function, a truth function that must precede any given social function. By serving this truth you are reclaiming your self. A strange feature of our existence today is that those who control it assert their independence by escaping and that those of us who cannot control anything have our licensed leisures, our controlled escapes. The reclamation of the self is a delusion, but delusions may be fruitful. On the other hand, you ask yourself, shouldering your pack, isn't this action completely absurd? That is why you are doing it, comes the answer; and you grit your teeth and set off up the track.

And that makes me think of other, similar things I had done. Years ago – I mean really years ago – I set out to ski from one end of the High Pyrenees to the other, by myself. What a crazy thing to do, at nineteen! I didn't get far because I soon realized it was rash. And then I'd done some huge solo treks in Norway, or around the Highlands. I was rediscovering myself. And so, if you like, the idea of traversing the Alps – my Grand High-Level Route – was a solution to a very common problem: renewal of youth. There was no way that I was likely to regain my former harder standards of technical climbing, so I was determined to do something different and to do it really well, setting my own rules and learning the wisdom of the tortoise and the old man of Les Courtes.

That was the general sporting reason that had led me there, to spend my third night in the dripping forest of Polset. Then there was also a more personal reason.

For years I had been working in an institution I had come to despise – one of those colleges that used to exist only in caricature but now appear before us in "reality". I was determined to leave but could not yet see how. And then, partly by luck, the occasion came for a real change of life – the sort of chance that does not come often, I took it with both hands, but before actually entering into a new life I felt I had to do something to shake off what the Poor Mouth calls the "fear and melancholy and disgust". It would have to be something of this kind, some experience that would rinse the brain clean.

And thirdly, the time and space came out right. My wife, who is an artist, was to work in Yugoslavia that summer, at the foot of the Julian Alps. A long excursion, ending there, seemed like a practical plan. Some dates were fixed, and some were free. Money was tight, but possible. Plans were changed and plans were changed again. But by April I could see my way through to seven weeks. What could not be done in seven weeks!

So I awoke on the third morning, in a mist-filled glade of giant pine-trees, damp but happy enough to see what might be done.

From the Polset alp a path leads up towards a saddle called the Col de Chavière. It is an old and well used track constructed for mules and often nowadays used by walkers and human mules making the circuit of the Vanoise National Park. It begins by some chalets and wanders up the old tree-crowned moraine above the valley floor until, after an hour and a half, it emerges on to a broad sloping moor.

I saw almost nothing of this but the track, since the mist was very thick. Yet it was a moving, shifting sort of mist that gave promise of better weather. From time to time slight breaks began to occur as I climbed higher, giving views of tree-crowned crags high above, outlined and floating as if in some Chinese painting. Once, even higher, there was a corner of snowy ridge and a patch of blue sky. I hummed or sang to keep myself company, no tune but a rhythm, to get the breathing and the footsteps right. When there were a few downhill yards, and there were from time to time, I would trot those steps. Rhythm; the continuous repetition of one foot placed before and slightly above the other, pressed down upon, lifted, repeated, provides the continuum. To be musical, the continuo; because music helps. To each his own tune and to me the kapellmeister's steady tread. Up these long alms the sheep may safely graze. Dah di di dah di di dah di di, ever upward. Absolutely safely and steadily at the gound level, foot to earth, so that high above the brain can improvise as it will. That's for the regular paths and slopes, the trods. In deep snow it's different because in deep, or even in quite shallow but loose snow one must pause, consolidate and move forward, and pause again. A regular pulse won't do in a long pull up deep snow, and when you are getting tired towards the top of the slope, when you keep breaking through crust or have to stamp or kick, then you need an air with an heroic shout to it. So that you can, if you have to, shout into the frost or mist. So a long pause between short hard movements is the style, and you can divide yourself between the beast who labours and the driver who lashes.

When the Alabama's keel was laid	(shout silently, tense for the next burst)
Roll Alabama Roll	(a hard driving step on each syllable)
It was laid in the yard of Jonathan Laird	(that's all in the head, that shout)
Oh roll Alabama roll!	(almost at a run)

> From the Mersey she sailed forth
> Roll Alabama Roll
> To destroy the commerce of the North
> Oh roll Alabama roll!

It has to be a shanty of this sort, a work song, full of pride and fate and a bit bombastic, to get moving at all on some hard mornings.

The previous two days had both been hard and long, and my limbs, cold from the damp, needed to be warmed. High up on the moor side I sat under a huge rock and watched the clouds roll back to reveal on both sides mountains, and in the middle the snowy *cwm* below the Col de Chavière.

The moment the clouds cleared the sun was very hot: the snow when I reached it was immediately deep and soft and wet. The struggle to the pass was long and wearisome and this day, I had promised myself, would be a day to take life easily. The sun flooded into the little valley that led up to the crest, and I stopped, now to lave my face with cream, now to pull on my sun hat, and now to readjust my sunglasses – and most of all to pluck up the energy for the next 50 yards.

And when I got to the Col the way down the other side was almost as bad, though the snow was a slight shade harder. A fine, broad valley greeted me with to the right a tall and jagged peak all covered in fresh snow, and to the left the broken crags of the Aiguille de Polset. I hoped to make this substantial mountain my next objective.

By midday I had crossed the pass and was sitting down outside the door of the Polset hut. This was a popular spot: there were youth groups and family groups, serious walkers and sunbathers. It was a holiday weekend – 12th July. For my part I celebrated the time by setting up my tent some distance away and laying out all my wet clothes and bedding to dry, and by having a very good wash in a little tarn. I ate and slept for most of the afternoon. Sometimes holiday-makers, seeing my extremely small tent would walk across to look at it, expecting to see a child within: they found my tent comic, for some reason, and wondered how – in God's name – could anyone live in a tent so small. And did I cook in it? And did I carry everything upon my back? And where was I going? By myself, *tout seul en montagne? Vous n'avez pas peur?* Yes, I was walking to Val d'Isère, but I hoped to climb some summits. And yes, I was all by myself: but it amused me, and no, the sack was not heavy, perhaps 23 kilos at most. Well, *bonne chance et bon appetit, m'sieu*.

Towards evening I got into a serious frame of mind again, and packed a sack for the morning with what I would need on the mountain: for these secondary purposes I had brought a very light nylon sack which I had used for running and which could hold minimal mountain gear. I spent a long while looking at a large scale map in the hut, and as long again reading the notes I had made back in England. Then slept.

Above the Polset refuge, to its east, are three summits. The Dôme and the Aiguille of Polset, and the Aiguille of Péclet, and each is just over 3,500 m. The standard best route is to climb them all in one long round: but for my part I was happy just to do the Dôme, which was nearest and easiest and a good enough morning's work. So the pre-dawn frosty light was on me, now, shuffling slowly up a little path, past and round a frozen lake (above which ice-cliffs could be discerned), and then up higher over screes and hard-frozen snow.

Somewhere up front a torch was flashing; I was to have company. Somewhere behind there was a glow of light over an extending floor of mist. And above the stars and rocks.

The route to the Dôme climbs up to a shelf of ice that overhangs the lake: walkers can take off here through a narrow col, but the climber has to clamber over some loose gritty moraines and on to the fringe of the glacier. Five folk were there, fitting on crampons and waiting for the light to strengthen. A rope of four and another soloist like myself, a big youngish chap. One weighs people up in these circumstances: one looks at how long it takes them to strap up their crampons and one listens to their chatter – or if they chatter. Well he, the other soloist, looked efficient enough; but I wanted to put a distance between myself and the rope of four.

So that's how it was: I got first on the ice and was well away. A wonderful hard surface on which the crampon spikes left merely their 24 points as a trace, with the odd drift of new powder snow, and the remnants of a line of footsteps leading over the snowy downs and upward. And it was also light, and set for a perfect morning, cold, windless and clear.

On mornings like this, and over easy terrain, one seems to drift upward: the panorama expands itself, the valleys drop away, new sights appear, new peaks over new ridges: the sun edges slowly nearer, down from the summits to the faces, from the faces (which glow red and biscuit) down to the glaciers which suddenly become incandescently bright. The other soloist and I were half-way to the summit when the light caught us.

Slowly he overhauled me, going like a big red engine. There was a bit of competition in me, but not very much, so I settled down to twenty yards in his rear. Once or twice, when we got closer, we exchanged a few pleasantries which slowly became a sporadic conversation. If a crevasse appeared – and there were a few slight fracture lines across the otherwise meticulously crafted curves of the ice – we would point them out to each other. He was a forestry worker from not far away; a skier and walker who had just taken to the easier peaks. That explained the fitness, I thought. This young chap was as fit as a butcher's dog! And I was beginning to puff as we toiled up a long steepening to emerge suddenly on to an upper-level ice-field, from which the

Dôme and the Aiguille rose (the Péclet summit was a mile away to our right, to be reached by a longish ridge of rock).

Later on I would become accustomed to extraordinary panoramas, would live with them and in them: but this morning, at nine, was my first of the summer and it stretched away over a cloud sea back south to the Barre des Ecrins (hunched and silvery), to the Thabor peaks (that rose but metres above it) and north to the further peaks I had to cross and very distantly to a high cupola that could only be Mont Blanc. That cupola was my goal for the coming week; I would see it each day nearer, larger, taking on form. To the east was the white whale-back of the Arpont; west the cliffs of the Péclet.

If the peaks of the Dauphiné have a neo-Gothic architecture, those of the Vanoise are Romanesque, vaulted and arched like Norman churches, very squat and sturdy. They have already fallen down as much as they can and so they just squat there, lumpy, but (one feels) fundamentally safe mountains. This was not, as will be seen later, entirely a reliable estimate – but the Vanoise is a welcoming area in character, with grand, broad valleys and high, wide snow-fields in between. And here we were on the top of one of the best of the peaks, and Andreu (for we had now exchanged names) was explaining how he had climbed the Dôme de l'Arpont the weekend before.

That had been my plan for the morrow; to reach that or one other of the Arpont summits by way of a little bivouac hut called the Vallette. But in the course of conversation, plans were changed. Firstly, I needed more food if I was to keep up my safety system of always having plenty with me, and secondly it seemed like a good opportunity to try something bigger and better.

To the north and east, partially obscured by a drifting cumulus, was the cubic block of the Grande Casse. I had decided, after reading Andreu's guidebook, that it wasn't a peak to solo. The book spoke of crevasses, of which I had a legitimate and fully prudent fear: but with a party of two things would be very different. So the plan emerged, in the way that Conservative leaders used to emerge – by an interchange of hint and gossip. We would descend at once, smartish, and continue on down to the village of Pralognan to pick up more food, and ascend at once, that afternoon, to the hut on the Col de la Vanoise, ready to climb the Grande Casse

in the morning. That would leave me perfectly positioned to
continue; and him perfectly timed to return to his car at Pralognan.

We descended from the Dôme de Polset at a wonderful speed,
passing the rope of four (who had barely started) and were down to
the hut again before eleven.

On the descent to Pralognan an event occurred that gave the lie to
my assessment about the peaks of the Vanoise. We had both just
paused to look at a herd of chamois, outlined against the sky on an
adjacent-ridge. Below us the path descended to the valley bottom
across a broad band of screes. And while we were both turning our
eyes from the chamois to the path, up which several gaily clad
figures could be seen ascending, we saw a large mass of cliff break
away high above and start to fall rapidly, bouncing and leaping,
towards the path. There were two very large boulders, big as transit
vans, leaping 50 yards at a time. Some of the figures on the path ran
up and some of them ran down. They had to run a long way because
the two great blocks kept changing direction, and were beginning
to scatter a number of smaller blocks, not to mention great clouds
of dust. What does one do, looking up and seeing something like
that approach? The really intelligent thing would be to get rid of
one's sack, at once, and then estimate which way the boulders
would bounce – and simply dodge them. But I was glad we were a
quarter of a mile away and not having to make those decisions. The
figures ran slowly, the blocks sped fast: but somehow, no one was
in their range. With a crash like thunder they vaulted over the path
and fell into the gorge below.

We went down a little further and found some rather shaken
walkers, and a little further still and discovered a crater like a shell
hole where one of the monsters had bounced. We did not wait
around for more to fall, but continued swiftly downhill, reaching
Pralognan in the early afternoon. We both agreed it had been a fine
and exciting day, and celebrated it with a feast of bread, cheese,
tomatoes, peaches and beer.

All through the afternoon and evening we toiled up the stony
track to the Col de la Vanoise: the mountains were hidden in a thick
cloud which, just as we arrived at the Faure hut, let loose a tempest
of hail and thunder.

Contrary to my plans I spent that night in the hut. The Faure
refuge is more like a small hostel than a mountain hut, and it serves

very good food. The weather had come on so hard and violent, and
the warmth and atmosphere within were so attractive that I could
not bring myself to pitch tent outside. Andreu, my temporary
companion, and I both managed to eat an enormous quantity of
food. He because he was very big and energetic, and I because I had
the beginnings of The Great Hunger that was to continue for the
next five weeks.

The dormitories of the hut were very crowded and hot; the
lightning flashed and the thunder banged and roared all night. Gales
of sleet and hail and horizontal rain slashed at the windows or
hammered on the roof. Sleep was almost impossible because of the
noise and the discomfort. In the morning, there was no point in
even discussing conditions, for the cloud was still thick and racing,
and the ground covered with an icy slush.

I gathered my gear together again as best I could, packed up, put
on my rain-proofs, said goodbye and "bonne chance" to Andreu
and put my best foot forward.

Descending down through the mist into the valley of the Leisse I
felt depressed and anxious. The decisions to team up for the day, to
go to the Col de la Vanoise instead of the Vallette hut, to press on
now instead of waiting around for the weather to improve, had all
been sensible or companionable. But they had broken the process of
inward concentration that I had set in motion, and which I knew
was absolutely necessary.

I had become convinced that I had mislaid my ring of four rock
pitons, and that became the symbol of what I regarded as my
mismanagement. The ironmongery was, in fact, in the bottom of
my sack. I also could not find my pen, so that when I stopped I
could not trace out my track or make any of the notes on the back of
the map that I planned to make. My son had given me the pen, and
that made me think of him, and my wife, and the loving pleasures
of home. I sat down on a rock and put my head in my hands, and I
sat there for almost an hour, I think, oblivious to the cold wind and
rain; I was experiencing a complete, though mercifully brief, failure
in confidence. I unpacked, and repacked, and found both pegs and
pen. The sky began to clear, and my spirits to strengthen.

Before I started on my way again, I made sure that the pack was
perfectly balanced and very neatly arrayed: I wanted to expunge the
sense of chaos I had been feeling. Then, to mark the occasion I built

a small cairn of stones and ceremoniously fed the birds with a large piece of bread. It was as if I were beginning the journey all over again, in a better frame of mind. Thereafter, at every rest I made a little cairn, perhaps no more than three pebbles high, and left some fragment of food for whatever creature might find it. By such little rituals is confidence maintained: and now there is a line of little cairns from the Col de la Vanoise to the Gross Glockner. I came to attach great importance to this little performance and on more than one occasion returned some distance to set up a cairn if I had forgotten one. The three stones corresponded to my wife, son and daughter; the scattering of food to my wife's ritual feeding of the birds every morning. The performance served to concentrate my mind on them, and on the task in hand that had to be done before I could see them again.

This may well sound absurd, or touching; but every lone yachtsman will recognize the symptoms.

Whatever the absurdity, the ritual worked; I never lost heart again. I came down into the valley, down a steep rocky slope, crossed an old bridge, and set off north-eastward under a bright blue sky. A sentence came into my mind and would not leave, a sentence which seemed to reveal something though I could not guess what. That sentence was: "And now the healing starts."

The valley of the Leisse is deep and broad and green. On its left the flanks of the Grande Casse and the Grande Motte – crumbling walls of shale and snow-filled ravines: on its right, the shapely peak of the Pointe de la Sana, set back across an alp. The path is narrow and beautifully cared for by the park rangers. There is an abundance of flowers, pools, little streams and great streams, broad snow-beds and pleasant meadows. As it rises higher, the path threads through rocks, which are inhabited by packs of marmots. There are many chamois. As it rises higher still it comes to a lake created by a small dam, set below the precipices of the Motte.

From the lake to the top of the pass – about three miles – was all deep snow again. Perhaps in other seasons, or later in the summer, the Col de la Leisse is an easy day. This time it was very hard work indeed, under a broiling sun, that slowly cooked the right side of my face and my right forearm till they were swollen and raw.

Snow thaws from the ground upward at this time of the year in the Alps. There are hollows you fall into, treacherous surfaces breaking into water or mud or ankle-wrecking boulders. The sack felt very heavy again, and each time I fell through the surface, the headband would slip or wrench my neck. Once or twice I was up to my waist in the snow, and the last time was one yard before the summit of the pass, where four Frenchmen, who had toiled up the other side and who had been watching me from an island of rock, were there to applaud and assist. (I later read that Martin Conway and party had a wearisome time in deep snow and thick cloud in this same pass, blundering about and getting lost. For the next three days our paths were to coincide.)

The path that follows the valley of the Leisse is one of the great "grande randonnée" footpaths (G.R. 55) that thread their way over the French countryside, and these four were on their way from Lake Geneva to the sea. We had a very good conversation, there on the security of our rock, before parting. They were not attempting summits, and so were equipped solely for hard walking: but their packs were, I thought, quite heavy enough. They too, had taken punishment on their side of the pass. While we were there, a party of skiers descended from the slopes of the Grande Motte and continued, swiftly and lightly, down towards Tignes in the direction that I was to follow.

After some more floundering, northward, I struck off sharply east, traversed some stony slopes, free of the snow at last, and crossed the grassy pass of the Col de Fresse, in order to descend towards Val d'Isère.

Skis would have been useful on the crossing of the Col de la Leisse. Skis are a wonderful means of travel. But in the spring and early summer, when the snow thaws off the vegetation, the skis' edges raze the first shoots of vegetation. Much skiing makes a desert of an alp. And then when hotel proprietors bulldoze the bumps away to make a fine, smooth run, and when the contractor's wagons have churned up the pastures and the workmen driven in the pylons for the lifts where before there was gentian and daisy – then the erosion sets in. At the Col de Fresse I left the scrupulous national park and entered a disaster. The cleared tracks of the pistes, the jeep roads, the delicate curves of the descending bowl of the valley below me, stripped of their topsoil, were turning into a stony useless wilderness. As I walked down through the runnels of the gravel gullies and across new screes, three boys on hired trail bikes rough-rode past me, scattering dust and pebbles. There was no sign of any cattle.

The lack of cattle brings another hazard to these slopes, for where there is vegetation it grows long, straggly and slippery: it no longer holds the first snows of October, but lets them slide valleyward, bringing about avalanches in places where they never fell before. Lives have been lost this way, and expensive hotels pulverized.

I was to pass several such resorts on my traverse: some dealt imaginatively with this problem; but at Val d'Isère I felt disgusted with the skiing industry, and its brutality. And when, after a long and wearying descent, I got to the valley bottom and found myself beside a huge and complicated array of apartments, surrounded by elegant and indolent persons sunning themselves, playing tennis or drinking under parasols, then I was in a paroxysm of disgust. I stripped down to my shorts and had a long wash in a stream under the disapproving gaze of an elderly couple who had, clearly, not paid their many thousands of francs for their apartment only to witness some *clochard* cutting his toenails and drinking soup directly out of the pan. And then, the camp site was miles up the valley, and it was only four in the afternoon . . . so I did an evening shift.

First I walked, dangerously, horribly, through or round a series of tunnels and avalanche sheds along a road noisy with holiday traffic. Then, by chance, I found a tiny path weaving upward through steep forest and across a chapel and a farm; and thence, by a small road, and by long grassy slopes, I came to the high open glen of the Sassière, where, just before dark I made camp. Camp 6.

It is very dark and a chill air shifts slightly in the broad glen. No moon, but a multitude of stars to light my way on the silver grey unwinding track and beside the silent slab of lake. A highland March, perhaps; with the skylines cut from black nothing and the sky itself almost as black except for the busy starlight. Still no sign of dawn as I search with my torch beam up and down and across the screes for the path, if there is a path, to lead me to the ice. Turn the torch off, and feel for the path with your feet: it is there, it will take you upward. White boulders showing grey; grey boulders black; The digits of the watch gleam green. You know there are rocks ahead by the feel of the grain of the land, though there is still very little to see. White sheens of snow to the right, black crests of rock to the left, take on texture; a trail of mist illuminates itself. This is the coming of the light. A last torch beam at the rocks ahead, but now you are better without it. A new skyline appears, white and high, and a new foreground of parti-coloured boulders, grit and snow. A shelf of rocks and a slope of ice. Pause, take out axe, look about carefully. Snow like iron, interspersed with crumbly ice, like walking on glass cornflakes. Treacherous ice on the rocks where by day water must have been running. Day? It is almost day again. There is a golden top to the snow ridge to your right and a strengthening glow over the glacier that rises up to the pass. Crampons on, at a boulder. Stop, adjust pack. Eat a handful of raisins. Consider the shining downs ahead. Fumble with cold buckles and stiff knees. Three stones in a pile to bring me safely down. Hocus-pocus, porridge and gruel, don't make this route too bloody cruel. Hocus-pocus, non compos mentis, back to the valley the good Lord send us. And where is John, that made the rhyme? At the bottom of a black crevasse; skiing alone, he was, and wasn't missed for two days. And who would miss me here?

It is wise to fear glaciers and to check those three stones and to scatter the remaining raisins as libation. Check crampons, check hammer, check gloves. And step out on to the adamantine snow.

This pass, the Col de Rhème Golette, leads up into Italy. A favourite in winter for the hardier skiers. Broad ice-fields up there, and a ring of little peaks: now bathed in light. The light is up there, waiting for you, while down here it's as cold as the Florentine hell. Cold toes; are my straps too tight? Cold fingers; why am I grasping this axe so firmly? Relax, but keep watchful, for this is what you came to do. Crevasses to the right, and ahead, but there's no problem here. Just be watchful. The slopes are steep, steeper than they looked from below, but slowly you rise. Then the next crest is fringed with golden fire and you step up into full blast of the dawn and into Italy.

From the summit of this pass, a broad, undulating snow-field stretches east and south. There are several summits worth a visit, and a team without a heavy sack would find the main peak of the Tsantaleina a very fine climb. I was quite happy to climb the little Pointe de la Traversière, which at 3,368 m is the last and lowest of the Sassière group. Steep snow and a bit of a struggle, with a pack, but what a place to be on an early morning before the sun has started to melt the snow, and while there is not a cloud in the sky.

The main peak of the Grande Sassière looks Himalayan from here. Great welts and bulges of ice. From the other side it looked more like a chocolate gâteau that's been kicked about a bit. And down below, a broad glacier basin, and beyond, more peaks. The map marks paths over the interconnecting passes hereabout, but there was no sign of them this year, though there was a small cairn at the top of the point to which I added my ritual three stones. Easy descent northward down a gravelly ridge, and then steeply into the shadow again down a broad gully to the level glacier where there was no sign of crevasse. Nevertheless, I kept in close to the edge, following round to the far side and the moraine that meant some kind of safety.

The map here showed a path descending by the glacier; and there was, indeed, a small cairn, and then a second. But the glacier here plunges deeply into a gorge crammed with very dangerous terrain. In so far as there is any track, it must go round to the right, over the moraine and across that shelf – I reasoned. So I spent a mile or two picking my way across more or less level ground intersected now and again by gullies running down left into the icefall. It was easy, safe going, but where was it going *to*? There were small glaciers coming down on my right and a fine peak emerging, but I still could not see any clear way into the valley. I found a third cairn. I found a fourth, so it seemed to be the right direction. But who knows?

This section would have been very tricky in bad weather; but at length I came to a broad ridge of blocks and snow descending leftward. It took care, and crampons, to descend it. But then, quickly, it ran out into grass, and a path that descended round a shoulder of green turf. At this point I began to feel very tired.

The long descent continued, and though I rested at the first opportunity, and though I bought a bowl of soup at the refuge called the Bezzi Hut, and though I sat down at the roadhead for an hour or two and changed into my lighter footwear for valley walking, it was a very tired man who finally set up camp about a mile outside the village of Valgrisanche. Three continuously hard days had taken their toll.

The valleys on the Italian side of the range are, on the whole, steeper and rockier in this region than upon the French side. Accordingly they have not been developed for skiing, nor even for general tourism, to any marked extent. When I strolled into the village of Valgrisanche in the morning, I found a working community, a square, an old fort and a church – and not much else besides. The people here spoke a Savoyard French, but their church was emphatically Italianate, full of elaborate detail, mixing real patterned marbles with their painted imitations, real modelled cornices with cleverly drawn illusions, and with ingenious perspectival devices that made the space seem much larger than in fact it was. What was not decorated was covered with fresco painting. It was altogether an imposing piece of building for so simple a village. Perhaps it had once served the garrison of the fortress that overhung the streets and square. There was a fine carved door of ancient cracked oak, set in a frame of coarse granite. The building from without was stark, even harsh; but within luxuriant and theatrical. I sat in a pew and tried to draw a plan and some details in my little book, but so clever had the architect been that my eye was frequently deceived: moreover, the outside form of the church seemed to give no indication of the inside space of it. My drawing was not successful. I could not draw it from without, or from within: and if we forget my very slight competence as a draughtsman there seems to be a moral there – that the Protestant demands a logical integrity, so that out and in both tell the same tale. But I am Protestant by habit, not belief.

I carried a loaf of bread and a pound of cheese and a quantity of fruit back up to my tent, and took a long and lazy lunch-hour. Once again I meticulously sorted my equipment, greased my boots, wrapped up my sack and tent as tight as possible; this too had begun to acquire a ritual quality. At these times, my movements were very slow and deliberate, so as not to waste a calorie of effort, so as to gain the maximum voltage of concentration. And when I started to move again, it was very slowly, tortoise-speed, up through the steep woods above the dam of the Val Grisanche lake, and up higher by a marked path to open pastures.

That night I made Camp 8 beside the moraine of the Morion glacier, and a huge moon rose slowly into a violet-coloured sky.

Once again, I rose very early for this was to be a serious day. The Rutor ice-field lies south of the Mont Blanc range; it consists of a broad plateau fringed with rocky summits and descending north-ward by a substantial glacier. Steep valleys lead up towards the group, which on the Italian side are unfrequented. The main summit of the group, the Testa Del Rutor, stands directly above the Val Grisanche, wholly in Italy; the other peaks, just a little lower, arrange themselves along the frontier or along the eastern rim of the ice-field. There are two refuges, one to the north reached from La Thuile, and the Scavarda hut to the south (some way below which I was now toiling). The main peak of the Testa is an easy climb by its normal route, but the other peaks – especially those on the eastern rim – are steep and rocky. The maps mark a path along the eastern edge of the glacier and the plateau, linking the two huts, but there was no sign of it when I was there. There is, however, the remains of a small refuge not far from the summit of the Testa that may have been used by hunters, or possibly miners, since there are traces of mining in the region. (I am giving this description because there seems to be no account of these peaks in English, yet they are excellent mountains of the smaller kind and well worth a visit.) The best base would be La Thuile to the north, where there is a camp site, and shops, and all that is necessary for a week-long exploration of the range. English visitors to the Alps confine themselves too much to established centres and waste time in waiting for good weather on peaks that are too large, when the smaller ranges offer good climbing even in bad weather.

The crossing of the Rutor plateau was my next objective, and a task that could not be avoided since there is no way round the group without descending out of the mountains altogether. I did not anticipate difficulty, but I did expect a very long day and an extended excursion across glaciers, so an early start and good weather was essential.

Once again, a star and torchlight stumble up the boulders, slipping on icy runnels; once again the fumble with icy straps in the dark, the adjustments to the pack, the mix of sweat and shivering. A few yards from the little stony bothy of the Scavarda Hut (which seemed to be deserted), the glacier flank gave an easy access. The torch picked out a line of old footsteps on the frozen snow and these I followed across a long slope and then when they gave out I took to a broad, steep area of bare ice, always working rightward across the glacier towards some rocky humps. The footsteps reappeared again as I passed between the humps, stepped over the bergschrund and climbed directly but easily up towards the crest of the ridge. It grew lighter all the time as I climbed, and I had plenty of time to watch the antics of a little cloud that kept forming and reforming around the summit of the Testa; circling around back on itself, dissolving and condensing again. There was something strange about the cloud, and about the cast of the light and the colour of the sky just above the horizon to the north-east. A strong wind was banging about above me, but not upon me. Damn strange morning, I kept thinking. Want to watch that sky. Want to get a look north-west. Come on, now, where's that sun!

The sun and I set foot on the crest of the ridge together and everywhere was suddenly bathed in a green-gold aura. Back south, the peaks of the Sassière that I had crossed, back further south the Arpont and the Casse. Off a few points east, the Gran Paradiso range where I had been four years before, and right around to the north and east the whole array of the Valais Alps, from Monte Rosa, to the Matterhorn, to the Weisshorn, to the bulk of the Grand Combin. And then directly in front of me the Vatican structure of Mont Blanc and its satellites. The sky about them green as a Granny Smith.

A sky that colour had to be bad news; and what were those black lenticular formations building up behind . . . ?

Frank Smythe saw a sky like that on the Schreckhorn, if my memory serves me well, and was subsequently hit by a very bad storm.

No time to waste. I left my sack not far from the ruined shelter and went as fast as I could, easily, up to the summit which consisted of a little turret of rock. Directly below and to the north the broad bowl of the plateau sloped away gently, still in shadow, surrounded by its rim of peaks and points. In so far as there was any track, a line of footprints – perhaps the same I had found earlier – went off directly down the centre of the bowl to where the level ice tipped over towards the start of the main Rutor glacier. Off to the east, under the rim where the path was supposed to run, were crevasses in all directions. The wind was strong and steady from the north-west, and the sky still livid green behind the summit of Mont Blanc. No time to waste.

The descent of the Rutor glacier was unpleasant and it was only because of the early hour and the iron-hard snow that I felt safe in beginning it. There were many crevasses that could not be avoided, long snaky ones a few inches wide at the top and heaven knows how wide or deep below. What I needed there was an old-fashioned alpenstock or some very long pole. My clever little modern pick was no use here because it was not long enough to prod and poke about around the edges of each crack. I took out my hammer for one hand and for safety pinned my gloves to my cuffs. If I did end up right down some hole, and still had breath in my body afterwards, I wasn't going to hang about freezing. I reckoned that, uninjured, I might manage to get out of most of them, because they were straight-sided: I reckoned I could climb out of those . . . but the others?

It took time as well, and the sun (which in these circumstances was an enemy sun) came sweeping down the glacier from between the gaps on the eastern rim, like a big blazing searchlight turning the crisp surface into slush the moment it touched. I zigged and zagged back and forth. One or two I had to jump across, and that was no fun with my pack: and then lower down I had to cut back right below a small ice-cliff that looked as though it might fall on me. I was very happy indeed to meet the moraine and to know I was on terra firma.

There is absolutely no way solitary glacier travel of this kind can be made safe: one must, simply, be very prudent at all times, and have eyes front, back, and sides, and in the soles of one's boots. A crossing like this, alone, is not fun; one justifies it with respect to the greater objective of a completed traverse, and one embarks on it knowing exactly the risk involved and having considered every possible variant or evasion. If not, not.

But the greatest risk in any mountain travel is the trivial one of a broken ankle or a shattered wrist, and that is what I nearly got myself, coming down the boulder-field toward the Margherita hut, when (relaxed and carefree) I fell heavily on mossy stones. It knocked the breath out of my body and gave me an enormous bruise on my hip. The only injury I have ever had in the hills was caused in exactly the same way – a broken thumb amongst mossy boulders. Toward the end of the traverse I made a mental inventory of its dangers, and these were, in order of magnitude:

1. New wet snow on steep grass

2. Frozen stream beds in the early morning
3. Mossy boulders at the end of the day
4. Crossing large streams
5. Crevasses.

I was to have plenty of number one, in the next two weeks.

There was less wind at the lower altitude, but now the sky over Mont Blanc was black, and a shining haze was beginning to creep southward at a very high altitude. The barometer in the hut was sinking fast, and the guardian (with whom I got into conversation) was reckoning on three days of bad weather. My plan had been to cross from La Thuile over into the head of the Val Veni by an easy pass, and to base myself there for an attempt upon Mont Blanc. But the guardian and I agreed that would be simply wasted effort.

He showed me in the hut book the signature of one Joe Morrigone of Genoa, travelling north three days ahead of me. He too, said the guardian, was going a long way; towards Austria, perhaps. We talked about this for a while, and discussed the problems and dangers: he clearly knew his mountains well. He and his family lived at the hut all summer and catered mostly to walkers, since few mountaineers visited the Rutor peaks.

The hut itself is set in a pretty corner between the end of the glacier and a region of barren rocky slopes. There is a lake beside it and another below it; small fertile meadows abound amongst the rocks, full of wild flowers and marmots. The peaks are neat and symmetrical and the broad sweep of the glacier is of the sort one imagines. These are the mountains at their daintiest, and of all the places I had stopped in so far, this was the one I most wanted to linger in and enjoy.

This, of course, was not to be. I had to take a long descent first down to a blue shining tarn and then down into glistening dark green pine-trees and then by a very steep path beside some huge waterfalls and at last to the valley of La Thuile where I made myself a substantial lunch and thought about what to do next and tried to shelter from the rising wind (on which large drops of cold moisture were being carried).

As already described, one does not have a strict plan to adhere to on such a journey: one has objectives to meet, by a variety of possible routes, and those objectives are main and subsidiary. I thought to myself – sitting under a pine tree with my back to the wind – that the first main objective had been attained. The only thing I had failed to do, that I could have done, was the crossing of the Thabor group in its entirety. Otherwise this first section had gone very well. Four of my eight days had been mountaineering days, and the other four days had been fine walking with good passes crossed. I reckoned that I was a day ahead of schedule, and in need of a day's rest. With at least three days of bad weather in sight (since in the Western Alps bad weather days usually come in threes), there was nothing to be done on Mount Blanc. It may be the biggest peak in Europe, but I had been up there before. Better, I thought, to attempt another peak in the range, my secondary objective, The Grandes Jorasses, which (in spite of three attempts) I had never finally and completely climbed. That peak could be climbed from the Val Ferret which runs up towards the Swiss frontier and which was the way I would have to go, whatever I did or whatever the weather. I thought it might be possible to "snatch" the Grandes Jorasses, since there is no long glacier walk, no arduous approach, no tedious descent; The Grandes Jorasses is a straight-up-and-down peak that rises straight from the valley in one bound. And so, at about two in the afternoon, on a day alternately hot and sultry and cold and windy, and with the wind beginning to rage and gust, I set off walking down the main road towards Courmayeur.

The route was not as bad as I feared, for it was downhill all the way and there was not much traffic: now and again it was possible to take an old track in the woods below the road, and here and there make a short cut through steep pine-woods. There was a nasty, noisy tunnel at one place, that coincided with the arrival of a vast truck bearing logs. But by five I had descended right down into the Val d'Aosta to the little village of Pré St. Didier, and had begun to walk slowly up the valley towards Courmayeur.

A pleasant path exists on the western side of the valley, running through dense woods, while the road bends wearily up the further bank. Slowly the main range of the Mont Blanc came into view, trailing mists and glistening in evening light. Great cracks of thunder were rolling round the peaks, their sound redoubled by the echoes: rain once again was threatening. Very heavy rain.

About two miles from Courmayeur, in a glade, I pitched my tent and spent a night listening to the downpour and the thunder and the wailing and crashing of the pine-trees above my head. Around midnight water began to flow in through the zip-fastened flap and collect in puddles and rivulets on the uneven floor of the tent; wet patches spread through my sleeping bag. After some time of this discomfort (who can say how long in the circumstances, since nights like this are interminable) I unfastened the flap and peeped out, with my torch. I seemed to be lying under a waterfall in the midst of the bed of a small stream; black and silver streaks of pelting rain were coming down on every side, and great globs of moisture, gold in the torch-light, fell out of the pine-trees at every shake of the gale: the bursts and streaks of lightning were blue as flares, lighting up profiles of lashing branches, and the heaving flanks of the forest. I took out the front pegs of the tent without actually having to creep out of doors, and tried to manoeuvre myself on to higher ground; once there I lay across knotty tree roots and the water collected in the bottom of the tent, wetting my feet which until then had been dry. The "new and miraculous fabric" out of which my shelter was made never let water in, but it never let it out, either. I finished the night sitting up against the bole of a tree with my head on my knees, and so passed the hours until dawn, when the rain relented and it was possible to creep out, set up my stove and make my morning brew of black coffee.

Chapter Three

THE VALAIS ALPS: BAD TIMES

ALTHOUGH THE TOWN of Courmayeur lives upon tourism, it is old
and substantial enough to have a character. The main street is a
long, winding alley, now full of expensive shops, but retaining a
distinct quality. The new buildings blend in with the old; there are
small courtyards, ginnels and an open terrace. There is also a good
bus station with a café that opens early and in which dishevelled
persons can sit without fear of being asked to move on. I sat there
and read a five-day old paper.

A picture of a street full of smoke; an overturned car; bottles and
stones. The caption read, "The city of the Beatles is in flames."
(Ten years ago I had sat in another café not so far from here and seen
a similar photograph. Troops had been moving through a street lit
by a burning factory and then the caption spoke of Belfast.) Well,
who, knowing anything, expected anything different? Why not
loot shops and stone the police, why not burn down the pubs? Why
not abandon work altogether and clear off to the woods, or maybe
the mountains? It doesn't matter what happens to "our" society, because in no sense is it ours: we simply inhabit it, like squatters.

Such a reaction may be worth recording, not because it was
sensible but because it was spontaneous. In any sustained physical
effort, thought is difficult to express; one's being is absorbed in the
action. But thought does not stop reflecting upon itelf and upon the
scraps of material that get thrown into its den. And so when action
is suspended out comes thought again, incoherent and hungry like a
dog too long in kennel. And if an educated, well-fed, comfortably
housed and supposedly intelligent man with what used to be called
a "stake in the community" can suddenly and spontaneously enjoy
the thought of riot and mayhem, then that is worth recording.

We do not assent to the world in which we live, and the mark of
achievement within that world is to be able to escape from it: to the
woods or the mountains, into activity of any private kind. The
formal structures of our world do not command assent; we merely

3. THE VALAIS ALPS

0   30 km

--- --- route followed
.... traditional high-level route
-·-·-· intended continuations
⑨ camp-site

⑮ Simplon Pass
Brig
▲ **Weissmies** 4023m
Saas Fee
Visp
Stalden
▲ **Allalinhorn** 4027m
Augstbord Pass
⑭ (2 nights)
Täsch   Zermatt
Meid Pass
▲ **Weisshorn** 4505m
▲ **Matterhorn** 4478m
Zinal
Dent Blanche 4357m
Dent d'Hérens 4171m
Sierre
Col de Torrent
Col de Valpelline
⑬   Arolla
Les Haudères
Chanrion
Sion
▲
Gr. Combin 4314m
⑫
Bourg St. P.
Aosta
Verbier   ⑪
Orsières
Martigny
Mont Dolent 3820m
Col Ferret (2 nights)
⑩
Courmayeur
⑨
Gr. Jorasses 4208m
Chamonix
▲ **Mont Blanc** 4807m

N

put up with them. And where there is no assent there is no thought for the shared future.

I am, of course, talking to myself now, in the corner of an Italian transport café, trying to make a cup of coffee last a long time and trying to read an old, damp newspaper in a language I can barely comprehend. Rain is falling again, a steady cold drizzle out of clouds the colour of cast iron, and I am waiting here for a bus to take me up to the Val Ferret, from whence I will be turning my face eastward.

The Val Ferret is a broad trench running south-west to north-east below the Italian side of the Mont Blanc range; the same formation extends over a low pass into Switzerland as the Swiss Val Ferret, and south-westward into the Val Veni – where I had planned to be – and thence further. On the one side, the successive spurs and buttresses of granite, like the blocks above Central Park; on the other, open grassy fells. Every mile up or down this trench brings a new vista of peaks and glaciers as each spur is passed; though today the cloud was obscuring everything above the level of the last pine-tree. The bright yellow post-bus swung and swirled its way around the hairpins and set me down at the highest inhabited spot, called Tronchey. Twenty years ago you never saw anyone there, but now each summer there is a substantial camp site, with all conveniences. When I first came there ours was the only tent in the valley, but there is still no sense of crowding, and almost no building.

I set up my tent, showered and did my laundry, and tried to keep warm.

I spent two nights at Tronchey, making myself comfortable and doing my best to overcome the real mountain hunger that had built up in the past nine days. I dried and mended clothes, and reproofed the seams of my tent; I slept and lazed about, though it was too cold to be restful. Though not much rain fell, a strong wind blew down the valley; when the clouds cleared for a minute or two, one could see the peaks deep under new snow. Once there was a vision of the big hill itself, Mont Blanc, Moby Dick, the big white one, trailing a great plume of blizzard. At other times, nothing but a scudding greyness. A party of French scouts was camping near me, and I drank coffee with them; they were following the path that circles round the range, camping every night, and they, like me, had got wet and cold in the great storm and were waiting for the weather to clear before crossing into Switzerland. I also made friends with an English couple from Hitchin; we gossiped about climbing, about which huts were good and which bad, about foreign travel, about epic bad weather, and we drank a bottle of wine or two. I spent some time trying to draw the landscapes, but they were never visible for long enough. On the second night there it came on to storm again, violently, and it became colder than I had ever known it in the Alps before at valley level. Even if the weather were to improve dramatically on the morrow, there would be no safe climbing for three days after such a weight of snow: morning revealed a snow-line down to within a few hundred feet of the valley floor.

It was Monday: my new friends drove down into Courmayeur and I went with them to pick up fresh supplies and mail: their little daughter prattled on about her toys. She made me understand her rabbit had gone up the mountains.

That midday we returned and I packed up, and all together we drove the last three or four kilometres to the end of the valley, and I started on my way again, up the easy path over the Col Ferret. Somewhere ahead was the party of scouts.

The last ten days had been like holiday; now it was for real, I thought. Now the greater Alps begin.

In order to explain my wanderings and miseries during the next week, it is necessary to describe a little geography.

The old and original High-Level Route was devised to give swift passage over the peaks and glaciers between Chamonix and Zermatt. It runs from Chamonix over one of three possible high glacier cols to the Swiss side of the Col Ferret (whither I was bound), and then passes over high hills to the village of Bourg-Madame just below the St. Bernard pass. It then crosses the southern flanks to the Grand Combin peaks – at this point reaching 3,600 m – and descends to the Chanrion alp from which a number of possible variants converge on the Col de Valpelline above Zermatt. This last section is all glacier travel, and needs good conditions underfoot and overhead. My aim had been to follow this venerable way, taking in one or two summits, and restocking supplies at the village of Arolla. The longest glacier section of the Col de Valpelline I planned to avoid by taking in the summit of the Dent Blanche. All this was entirely feasible and well thought out. Moreover, I knew the way well, having traversed all parts of it at least once, and, twenty years before, having done the whole High-Level Route in the reverse direction with my wife. One secret aim was to visit the places where we had made camp and see how I could recall them, and to write to her from them.

The Valais Alps fall steeply down into Italy, with short glaciers, steep stony valleys and precipitous forests. The crest of them provides the linked section of easy glacier passes that the High-Level Route employs. To the north a series of long spurs, each a mountain range in itself, projects towards the wide and deep valley of the Rhône. There are five of these spurs or ranges. Therefore the easiest way between Chamonix and Zermatt is the most direct: to diverge off into Italy means a great loss of height to be regained and only a few decent crossings back into Switzerland; and to diverge off northward means five successive mountain crossings, each problematical, and each involving considerable effort. Some of these five successive crossings are high and icy, and all are hard work. Imagine a hand, a right hand laid flat on the table, fingers outspread; now imagine a beetle crossing that hand from left to right. The wise beetle will take the high road over the knuckles; the foolish or unfortunate beetle will toil up over the thumb down to the level, up over the first finger and down, up over . . . I ask the reader to remember that hand and that wretched insect. This chapter is in five parts – one for each digit.

Rounding the thumb.

The crossing of the Col Ferret is similar to crossing from Langdale to Wasdale in the Lake District. A good walk on a decent path, over grassy fells (in summer) or a snowy trek (in winter). Now it was winter, or as good as. The great smooth sweep of steep grass that runs up to the pass on the Italian side was covered with several inches of damp snow lying on wet vegetation. Several snowslides and miniature avalanches had occurred and were occurring as I crossed. Nothing in themselves to be concerned about; but I had a heavy pack on my back and at times the path wound above steep gullies into which a fall was not to be considered. You only have to be knocked off your feet in such circumstances to be in trouble. And as the weather improved and the fitful sun grew hot, the snow grew wetter and more slippery. Several other parties were descending towards me, from Switzerland, moving cautiously.

The sun came out more firmly for a while, and there were views of the Dolent ice-fall, and of the ends of long steep ridges: but the summit of the pass was in thick cloud. I passed over into Switzerland in a squall of hail. All down the long descent it hailed, or rained or snowed, and the path from being icy became muddy and the hillsides treacherous. I would vary the balance of the pack, from headband to shoulders and back to head, but whichever way it was, it hurt. But this, I assured myself, was what it was all about.

The path descended to some chalets and here it coincided with the old and original Route. To follow that – on towards the knuckle of the thumb, so to speak – I would have to climb up over another pass and continue toward Bourg-Madame and the great mound of the Grand Combin. But this, I had already decided, was out of the question since a full metre of new snow must be lying on the high Sonadon glacier: that, I knew from the past, was not a place to fool with in bad weather. In so far as I had any plan at all, it was to round the point of the thumb to see what weather the next day brought with it.

But here, if the physical conditions were bad, there was a pleasure. A new map, and a new vision.

A map is a language, and it must be learnt. The French 1:100,000 map is a good practical thing, but it wholly lacks style when set beside the Schweizer Landeskarte of the same scale. Each sheet of the Swiss map is a wonderful communication, a heavenly telegram of compressed information. It is the only shaded map that does not obscure its object – the real terrain. Though the old British Ordnance Survey is the most informative of all, the new shaded tourist maps are clumsy instruments beside their Swiss equivalents. The delicacy and finesse of the drawing is surpassed only by the very best Italian maps – but these, alas, are almost unobtainable.

And the change of map was also symbolic of my progress, since the peak above the Col Ferret is the peak where the frontiers of three great nations meet, and the slushy water running at my feet was to descend into the Rhône, whilst that behind me ran into the Po; and although I was still walking northward (now down a jeep track toward the head of the road at La Fouly), yet in an important sense I had turned a corner and was on my main highway, strutting like a sparrow on the roof-tree of the continent.

This appealed to my sense of topography, and in spite of the cold and sleet I was immensely cheerful and determined. I had in my mind – almost like a physical form, it was so vivid – a model of the whole of the Alpine region. Any part of this model I could suddenly enlarge, or bring into focus: it seemed I could pick it up and turn it round, it was so present to me. And this model was not simply concerned with the surface of things but was conceived like a geologist's map, of strata upon strata of rock, like a crumpled bed, planed off by glaciers old and new, faulted and crushed, but always logically and inevitably constructed. On my left now, the huge granitic intrusions of Mont Blanc – here breaking up into meta-morphosed shales: and on my right the shales and schists and burnt up limestones of the Valais Alps. This valley was their demarcation.

I went cheerily down the track, enjoying the sense of having started the second major section of my Grand High-Level Route. I met the French scouts again, pitching their camp at La Fouly, and talked with them for a few minutes; and then began the long descent of the Swiss Val Ferret.

A very pleasant path, now narrow and now almost a road, runs down the western, left-hand bank of the river. Sometimes it is in open scrubland, at other times in thick forest: once or twice it is high and narrow above a gorge. I think I met no one in the whole long ten mile descent. The weather now was cold and windy, but dry; and I went at the task with speed. My aim was to reach a camp-site at Orsières where my wife and I had camped once, twenty years before, and from there to improvise according to the weather. At length the path divided, and a small signpost directed me rightward across the top of a heavily forested and very old moraine ridge back to the road. Here, to spare my feet, I changed into my light training shoes, and with boots fastened to my pack, went steadily on down the road. (All through the whole traverse I was constantly changing my footwear in this way, and I am quite certain that it prevented ankle or tendon strain.)

But when I got into Orsières, well tired from a good 25 mile march, there was no trace of the former camp-site. I remembered an open field beside the railway station, and a wooden barn, and a

steep bit of hill above the town. None of this was there (though
there was a large hotel, a woodyard, a bar and a row of houses). I sat
in the bar and drank a large beer, disconsolately. There was, I was
told, no *camping* in the town.

The trouble with the Swiss valleys is that you can't just doss
down anywhere, because the least bit of decent ground is used.

So I had another long four or five miles down the main road to
the village of Sembrancher, where (oh miracle!) beside the bridge
was a pleasant site, with a small restaurant. The site was run by
three old ladies, sisters, who were very cheerful cooks, and loaded
up my plate with as much veal and chips as I could eat, and then
laughed and exclaimed at my tent. All around were brightly-
coloured canvas pavilions, with lamps and cookers, electric irons
and television sets.

The first finger.

Sembrancher is the point of the thumb of the outstretched hand
of the Valais Alps: at the head of its valley lies the Chanrion hut
through which all variants of the High-Level Route must pass. My
task was to get from Sembrancher valley over to the Arolla valley,
which would take (I reckoned) a mimimum of a day and a half by
way of Chanrion. The hut and its meadows can only be reached by
a very long walk up the valley road, up which there is no public
transport: my "ground rules" allowed me to use such transport if it
existed, or to hitch my way. But in the morning it was still heavily
overcast, and the prospect of the glacier crossing in deep snow and
bad weather was not attractive. In the Appendix I have set out a
range of possible alternatives, but all of those passing through
Chanrion seemed at that moment out of the question. In retrospect,
I think I might well have successfully done the easiest crossing by
way of the Dix hut and the so-called Pas de Chèvres, the way I had
gone so many years before; but hindsight is a comfortable sort of
vision.

I determined to cross the tip of the first finger by a roundabout
low-level walk over a series of supposedly easy passes, starting at
the ski resort of Verbier. To make the going lighter I also decided to
send a quantity of equipment round by post-bus to Zermatt to
await arrival.

Verbier was reached first by a little train and then by the post-bus:
it is a colony of hotels and chalets climbing up a huge smooth alp

and a place of no interest. After depositing my lightweight sack, containing my trainers, spare clothes and some other items, at the post office, I went out and found a bookshop where I, rather surreptitiously, made a quick sketch map of the twenty or so miles beyond the reach of my map. I discovered that the immediate task in hand was to get into the head of the little Val de Nendaz; but thereafter, all was vague.

By midday I was following a path above the resort that was marked to the "Col des Mines". No such place existed on my map, but it "looked right". I was seeking to find a line or a linked series of paths that I could follow without much loss of height, and without having to attempt the snowed up ridges around the peak called Mont Fort. The peaks round here are steep and grassy, and that was what, in these conditions, I wanted to avoid. This path led me round into a deep corrie or cwm below what were evidently old mine workings, and from here, without benefit of path, I had to work my way up a steep but snowless hillside on to a further ridge. The weather was misty but pleasant, and was just clear enough to make out below the vineyards of the Rhône valley and the steep forested hillsides that descended to it. Round the corner of this ridge I could see no good way directly forward, so I cut back up into thick cloud and came out on the shoulder of what I think was called Le Parrain – on the first joint of the "finger".

Up here I was on the snowy ground I had meant to avoid, but at a level stretch – a sort of plateau that seemed to extend eastward.

In the first chapter I remarked that one may not know where one is, without being lost: that was my position at that time. Being well-equipped with food, it hardly mattered what I did so long as I didn't injure myself; so I took an eastward compass bearing and set off along it. Just plodding along in hope over the boulders and snowdrifts. As I did so I encountered another path travelling more or less the way I hoped to go, so I followed that path; it led me across some hummocky hills and once again to a crest overlooking a hollow. Some way across, perhaps two miles away, a line of pylons ran up the hills and over: one of the ski-lifts that I had on my surreptitious sketch map. I crossed down to this over some steep ground, very slippery under the wet snow, and came out beside a pretty little tarn and at the head of a track descending into the head of a valley. This was, certainly, the head of the Val de Nendaz.

By now it was a pleasant evening, with the cloud clearing off the little mountains I had crossed, and a balmy breeze wafting up from the depths of the Rhône trench where a late sun was still glowing on the vineyards. A boy was herding cattle down below me, and their massed bells seemed to hum they were so many and so continuous their ringing. I made camp beside a cleared ski-trail and tried to sleep for as long as possible, not knowing what the next day might bring.

A high pass links the Val de Nendaz with a swift route at a higher level to Arolla, but the persistence of the mist made me continue at this height when the day broke and when I was once more on my way. The upper Nendaz valley is occupied by a purpose-built ski resort; two tower blocks called Super-Nendaz. They seemed, at this time, to be deserted. From this place climbs an array of ski-lifts and descends a multitude of ski-tracks – a kind of snakes and ladders landscape now devoid of players. I walked slowly and steadily along a track that traversed above the resort and which, after a full hour or more gave out on a broad shelf of alp overlooking the Rhône valley.

The weather, at last, was fine for walking (though uncertain for climbing). Over the Bernese Alps the clouds had cleared away to give a wonderful panorama; I amused myself by imagining a second long traverse to be done, along their crest. Martin Conway and party had gone that way in the course of their journey. They had made a traverse of the whole Bernese Alps in admirable style, but then taken a rather eccentric meander through Central Switzerland. I was only to meet their route again in Austria.

I found that what I was following was a track cleared by the hotel companies in order to service their ski-lifts: every now and then I came to the head of a descending row of pylons, now cableless. Up to my right there was a rock ridge, powdered with snow: down to my left, a mile away, the edge of the forest falling off into the deep valley. Far down on the left, vineyards and villages and the entrenched banks of the mud-coloured Rhône. The track was almost level, and I was making good progress, now gently up and now gently down, following the grassy shelf and contouring round the end of the "first finger". To find this track was a piece of great good fortune. At one place it gave out, and I had to descend into another bowl and climb out the other side of it over steep scrub; but it led me steadily on, in one form or another, almost uninterruptedly round headland after headland till I suddenly, around midday, emerged overlooking the Val d'Hérémence, at the head of which Arolla is situated.

This was a wonderful lookout point, with views over the Bernese Alps to the north and to the east and south a splendid panorama of all the great peaks of the Valais Alps, free of cloud at last. I sat down to identify them – from the notched pyramid of the Weisshorn, to the gables of the Rothorn and the Gabelhorn, to the crooked spire of the Matterhorn, to the humpbacked Dent Blanche, to the array of lesser but still inspiring mountains around Arolla. They were all clearly visible, glistening with a silvered or metallic shine under a hazy and uncertain sun. At my feet, the slopes ran down steeply into a thick forest that continued down into the depths of the valley; up to the right, at the end of one branch of the valley was the huge wall of the Dix barrage, that is the centre of a vast hydro-electric complex. (Had I gone over the range that morning instead of coming round its end, I would have descended to the dam.)

A ski-lift ran up to this balcony and there were many people about in the lightest of summer clothes. Although the lift was not working, it was clear these elegant and above all clean *personnages* had not walked there.

This problem was solved in the next hundred yards, when, climbing over a little rise I found myself looking down onto a huge complicated building, surrounded by tennis courts and swimming pools. Balconies, verandas and patios were stacked one on the other in interlocking and ingenious patterns; there were bright awnings, amber-coloured brickwork and massive timber beams. This construction, I soon discovered, was called "Thyon 2000". Three weeks later I was to encounter another, even more remarkable one-piece resort, called Kurzras, on the Austro-Italian border. I walked all round the building and took photographs of it from several angles: my conclusion was that such resorts offer an opportunity for the realization of one of the dreams of the modern designer – that of the totally contained community. This place was a small town under one roof, devoted to pleasure and health; a sort of healthy-life utopia. The site, of course, was magnificent; but the architecture measured up to it.

It is hard to compete with traditional Alpine architecture for correctness and efficiency of style: most new buildings simply fall in line and imitate the vernacular as best they can. At times they do this well, since some modern techniques and habits, such as rough walling and long eaves, fit well with the traditional – are, in fact, an extension of the traditional; but at other times the effects are of extreme vulgarity – over-varnished and over-decorated woodwork applied to the outside of an urban tower-block. Here, on this coign of vantage, overlooking the finest view in Europe (well – possibly!) the architects had put together what was mainly an urban style. There was nothing nearby to make this seem compromised or ridiculous.

My opinion, after a good few years watching tourism spread over the Alps and our own mountains, is that centres like this act as condensers of activity and are much to be preferred to the sprawl of the unplanned resort. They make more human sense, since for the most part holiday-makers want to have facilities easily to hand, and rarely walk very far from them. And they make good ecological sense in that the damage to the natural fabric of the countryside is within a controllable compass. I had noticed, as I had walked along the grassy slopes during the morning, the great care with which the ski-runs had been treated. A fine mix of chopped straw and tar or some similar nutrient but bonding material had been sprayed over surfaces denuded by clearing or by steel edges of skis. In some places, nylon nets had been set into the ground to retain topsoil. As a result, no erosion was taking place. The immediate area of the resort was being trimmed into a parkland.

This was so much an improvement on the desolations around Val d'Isère that I had to praise what I otherwise wanted to blame. Those who, so to speak, work for their pleasures in the mountains (and I reckoned I was one of them) always are tempted to resent the idle sort of tourist, and it is very easy to get into a superior frame of mind.

From Thyon I set off downhill, still not knowing exactly where I was or which direction to take. The weather was, it appeared, about to improve and so it was essential that I should be back more or less on my planned course by that evening. I had now gone well off my map, and had to work partly by guesswork. Fortunately the valley in front of me – the Val d'Hérémence – was open as a fallen book.

A bold new road descends from Thyon, but not (so far as I could tell) in any direction useful to me. I did not want to take a ride back down into the Rhône trench only to have to climb right out of it. So I walked straight on down through the pine-woods and steep meadows, aiming for what I thought would be the most appropriate place, at an intersection of the main valley with the valley leading up to the great Dix barrage. Here I would meet the main road up the valley and hope to take a bus. The pleasure I found in this descent was increased by a sense of relief – I had actually found my way around the top of the first finger without getting lost or wasting time. After an hour or more of descent, singing cheerfully to myself most of the time, I came upon another small resort – a colony of sanatoria and villas. Here a shop was *giving away* food. Yes, a huge box of bananas stood by the door, for anyone to help themselves to. They were old and brown-skinned, certainly; but there was nothing wrong with them. It may be that the sort of people who live in such places prefer their bananas with fresh yellow skins: but after two weeks of hard grinding work one loses pride in such nice matters. To the amazement, and I think the disgust, of the girl at the till I filled up the top of my sack with them, then filled a plastic bag with more and went on my way rejoicing.

Below this colony the hillside grew steeper, and interspersed with farms and chalets. Little paths could be followed down terraced meadows and beside irrigation channels, past barns and small farms. Sometimes I crossed a narrow winding road, and sometimes I followed it; but for the most part I went straight on down the hillside by these paths till I came to the village of Hérémence, which hangs on the slope rather like a swallow's nest on a farmhouse wall. Beside a water spout I sat and ate my bananas; or rather, all those I had not already eaten whilst walking and singing my way down there. Some village children came out to look at me, and this is what they saw: a stringy sort of fellow, almost bald, wearing a pair of old patched shorts and heavy boots, with a dirty cotton cricket-hat on his head. This person was very badly sunburned all the way down his right side and not burned at all down his left side; he was not very clean and he was very sweaty, and his nose was burned as bright red as his sack: and he was sitting there, in the middle of their pristine street, thrusting bananas, whole, one after another, down his throat. From the appalled expression on these childlike faces I knew that I had become the sort of person my parents told me to avoid.

I had now descended 3,000 feet, and the climate and vegetation had changed accordingly. It was very hot, and the undergrowth in the steep, even precipitous woods below Hérémence was thick and thorny. Rank nettles grew chest high among the bramble patches; stinging flies assailed me. The little road I followed dwindled first to a track, then to a path, then to a line of broken stems in a jungle of spines and scratches. I forced myself through a cliff-steep maze of dogwood and thorn-trees, and at last fell, rather than stepped out on to the road, about a mile from the village of Euseigne. Euseigne is noted for its famous pillars of eroded clay, that feature in all geology textbooks: but I barely noticed them, since a bus arrived at the same time as myself.

My fourteenth night I spent outside the village of Les Haudères, just down the valley from Arolla (where I had first planned to be). I was now in the gap between the first and second fingers of the "hand", well placed to avail myself of good weather, if good weather came.

Les Haudères is another village overtaken but not spoiled by tourism. There are some quaint streets between high walls of black-brown timber, there are whitewashed stones, a few shops of a practical kind and a pleasant square. There is also a large restaurant that served an inexpensive meal.

As usual when in a Swiss valley, one asks for directions to a camp site: here it was expensive. What was the alternative? "Ah," said the lady in the tourist office, waving her arms expansively at the forests and the mountains, "*Il faut aller dans le sauvage.*" That meant, on this occasion, walking half a mile out of the streets and up into a valley and finding a stretch of level gravel set around with willowscrub and thistles. As I pitched tent it started to rain and to thunder again, and to come on dark and stormy very quickly. Not wanting just to lie there in the two or three hours before nightfall, I walked back into the village.

Whoever traverses the Alps does more than take a cut through the many-layered and much folded pastry-cake of their physical geology; such a person cuts through an equally intricate, many-layered, enfolded and crumpled landscape of languages. Here, in the Val d'Hérémence, we are at the fault-line between French and

German. The names on the shop-fronts are, more or less, Germanic; but the villages are named in dialect French, which is overlaid with standard Swiss French – rather like custard over pudding – to make it go down easily. It is also, though Catholic in liturgy, Lutheran in style. The little church just out of the village, was plain, even severe, in its decoration. I sat there partly out of curiosity, partly to get out of the rain, and partly out of respect. Plain wooden pews, a renovated structure, decorative arts that were not quite traditionally peasant, not quite modern but some quite effective mix between. Some new glass, too. While I was sitting there, completely silent, and in a sort of daze, I heard footsteps in the organ loft over the door. There were the sounds of a case or cupboard being unlocked, of paper being shuffled, of a stool being pulled up to a table or a keyboard: and then, hesitantly and with several revisions, the sounds of a Bach Prelude and Fugue. Which one? No idea. But to sit there, listening to that grand intricacy . . .

The playing slowly improved and strengthened and grew in confidence. Really good music – and really good plays, for that matter – can survive almost any performance. Quality pardons ineptitude and exposes and transcends pretentiousness. Whoever was playing in the organ loft was no more than a competent amateur, stumbling over the tricky passages and far more concerned with getting the right notes than with the problems of expression; and yet the wonderful engine of sound began to move under its own power.

Outside the rain continued to fall, not heavily but steadily and without even the slightest intermission. Night and darkness, lit with flickers.

I went into the bar on the square and sat with my maps for the next hour, planning some sort of strategy. There at Les Haudères was the best possible place for a crossing over to Zermatt. A long steady day up to the Rossier Hut on the Dent Blanche and a second half-day crossing over the shoulder of the Dent – perhaps with a visit to the summit – before descending easily and safely into the head of the glacier basin at Schönbiel. This is the best way for a soloist, certainly, for there are no extended glacier crossings. A long glacier crossing was to be avoided after almost a week of snowy weather, for any tracks would be hidden and the small crevasses covered up. In such conditions, going high is going safe. But to go high one must have decent weather: at least weather you can stand up in. The way conditions were now, there had to be a great storm ranging around the Dent Blanche – a full blizzard, lightning, gale, the lot. What other alternative did the map offer? Well – I could go up to Arolla and take the easy Collon Pass over into Italy and work my way around by some lower peaks and passes on the other side of the Val Pelline, so that somehow – sometime – I would get to Breuil which was on the other side to the Matterhorn to Zermatt; and then hope for decent weather to get over the frontier. But that would be a frightful trek and of uncertain outcome. The next best thing would be to cross over to the head of the Moiry valley, reach the Cabane du Moiry, and from there descend to Zinal – a very long day – and follow that with a traverse round the north flanks of the Weisshorn, arriving three days later at Tasch. That interested me most, because it was at Tasch I proposed to camp, and it would give me another day before going high in which the weather might – just might – improve. And then there was the third possibility; to cross the Col de Torrent and come down to the Moiry lake and get round into the Zinal valley by a lower line. From here, on the following day if there was no improvement in the weather, I could continue with a similar long trek over the Meid pass into the Turtmanntal, followed by another great flog over the Augstbord pass to the foot of the Zermatt valley. To take the image of the hand again; I was at the top of the gap between the first and middle fingers. To cross the middle finger, since the "knuckle route" was impassable, I would have to take the first joint or the second joint.

Once again, I would be going off the map. And that suggested a final alternative: to stay where I was until good weather came. At another time this might have been good counsel, but this season the weather was so cold and so persistently bad that I felt sure at least two more days of it were bound to come. Moreover, there is a certain matter of morale and impetus to be considered. I was now beginning to feel very fit and had gathered up a great steam of enthusiasm; to pause now might waste that valuable asset –confidence. I decided that whatever the weather did next day, I would set off in one of my three directions.

By torchlight I sought out my tent "dans le sauvage" and spent another restless, thunder-woken night.

At four in the morning it was still raining, and my automatic alarm clock would not stop ringing: I mean the automatic self-awakening and adrenalin-dispensing system that comes with every brain but only gets used in unusual circumstances. I made my coffee, ate a handful of oats (uncooked) and then, rapidly, uncocooned myself from bag and tent and, in the half-light and the drizzle, packed my sack. The weather had made the decision for me: it would have to be the Col de Torrent.

Just outside the village a sign post said "Col de Torrent 4 h. 45 min." The Swiss are a precise people.

The path over this pass is an old mule trail, well marked and easily found: mostly at an easy gradient, passing farms and chalets and winding its way up a huge grassy hillside towards a rocky crest. It was, this time, invisible in thick mist: but because the path was well marked I was able to hand over to my other self-regulating mechanism, the automatic pilot. The automatic pilot takes you wherever you want to go, at his own pace, leaving the passenger free to reflect, doze, admire the scenery (when it is visible), and abstract himself from the immediate task in hand. The wise passenger leaves the automatic pilot to get on with the task, and does not question why the journey stops from time to time, or why refuelling takes place here and not there. The foolish passenger interferes with his pilot and says: "Stop at that point for five minutes," or "Now it's time for a bite." The automatic pilot never listens to a foolish passenger, except now and again to a bit of music. Bach is good, and since the night before I had had Bach on the brain. A clear, steady continuo to help the legs. Jee-eesu joo-oy of *man's* desi-iring da de da de dadada. At other times, it may be nonsense chanting, and I had developed one or two good pieces of jabberwocky. One was in a species of French and had some reference to life assurance – perhaps suggested by an advertisement I had seen. Others were counting chants – *one* two three four *one* two three four. And so on, for four and three-quarter hours.

The rain ran down my cape, the long grass wet my boots, the mist gave way to impenetrable cloud stirred by a sluggish breeze that was more a shifting of the air than a purposeful wind. At length I was on the boulder-strewn moor, treading on a thin crust of snow, with a light sleet falling past me without aim. The cloud was still impenetrable, though the path was always clear and always straight ahead traversing left and traversing right. I met no one.

After four hours of this there was a certain lightening and one began to see forward and upward: I seemed now to have climbed to an altitude between the valley cloud and the high storm clouds. Now it was snowing steadily and all the ground was white. Snow at 2,700 m. Bad sign. And there was a hole in my cape where the point of my axe had torn it. Rain came through, and then snow.

A long last slope of snow-covered scree led to the Col – a miserable place, where I crouched out of the wind, switched off my automatic pilot and considered again what to do. From here I could descend southward to go round the head of the Moiry lake and seek out the hut, or I could descend northward, to the left, to the dam that held the lake, and from there improvise a way around to Zinal. Or so I thought.

The descent was harder than the climb, in deeper snow and in the teeth of the wind. My cape tore still further, so I took it off. I scrabbled down steep and slippery grass toward a level shelf, and then around and down a muddy trail. The sky was grey and the ground was also grey – a mixture of slush and faded grass.

And then, as I descended, the greyness became suffused with the colour of lapis lazuli dissolved in milk and, very faintly at first and then steadily louder as the colour spread and swelled, the steady roaring of a flume. The colour stretched out beneath my feet and seemed to rise up before me, deepening and strengthening, as did the roar, the full-throated roar of the water. The whole valley below me and across was roaring lapis lazuli, without outlines or shapes or any sort of distinction. And then in a few yards I came to the edge of the mist and saw I was looking down on to the blue, the deep milky blue of the Lac du Moiry, and the great roaring was of its waters falling into a shaft beside the dam, that stretched as taut as a rope across the valley's throat. I was standing on a grassy spur looking down on to the lake's surface, while across from me a break in the clouds revealed the easy grassy pass that would lead over to Zinal. Once again my mapless wandering had led me to the right place.

There are parts of the Alps, and this was one of them, in which water has an adventurous existence; though Nature may intend some single molecule to make its way to ocean by way of the Po and the Adriatic, man's intervention so organizes affairs that it finds itself bound for the Rhône. Rivers are reversed; lakes engulf themselves and reappear spurting from a mountainside beyond the next valley, glacier torrents are spiralled back through the peaks that gave them birth, prodigious pipes rise and sink out of the earth and, most unexpected of all, a stream may suddenly be swallowed into a shaft and never be seen again (except on the other side of the range). For this reason it is important to have an up-to-date map, that shows the lakes that have valleys and the valleys that have lakes, that shows just what might happen next year as well.

So it is that you encounter, in remote places where the tracks if they exist are faint and where you expect no trace of human activity beyond that of shepherds, massive bulwarks of concrete, echoing tunnels reamed out of the granite, projections of iron having an obscure relationship with certain pieces of modern sculpture. Because they have no obvious use, these *travaux* are as much like art as industry; we sense their connections with immense forces and purposes unknown to us, like barbaric fetishes; they hardly belong to the human culture that we experience. And the adventures of water, too, become for us a complicated analogy to the spirit – damned, diverted, drawn back into itself, made to go whither it was not intended, set to complicated works to purposes hidden underground – and then suddenly emerging with a shattering energy in the most unlikely of places.

On the dam there was a large board that described how water was brought underground and over mountains to the Lac de Moiry, and thence to some other place. Beside the board I peered over one side and looked down a cliff of gleaming concrete for 600 or more feet to the grass and rocks: on the other side I looked over into an enormous, sucking plughole. The water raced around it with a steely smoothness before vanishing, and the sound it emitted was as palpable as granite. Imagine a volcano *in reverse*; such was the source of the noise that filled the valley.

At the far end of the dam was a café and a road-head (the road emerging from a dripping tunnel). I sat in here a while and drank a glass of lemon tea: there was a large map to study. The café was empty except for the waitress and a couple, who sat silently some tables away; the rain dripped from me and made a pool at my feet.

Paths in plenty led into the valley, and, yes, certainly there would be no trouble in reaching Zinal that night.

But to what purpose? The rain came down with redoubled force outside and once again the thunder was roaring and the sky utterly black. My plastic cape was now useless and the rain had got down my neck. If I got wet now I would be wet for three days till I could get round to Zermatt.

I now regretted having sent my spare clothes and gear to Zermatt by the post bus, since it meant a long (and possibly expensive) journey. With that bag of stuff, I would be once again footloose. I could stay here, if I wanted, with plenty of dry clothes to change into, and spare footwear, and above all my extra maps for the next section beyond the Simplon Pass. But now I was committed to Zermatt. It had been a bad mistake.

I made a decision to improvise: I would set off down the road into the Val d'Anniviers. If I managed to get a lift I would go as far as I could; but if not I would stop at one of the villages on the way down, and start working my way up over the Meid Pass. An hour later I was clumping down the innumerable hairpin bends through the forest above the village of Grimentz when the first and only car that passed me, stopped. It was the couple who had been sitting in the café at the dam. This was a real stroke of luck and such that was needed, for they took me down through the torrential rain and through the clouds, down through the gorges and windings of the valley, right down to the vineyards and melon-fields and motorways of the Rhône valley, dropping me off in the station courtyard at Sierre.

It was still raining and cold, even down there, 6,000 feet lower.

That evening I arrived at Täsch in the Mattertal, about four miles below Zermatt, walked through the dripping woods, and found my appointed camp-site. Camp 14. Under an overhanging boulder. Once again, it rained all night. It rained all the next morning, too, and most of the afternoon: and what fell as rain in the valley, fell as snow above tree-level. Between the third and the little fingers.

But it was not all bad: I walked up the valley to Zermatt in my wet clothes, to collect my dry clothes, and walked back. I cooked and ate several large meals one after another, squatting in the shelter of my rock. I held converse with two rats that shared it with me, and gave them crumbs and bits of sausage-skin. I talked with a Dutch family, camping nearby, and drank some coffee with them. I had a warm shower and did some necessary laundry and repairs.

I was at Täsch for two reasons: the first because there is the best point from which to set out for a crossing of the Allalinpass to Saas-Fee, and the second because fellow-members of the Alpine Club were to arrive there as part of a club meet. The chances of crossing the mountains looked remote, and I was now five days ahead of schedule and not expecting to meet anyone I knew – so I greeted a British car with pleasure. It contained two tough-looking, elderly men and a heap of gear. Together we listened to weather forecasts, drank tea, and gossiped about high-level routes. They had done plenty of those, over the years, and had visited most of the places I had been on winter ski tours. One of them had, in several stages spread over several winters, done a complete traverse much like mine. We all three had an enjoyable meal together that evening, at a restaurant in Täsch village.

I spent that night gathering up my concentration again for the next task in hand – reaching the Simplon Pass. The last few days had been continuous friction.

Between the Saastal and the Simplon Pass is an area of ridges and moors that, as it goes south, develops into high mountains. There is one broad, easy pass – the Zwischbergen Pass, well to the south, and two high mountain crossings. But there is also a complicated connection of valleys well to the north. I had a description of this crossing copied from the English language guidebook: the book describes it from east to west, so I had attempted to transcribe it west to east. With this description I left Saas-Balen, a little village and hotel centre, and started climbing an endlessly long steep hill of pine-trees. The path was marked with the usual red and white flashes of paint: but when (around ten in the morning) the trees ran out and great grassy hillsides swept with cloud succeeded, the marks grew fainter and fewer. I followed a valley eastward on a narrow path that was sometimes hidden in snow, and then a shade northward and then due north up yet another steep hillside. Though not lost, I did not know where I was with any accuracy; my map had nothing like enough detail for such a crossing. But I went by dead-reckoning and guesswork and crossed the first ridge into the head of the little Nanz valley.

Unfortunately I came over the wrong pass – or rather, over no known pass at all – and came down on the western side of the river instead of passing round its head on to the eastern side. The river was in a deep cleft, and I had to descend the valley for a long way till I encountered a track and a bridge. Here I was out of cloud and snow, and could see my errors plainly: but here also was a little signpost with the legend "Simplon Pass".

I soon made up the height I had lost, and by mid-afternoon, under a clearing sky, was walking over yet another huge, green, snow-streaked hillside towards yet another saddle. And from this saddle, called the Bistinen Pass, I could look down on the Simplon road and the snowy bulk of Monte Leone. A very large cairn had been constructed here, and I added my three stones to it thankfully.

By six I was threading my way through some little meadows and beside dry-stone walls and dry-stone barns such as one might find in any Lakeland valley, and finished my way to the crest of the pass up the old medieval pavings of the ancient track.

Now there was sun, strongly though intermittently, and there were views of portions of great peaks. Bees were busy again in the clover and scabious. I reached the crest of the pass and the main road, looking down one way to the old hospice on the descent into Italy, and on the other, past a new hotel, into Switzerland. The wind was northerly, strong and cold; but finally, it was a dry wind.

About a mile above the road on the eastern side I found a level stretch of turf beside a watercourse, set up my tent and cooked and ate in the evening sun. A man came walking up and talked to me; he and his friends had plans to climb the Monte Leone if the weather held next day. We talked about the route, and my route over the Kaltwasser Pass. I told him that I hoped to reach Austria within three weeks; and we wished each other well.

This camp on the Simplon Pass, my Camp 15, was the first warm dry camp since the Val Grisanche, ten days before.

And thereafter, with only two exceptions, all my camps were warm, dry and cheerful.

Chapter Four

LEPONTINE AND ADULA: HARD POUNDING

CAMP 5: THE Simplon Pass (exact location: one mile uphill from the New Hospice, at the point where the water channel from the Kaltwasser stream bends south, on the last patch of level turf). From looking at the grain of the land I deduce that before the Alps were Alps, a huge glacier flowed over this site, between Monte Leone (on whose flank I am camped) and the Saas and Weissmies peaks. The area here is scooped out and smoothed off just as a modern miniature glacier grooves up the ground. In the ice-age, perhaps, a huge snow-cap extended northward over what are now the Bernese Alps (which I can just make out through the evening clouds); and it was over this ridge that it flowed southward into Italy, carving out the trench of Lake Como. An ice-fall of Karakorum proportions must have been falling down from here into what are now the Gondo gorges; all to the north would be sledging country. The Lagginhorn and Fletschorn, across the way there, would be nunataks sticking up out of the mantle. Here, just where I am camped, would be under a couple of thousand feet of compressed and twisted ice and would be the interface of the rock and the mantle – a zone of crushed boulders, slurry and granite flour, like a gargantuan cement-mixer, rubbishing the ranges and slurping them out towards the Adriatic. And somewhere down there, well to the south and hiding from the freezing mistral that flowed down from the north like an invisible ice-fall, there would be human creatures making out as best they could. They would be Magdalenian men – no different from us, with an Eskimo technology that is one of the best that was ever devised (all things considered), and with plenty of understanding. Good painters, so presumably good thinkers. It was probably a good time to be alive, with the land warming up and you pushing northward following the bison and the deer or whatever, and retiring southward down a chain of established camps when the winter drew in. And after a few centuries some of you would move up into the Como valley –

to Juf

Hinterrhein

S. Bernardino
Pass

Läntalücke

(21)

Soreda Pass

(20)

Adula 3402m
(Rheinwaldhorn)

Luzzone Dam

Campo Blenio

Olivone

Disentis

Col del Sole

Lukmanier
Pass

(19)

Lago Ritom

Piotta

Andermatt

Airolo

St. Gotthard
Pass

(18)

Passo di S.
Giacomo

Basodino
3273m

A. Toggia

Col de Nefelgiu

Nufenen
Pass

(17)

Scatta
Minoia

Gletsch

Ofenhorn
3235m

Alpe Devero

Domodossola

(16)

P. Cervandone
3210m

Passo di Valtendra

M. Leone
3553m

Kaltwasser
Pass

N

(15)

Simplon Pass

Brig

0   30 km

– – – – –   route followed
. . . .   possible alternatives
(15)   camp-site

perhaps as soon as the lakes could keep fish – and then (because the ice would have crept right back up to here) further up still. Perhaps it was getting crowded down towards Como, so you moved to the head of the lake where there was a chance of clearing some pasture land. And then the Como men started moving in on you because they were being jostled by population movements down in the Milan area; so you followed the deer-hunters' trail through the Gondo gorge and established a summer settlement just down the road there and were safe and quiet for a while. By this time, of course, you knew that the snow to the north was not the rim of the world because one or two people had come over the top, surprising you; and they had been carrying amber and flint and just possibly metals. What had been your back yard was now becoming a public right-of-way. The family down the path had taken up banditry because that was easier than farming; but that meant a visit from the people down at Como (where they lived in houses, set in rows!) and those lads had iron spears and heavy manners. They were having problems too, from the tribes down at Milan and one day a whole different team arrived, with woven cloaks, riding on ponies and talking posh: and the difference was that everybody obeyed them. And all these layers of people passing down what was your old valley, silting it up with their foreign words so you yourself hardly knew how to speak to anyone and your head was a jumble of their foreign sounds. Then the only way was to keep still and say nowt and act dumb and daft, like a stone on the road. That was the only way to remember who you were and where you came from, and to keep a picture of that time when the world stopped at Simplon. And that was how you meant to keep it, in your head, because the old times were always the good times and tomorrow was another insult.

The very first English language mountaineering guide to the Alps has this to say about the Lepontine range. "The Lepontine Alps are not suited for the purposes of the gymnastic climber and do not offer the comforts demanded by the centrist, but . . . they are admirable for the wanderer." With that in mind and observing the change to a cold, dry weather that had come about, I felt confident of doing something worthwhile in the next week.

The section from Courmayeur to Simplon had been a complete disaster, from the mountaineer's point of view. It had been a defeat:

the highest and the best had been impassable. And then to be forced out of the mountains altogether, and to be forced to take a train! I consoled myself with thinking that I could not have done anything else in safety.

I was now at one of the rather few places where I had no alternative but to go straight ahead: over the high Kaltwasser pass between Monte Leone and the main chain of the Lepontine Alps. If pressed, one might descend from here towards Brig and take a lower line on the Swiss side of the range; and if desperate one might also make a long tour round the southern side of Monte Leone; but only at a cost of effort and trouble and indirectness. The only real way was straight ahead, into the clouds. The guide book says that the Kaltwasser Pass is "quite often traversed"; there are narrow but good paths on either side. On this occasion it was remote, cold and snowy. A strong northern wind was chasing clouds over the long stony slopes, and the grey light hardly distinguished the grey boulders.

I followed the little path along beside the water channel, traversing the hillside, crossed streams and a wide hillside covered with moraine and streaks of snow. Up above were the ridges of Monte Leone, directly ahead an S-curve of moraine ridge leading up into the driving cloud. My sack was heavy with a good four days' of provisions, so I went as slowly as an old tortoise. At one point I missed the track, but found it again: everywhere was grey or white. At length I found a very large cairn and the way ahead led across some slabby rocks and up into the murk.

I followed the moraine ridge upward along a path almost hidden in new snow; a glacier appeared through the mists on my right. A few flakes of snow were blowing past and frequent little squalls of spindrift. The path emerged on to an extensive and apparently level snow-field; its termination marked by a large wooden stake. Here the map marked a lake, and the path passing to its north: but so thick was the cloud and so white the ground and sky that nothing of any kind was visible. I took one cast towards the north and found myself floundering in deep powdery snow amongst boulders and breaking through the ice of little pools. I had a great horror of falling through ice into something deeper, and began to imagine, vividly, just what sort of death that might be. I returned to the stake by following my footprints.

For the second attempt I took a careful compass bearing – as careful as one can with a 1 : 100,000 map – and set off directly towards somewhere. I felt safe from drowning because I was traversing an easy slope; but in danger of walking over a cornice or an ice-cliff at the other end of the pass. For the next mile I practised the three-snowball trick – throwing snowballs ahead of me in a straight line. If I could see them, I knew there was some sort of ground ahead; and if I placed them carefully, fore and aft, I could keep a firm straight line. This technique I devised for myself coming over Mont Blanc, many years ago, and I have tried it out on a few bad days since: it is not to be encouraged.

The wind was very strong now, but for the most part coming from behind; only the really knock-down gusts came sideways. I got up a pleasant rhythm, making my snowballs, tossing them ahead and moving step by step; then pausing, scooping and pressing and throwing again. I kept thinking to myself that the top of the pass had been reached. I was confident that there were no crevasses here, for the ground was gently concave, and I was contouring across it on the safe line. It seemed to be flatter and more level to my left and I took that to be the site of the frozen lake. Then I found I was slowly climbing. I checked my compass and my map and kept on moving slowly in the same line. This must be near the top, I was thinking; when, quite suddenly, rocks were visible on either side and there was a slight descent. Had I done it? Now was the time for the greatest caution, because from here on down there was a steep little glacier. I worked over to the right-hand rocks; the snow now knee and thigh deep and blowing all around me in stinging clouds. Somewhere ahead, below, was a faint sky-line. This time I threw my snowballs well ahead, and their position showed a steepening descent. Now I moved right over to the rocks, which were high and covered in ice; I skirted around them, looking down a steep slope. This was the edge of the pass and it looked nasty. A moment of clearing showed, or seemed to show, much easier gentler ground to the far left, but I thought I would work a little further on this rightward line. I scrambled up on to a terrace of rock and walked gingerly along it, looking down into the mist, which here was brighter and thinner. I found I was peering on to the upper slopes of a descending glacier, with a large corniced ice-cliff about 80 feet high straight below me. And yes, there was a way over on the left hand side, if there was no crevasse in the hidden ground. I worked back along the terrace, almost crawling into the fierce wind as if I were back in Scotland. Then, looking up in a direction I had not looked before, hidden in a corner of the rocks I saw a tiny bivouac hut. The damn thing was I could not get to it because of a ten foot wall of iced rock that I could not climb. I had to trek and creep back into the wind for a hundred yards to get on to the crest of the rocks and then scramble back along them before I stood at its door.

I was relieved to be inside, and even more pleased to find a gas stove, coffee sachets, old sugar lumps and a tin of pineapple. There I sat for about an hour, while the weather slowly improved, drinking coffee, eating chunks of fruit and looking through the hut book. No English; so I signed myself in and by way of a flourish added "Ecrins to Glockner Traverse". It was a good little structure, anchored down hard against the wind: most people who had visited it were *en route* for Simplon but a few had climbed Monte Leone. Had I known this hut was here, I should have used it (or planned to use it) as a base for climbing the Leone. But it was only ten in the morning, and there was now a clear view down the glacier.

I left the hut, having carefully tidied it, and lowered myself down some steepish rocks into a gully that led down to the snow below the ice-cliff. The descent of the glacier passed without difficulty, though I took it at speed because up on my right were great towers of seracs and there were signs of a recent avalanche. Sitting down on the moraine and looking back up at the Pass and the faces on either side, I thought it had been quite a crossing.

From here a pleasant path led down a steep hillside to the Veglia alp, where there are several barns, a chalet, a mountain hut. The views back up to the faces of Monte Leone were very impressive – this side of the peak (its east and north-east pillars) is one of the biggest mountainsides in the central Alps. Clouds were still trailing from its summit, and the main Lepontine chain on my left – of steep, broken rock peaks – was hidden completely; but the sun had warmth in it at last, and after a meal of tinned fish and cheese and bread I set off at a good pace for the Passo da Valtendra.

The Lepontine Alps have a very strong grain to them, formed by folding and bending movements: the strata give steeply scarped and turretted outlines to the peaks, and broad terraces of forested alps. The rock, for the most part is a shattered and brittle limestone, with areas of slates and schists, and lumps of harder stuffs. On my side, in Italy, these peaks rise up suddenly from almost level pasture; but on this day they were scarcely visible. Paths, sometimes rather sketchy, link the little valleys. The three days I spent among these peaks and crossing the steep passes were amongst the very best days of the whole traverse. The weather continued very cold and windy, with low cloud, and it did not relent until the third day; but simply to walk there was a perfect, though hardy, pleasure.

From Alpe Veglia a short walk led to a farm lodged in among some enormous cracked boulders, and then up vaguely through open forest to a group of chalets where two men were gravely splitting logs. What language were they speaking? This was no Italian that I had ever heard, nor was it Germanic. We acknowledged one another, silently. At length the forest yielded up a small path that led in an upward traversing line, with views down on my left to a tree-filled valley and beyond that to a steep and impressive line of peaks. Somewhere up there a pass led over to Switzerland; but the path I was taking was parallel to the main crest of the range, leading over a succession of lower passes. And here was the first one, suddenly rearing up in front of me – a very steep slope of grass and boulders, with the steep walls of a rock peak on the left. My automatic pilot took me up.

The other, eastern side was more problematic. My map indicated two choices, but was not detailed enough for the intricate manoeuvre that I had to follow. One path plunged off down a long narrow valley, losing height all the way; the other cut across and doubled back to take another pass called the Scatta d'Orogna. A "scatta" in this region seems to mean "an oblique way through". The strata of the rocks is so uniform along the Italian side of the Lepontines – horizontal but tipped quite sharply into the mountains – that long oblique and narrow ledges are to be found everywhere. The Scatta d'Orogna was such a way through.

An arrow painted on a rock showed me the way – "To Alpe Devero". A very narrow path led horizontally across a very steep slope of grass, earth and loose rock: I slipped off my headband for this section, wanting to be freer in movement. The grass was dry and the earth firm, fortunately, because some situations were airy. Axe held at the ready, I trotted daintily across this slope, down round some spurs of crumbling limestone and up steeply through a line of cliffs by means of a narrow gully and ledge. This gave out onto an upper, broad shelf at an altogether higher level: there was a curiously formed theatre of rocks through which the path, which was now marked by paint-flashes every few yards, took a circuitous route. By means of scrambling over boulders a further ledge or terrace was reached that led round the end of a ridge and gave an abrupt and astonishing view forward down the full length of the range and into the forested trough of Alpe Devero. The wind was roaring over this ridge straight out of the north, bitterly cold: and I knew I was tired. A long descent of snow and grass and watery gravel led down to a fine camping site beside an old stone hut, marked on the map as Alpe Buscagna. Camp 16: at the end of a long day.

That had been a very successful day; the first part a trying piece of mountaineering judgement and the second part, tough and exciting walking. All of it had been, or felt, remote and serious; and all of it had been in territory completely unknown to me, with utterly new vistas at every turn. Sitting in the doorway of the stone hut and watching the clouds thrash round the pillars of the Helsenhorn, I felt I was well on my road. I discovered that I had unconsciously clenched my right fist and that I was pounding it into my open left hand.

Above Alpe Buscagna was one of the peaks I had been intending the climb – the Pizzo Cervandone; but in the morning it was invisible in the racing cloud. Accordingly I altered my objective to the Ofenhorn, to be reached by evening and climbed the next day. Such was the constant changing of objectives this weather forced upon me.

A pleasant walk down beside a reedy tarn led to a steep path descending to the little village of Alpe Devero. Like very many of the upper valleys on the Italian slopes of the Alps, local population has shrunk and productive farming departed. Where there is work it is in forestry or hydro-electric schemes, or in the tourist trade. Twenty years ago, walking in the hills about Domodossola one found whole villages abandoned, desolate, and ruined farms. But in the times since then these upper valleys have revived and the farms been converted into holiday cottages and weekend homes. It is the familiar story that we have seen repeated all over the wilder parts of Britain. Alpe Devero was such a village, in the throes of revival. Its simple but noble little houses were no longer facing dereliction, and though they were not being put to the use for which they were intended, the stone barns and courtyards had life and a little colour. Small and remote mountain settlements such as this have a fitness of design that makes them well worth preserving.

I made one mistake here, which was not to buy more food at the village store. My sack was heavy enough and my shoulder and neck had been feeling sore. That laziness cost me a good day, later.

From Devero an enjoyable walk takes one up to and then along the side of a substantial lake: this, like most of the Lepontine lakes, has been enlarged by a dam and set to work the sluices of a hydro-electric scheme, but that does not spoil the view. A bold, flat-topped rocky peak stood out beyond it; then came a pass – the Albrun Pass – that led over into Switzerland, and then the large and cloud-obscured bulk of the Ofenhorn that was my goal for the next morning. I had to find some suitable camp site from which to tackle it and had chosen the Forno chalets above the head of the lake.

I followed the track around, passing a few fishermen, and came at last to the head of the lake. It was beginning to rain, so I put on my waterproofs and started the steady walk up, keeping the same automatic pace that had brought me there.

By now my mental state had become something similar to that experienced by lone yachtsmen: a curious blend of the very practical and the quite fantastic. I hope the reader will not think it ridiculous if I tell of mine. Somewhere in the Lepontine Alps I became very interested in the activities of marmots. Now the marmot is a vegetarian rodent that looks something like a beaver crossed with a rabbit: it lives in burrows in the rocks, in colonies, and spends most of its time eating or lying about in whatever sun it can find. Each colony protects itself with a ring of look-outs, and the commonest sound in some valleys is the piercing wolf-whistle that these sentries give out as a warning: then the feeders and the sunbathers lollop and scurry off into their dens, and the sentries, after a last look about, dive down after them.

Ever since I had cleared the rubbish out of the marmots burrow while crossing the Thabor range (as recounted in Chapter One), I had been observing their habits and enjoying their company. Sometimes they were the only company I had, and so I had begun talking to them, in a harmless fashion. I would give a sharp whistle

in passable imitation, and shout out "Hi", or sometimes (and this
was a little odd) I would address them quietly and courteously with
"Good morning, marmots" and suchlike. If I saw one standing on a
rock, I would wave to it.

But in the Lepontine Alps the marmots began to answer back. At
least I think they must have done, because I was able to have short
and lucid conversations about what I was doing, about the way I
was going, about the state of the weather, or indeed about whatever
was in my mind. I developed the childlike fantasy that they were
accompanying me, or at least, cheering me on in some way. For
instance, I would find myself saying "Look, here I am. This sack is
bloody heavy. How far is it to Forno, now? Look, why don't you
go on ahead and get the kettle on. I'm croaking. It's all very well for
you. Will there be crevasses on the Ofenhorn? Perhaps it will rain
tomorrow as well, and then I won't have to do it. Anyway, how are
you keeping?" And similar prattle – out loud. I think it was out loud
. . . but it may have been silently.

From around this time I added to the ritual placing of the three
stones in a cairn a special morning and evening greeting to the
marmots.

If every fantasy was as harmless as this, there might be fewer
troubles in the world.

Around two in the afternoon I arrived (with a little help from my
friends) at the Forno chalets. These were sturdy bothies built of
massive stones, with tables of stone and chairs of stone. It was very
cold and raining outside, and cold and drizzling inside; no place to
make a camp. I sat about for a time, getting ever more chilled,
before making the decision to push on over the Scatta Minoia. I had
observed on the map that from the other side of the next pass it
would be possible to climb the Ofenhorn, though I had no
information about this route.

The Forno chalets are on the edge of a wide, sloping moor, much
like a Pennine moor; unusual country for the Alps. The Scatta
Minoia appeared to be, from my map, another oblique way
through between the Ofenhorn and its southern subsidiary peaks.
A path was marked, but its start across the moor was very faint. I
took a compass bearing and set off into the mist. The rain now
began to move away, the cloud to break up into drifts and banks.
My bearing was true and took me into a narrowing valley full of

snow-drifts, where I found a line of cairns, and at length to a short, steep hillside of rocks and crags up which, following the oblique strata, the path debouched on to the col. There was an old half-ruined hut here that looked as though it might once have had a military purpose. A short way beyond this, a steep snow gully led downward without difficulty into a little grassy cwm; and suddenly the weather became clear and sunny. Two lakes were below me, grassy hollows and knolls and a convenient traversing line. That evening, as the sun went down, I reached the upper of the two lakes and found beside it a small stone hut. This was my Camp 17, and among the finest of them all.

The hut had clearly been made for the engineers who had built the little dam; it had a cold concrete floor and no glass in its windows, but it looked out across the rippling and brilliantly shining surface of the upper Vannino lake and up at the wide, high, snowy saddle that would give, I believed, an easy way on to the upper snow-fields of the Ofenhorn. On either side of this saddle there were shattered rocky ridges glowing a golden biscuit colour in the evening light. Looking further round to the right there was a steep valley leading up to a narrow pass, and further right still the steep rock spire of the Nefelgiu. This very elegant little mountain stood directly over the larger and lower Vannino lake which I could look down on by walking over the grassy ridge behind the hut. Over to the left of the saddle, the steep rocky ridge went up higher into a meeting of ribs and gullies that marked one end of the Ofenhorn massif; to the left still further was the nick of the Scatta Minoia through which I had come and beyond that an enclosing rim of high hills and precipices that came round almost in a complete circle. The Vannino lakes gave birth to a steep stream that descended into a mist-filled valley through a deep gorge.

The lower lake and its dam and installations can be reached by a rough track; there is a mountain refuge there, and engineers' huts. I could see a few figures enjoying the evening (though they were in shadow long before it reached me). The wind was still strong and cold, but before it got dark the sky had cleared. I made myself comfortable inside the hut, sorted out what I would need for the morning and packed my light sack; then slept very soundly, trusting to my automatic alarm to wake me around three in the morning. Which it did.

The author, with a heavy pack, crossing the
Col de la Leisse on the sixth day.

At the Plan de Valfourche, with the peaks of
the Ecrins massif behind.

Early morning; and crossing through the intricate passes of the
Thabor range on the third day.

The Val de Leisse, and above the peaks of the Grande Casse (*l.*) and the Grande Motte (*r.*). One of the few valleys that goes the way you want to go.

The Rutor peaks, and in the far background the Valais Alps with the Matterhorn on the far right.

Storm and much new snow on Mont Blanc.

The good track that I followed above the Val de Nendaz –
behind, the peaks that I crossed in cloud the day before.

A break in the weather on the trek over to the Simplon Pass.

Camp 15, under the boulder at Täsch; with the smallest tent
in the world, my home for 44 nights.

Monte Leone from Alpe Veglia; the most impressive peak
of the Lepontine Alps.

Alpe Devero; a half-abandoned village restored for holiday
cottages – just as with hill-farming villages everywhere.

The Ofenhorn, above the upper Vannino lake.
I was able to climb this peak from the snowy saddle
to the right – all except the last few metres!

On automatic: shivering in my shelter just below
the summit of the Ofenhorn.

In the Lepontine Alps. The beautiful Nefelgiu col which I
crossed on the twentieth day after climbing the Ofenhorn.

The early morning was extremely cold and still and the sky shimmering with stars. A little path, a footstep wide, led round the side of the lake and up into a slope of moraine and snow-patches; every little trickle of water had frozen hard, and every breath chilled the throat. A very slow dawn came up as I steadily ascended the steep but easy ground to the saddle above the lake: I was aiming at its lowest point, beside which there appeared to be a large metal post. As I got nearer, the first rays of light touched the post and revealed it as a cross; I later discovered that this pass was used in winter as a ski-crossing, and that the cross served both a useful and an emblematic function. A very large cornice extended most of the way across the top of the saddle, except at the extreme right-hand end where I could walk up easily on to a broad plateau. As expected, the summit of the Ofenhorn was about two miles away across an easy undulating snow-field that rose up steadily to the narrow crest of the peak: there were fine views northward and eastward, though a bank of clouds seemed to be trying to push its way over from Switzerland. They would need watching. There was also a cold strong wind, that was raising a long plume of blown snow off the summit.

The crossing and ascent of the snow-field was simply a matter of walking over very hard *névé*, keeping a sharp look-out for crack-lines and avoiding occasional drifts of powder snow. The surface was aerodynamically smoothed and trimmed and the steady wind passed over it without interruption ; the sun was very bright but without warmth.

The actual block of the peak is a crescent of ridge rising out of the snows: on the right it was steep and rocky, but on the left an easy detour led round on to an upper shelf of glacier: a fine, icy, sparkling dust was swirling about me when I reached the topmost island of rocks and crouched in a wind hollow to reconsider the last 200 feet.

The actual summit was defended by a long and very thick cornice of new snow extending about 200 metres horizontally. I had one plod up to the right, into the wind, to get around that way; but this led out over a steep ice-slope exposed to the violent wind-tunnel, shot-blasting effects of the spindrift. Turning my back on that I tried left, with my back to the wind. Very deep, loose snow, lying on hard ice above a huge crevasse; damned unpleasant. I went back to my hollow, to warm up a little. Peeping out, in between gusts, I was able to admire a magnificent snowy panorama over the Bernese Alps, but it began to look as though I was not going to get the vista I wanted to see – that of the way I had come, along the backward crest of the Lepontine range. I had a third attempt, directly upward towards a nick in the cornice. 50 feet below the summit and I was up to my chest in shifting, sliding powder snow on a 50-degree slope. The cornice was 15 feet thick, and sheets of spindrift were pouring over it on to my head, into my eyes and nostrils. I tried a few more steps, but started sliding back, with a few hundredweight of snow for company.

In other circumstances I think I would have pushed my luck on this slope, and would have made the summit (which was just there above me); but I was mindful of my rule of safety. And what was the point in building little cairns, and talking to the marmots if you didn't heed their advice. I slithered back into my hollow and ate a bar of chocolate. I had all my clothes on, and had been expending a lot of energy, but my jaws were almost too frozen to eat. The way down began signalling at me. Such is mountaineering: such is "friction".

On the way down, walking steadily and carefully and following the 24 punctures of my crampon points (that were the only flaw on the surface of ice) I decided that, broadly speaking, I had climbed the Ofenhorn and had achieved that objective. And if I missed it by 50 feet, well, what was 50 feet in the thousands I had plodded up already.

When I got back to the lake it was still barely ten in the morning. Three hours up, half an hour fumbling about below the cornice, and an hour and a half down: yes – I was getting fit. I made myself an excellent early lunch, sunbathed for a while, and then set off again. Before leaving that place I built a fine little cairn in celebration.

The Passo di Nefelgiu rises from a steep valley overhanging the lower lake, but with a little care I was able to work out a scramble across steep grass that led into the upper half of that valley without any loss of height. I had got a great deal of hatred of unnecessary loss of height by now. A long, steep snowbed led up to the pass, which is the last of the "scattas" along this side of the range. As I started at the bottom of the snow, a young couple came down it, descending to the Vannino refuge – these were the only people I had met in the whole of my crossing from Simplon, except those in inhabited places. We waved cheerily.

The crossing of this path was another delight, celebrated with another fine cairn; the descent on the eastern side was an immense glissade down to green pastureland, full of flowers. The sun was now high and hot and brilliant; there was a fine new vista of the Basodino peaks and of the rear of the Nefelgiu and of this side of the Ofenhorn ridges, all hung with new snow. A pleasant easy walk led down to a farm track, which in turn led down steeply to another dam and the head of the road.

Once again, loath to lose height, I struck off up and across an immense, and very steep, slope of grass and shrubbery; I did this to avoid the descent to find the foot of the track to the Alpe Toggia, which was my objective for the night. By following sheep-tracks I made my way safely through some precipitous ground to another area of knolls and little valleys, where the Toggia Hut is located.

This is a very fine old hospice of the ancient Alpine type, established long before there were mountaineers and skiers: it was built for travellers between the north and south, since it is near the summit of the broad and low San Giacomo pass, which in turn is linked with the Nufenen and St. Gotthard passes. Anyone wanting to get to the Como valleys from Eastern Switzerland would pass this way in the olden days. The building there now is an Italian Alpine Club hut, full of very dark wood panelling, old photographs, ski-racks and decorated wooden fittings. There were plenty of people there, since it was at the head of the road out of the Formazzo valley and an excellent walking centre. I found myself in conversation with a Dutchman, who was waiting there for friends who had been climbing in the Basodino group on the other side of the valley. I bought myself a large plateful of pasta and several glasses of lemon tea. The Dutchman was rather concerned about his friends who had been out a long time and not returned; and I explained that with the new snow, any rock climbs would be slow and cold. I did not tell him where I was going; I had become shy about it, once again.

My plan had been to make a camp not far from the hut and the next day to cross a pass in the Basodino ridge, climb a peak called the Cristallino, and descend by way of another col to Airolo at the

foot of the St. Gotthard pass. But I had had four long and hard
days over the Lepontines and my supplies were almost finished.
To complete that next section would mean coming down to
Airolo, very late, very tired and very hungry. That was just the
sort of exhausting experience I wanted to avoid, and had managed
to avoid so far. The pace I had established was as fast and hard as I
thought right; but it meant that every third or fourth day needed
to be gentler. Tomorow, then, I would go to Airolo by an easy
valley route, change money, stock up on provisions and take life
easily. That meant the effort of an evening shift over the San
Giacomo pass and back into Switzerland.

At five, as the sun began to lengthen, I set off up the track beside
yet another lake formed by a dam, to the summit of the pass; to
my left the main Lepontine range crumbled into shaly hills, on the
right – beyond the lake – a line of easy but attractive rocky peaks:
at the head of the lake there was a Dutch car, with climbing
equipment inside. I scanned into the slanting light, but saw
nothing.

Towards the pass, which was a little way ahead, I passed an
abandoned customs office; then set off walking over a short, level
plateau of turf covered with mixed flowers. The path, though
narrow, was certainly very ancient, predating history. Within
twenty miles of this spot, I thought, are the Gotthard and
Nufenen passes, that link in their turn with the Grimsel and Furka
passes, and roundabout back to the Simplon. This is one of the
great ganglia of the body of Europe, through which for millennia
men and goods and men and weapons have passed. Now all these
other passes are crossed by roads and all but one are pierced with
tunnels, and this is the only one of six that one must still cross on
foot or on horseback. Here I come, back into Switzerland again,
by an unmarked and undefended frontier; life is safer than it was,
if less adventurous.

I passed over a little crest and started walking gently downhill
towards a group of chalets that stood at a mile's distance; their
style was typical of the district, low-eaved upon a sturdy base of
stone, with fretted shutters tightly-closed against the night air and
the shadows that were beginning to rise up out of the valley
below. A small notice or signpost attracted my attention and I
began to walk towards it. As I did so, I noticed curious features

about this chalet. It had no yard or garden beside it, no enclosure, nor any track leading up to it. It appeared simply to have been placed there without function.

And as I got closer still it seemed to me that the style of this building was not as elegant as I had thought, that in fact it was needlessly sturdy, even massive, and lacking in the random sags of roof or bow of porch that one expects in buildings of old timber. And that there were curious mounds in its vicinity.

The notice said: It is absolutely forbidden to take any photographs of this and other structures.

The "chalet", when I got there, was composed of thick concrete and its shutters were of heavy steel: sinister slots were cut in the steel and at intervals in the concrete walls below. The grassy mounds were evidently hollow, since little doors were set into their farther side. A ropeway led up to this outpost, from out of the valley.

It is quite clear that this delicate spot on the continental spine is still thought to be vulnerable; and the question occurs to me in writing this, whether or not I can be prosecuted. I did not take any photographs. Suppose I had drawn the installation; would that have been an offence? I have certainly been describing it in words; does that render me liable to prosecution? I think not, for since the invention of the camera, no one seems to believe that drawing can tell the truth! Or that you can describe something or someone accurately with words. Imagine what a passport would look like, without the photograph. Does my photograph resemble me; or yours you?

I walked on for another mile or so, down into a grassy cwm full of streams and found myself a level lawn. While the pot boiled I tried to draw the folding strata of the Pizzo de San Giacomo, that stood directly up into the evening air above me – but I couldn't believe that my marks had any real connexion with those buttresses, those scalloped gullies and cones of scree. Camp 18.

In the morning I got up later than usual and walked gently valleyward, coming down by various pleasant paths to a bridge a short way above the village of Bedretto; after sitting for an hour in the sun I got a post bus for the four or five miles down to Airolo.

Airolo must have been a pleasant town once, and has good corners still, but its character has been overwhelmed by its location on the southern side of the St. Gotthard pass motorway: vast flying bridges overshadow it, a swath of concrete has lobotomized it, its centre is a den of souvenir merchants. I restocked my sack with food, ate a vast meal of fruit and bread and cheese in the main square and drank a cup of coffee in a bar, trying not to hear or see some elaborate state occasion that Britain was broadcasting to the world. In the early afternoon, under a burning sun, I walked down the valley a short way and took the mountain railway up to the Lago de Ritom – a large lake and tourist location on the hills above the town.

I can see now that a more adventurous line would have been to climb from Airolo up to the Cadlimo Hut, and from there next day I might even have climbed a small peak: but I was determined not to over-exert myself in the now extreme heat, and to husband my resources of energy and will-power for the remaining half of my traverse. For this point, I calculated, would be the half-way stage on the Grand High-Level Route. Perhaps for that reason I slept badly, through undischarged energy.

An enterprise such as this, I was discovering, required no very great skill; but it did require two sorts of judgement. The first was a judgement of mountain conditions that had to be more exact than usual because of my isolated position; the second was a judgement of my personal condition and energy. This, in effect, was keeping a very firm discipline, a controlled and careful discharge of energy such as you must attain in long distance running (only, of course, in this case very long distance, and no running). I would like to describe this as the controlled release of aggression, except that *aggression* has implications. One can only be aggressive against something or someone. Yet I had got a habit, at pauses, of pounding my open left hand with my clenched right fist, like someone considering a fight. I am quite unable to find any single word to describe this aggression-like deliberate and hardened state of mind that I needed to maintain, but I think it is a state of mind similar, in a slight way, to that experienced in battle. I had concentrated every thought into the completion of each and every part of the traverse and had no thought left for anything else: at times it seemed as if the crannies of my brain actually imitated the foldings of the peaks, so intensely had the image of my route become imprinted on my consciousness; everything I did or thought or even momentarily considered had to be relevant to the task in hand.

This is not a very attractive state of mind, but it is efficacious. After quite a lot of experience I have come to the conclusion that people who go in for extreme pursuits (and I seemed to be getting to be one of them) are not very attractive people. In the course of research that I did for working out my itinerary I read through most of the *Alpine Journals* of recent years and some much older, and I came across a summary of research that had been done upon such paladins and – not surprisingly – they turned out to be a bloody-minded crew. One test suggested that they were "shown to be opportunist, evaders of rules, disregardful of obligations, often casual and tending to lack the type of effort needed for group work and cultural demands".

Enough said on that matter: anyone who goes off to the wilderness for 40 days is up to no good, by the common lights of life.

In some quarters, mountain activities are supposed to be character building!

At length I got to sleep only to be awoken by a continuous humming, jingling sound that gradually grew nearer and louder. I knew, of course, that this was the sound of cow-bells; but there were so many to be heard I thought I should look out. (I was camped for my 21st night on a broad meadow about a mile beyond the Ritom lake). Creeping out of my sack and fiddling for my torch took a little time; when I emerged and shone the light I saw that I was only just in time. A very great herd of cows was wandering slowly up the gentle slope towards me; just dim white-and-mottled shapes in the night. The noise of the bells had blended into a continuous melodious roar, the tearing and grasping of a thousand mouths at the lush grass was like the noise of some immense mowing machine, the massed breathing was that noise I used to hear many years ago when there were still steam trains and they puffed and shunted all night long in the marshalling yards near home.

Stark naked I leapt out and ran up and down fending them off, driving them away from around my little and immensely valuable tent. I trod on sharp stones and got my feet full of thistles; I threw pebbles, waved my torch, hooted and yelped. The great bovine tide parted only at the very last minute; passing within a yard at either side of all that I possessed, without trampling anything.

I spent the hour of dawn warming up and picking the thorns out of the soles of my feet.

I spent the whole of the next morning and into the early afternoon walking over a huge area of grassland ringed by little limestone scarps, crossing one pass (the Col del Sole) and coming down yet more grassy slopes to the road over the Lukmanier Pass; and then yet again up over another great grass-covered mound to the top of the col called Gana Negra. This was a fine and peaceful excursion through the most beautiful green pastures, on good paths, with (once again) not a soul to be seen. It was immensely hot, and I stopped often by streams or in the shade of the infrequent pines. The lower valleys were filled with a dusty haze, and the summits silvery through a very thin high cloud. Another long valley led me down to the hamlet of Campo Blenio, in a fine bowl-shaped hollow set around with steep pine-woods and crags: and thence by a very steep road up to the Luzzone dam.

Of all the dams encountered on the traverse, this is the most sensational – a white curtain of concrete that seems from a distance to be as thin as paper, swelling across the throat of a deep gorge and holding back an immense weight of milk-blue water.

The Luzzone dam represented yet one more important point; for it was the starting point for my crossing of the Adula or Rheinwald-horn. This group of peaks, like the Rutor of the first section, or the Kaltwasser Pass, has to be tackled by anyone making the Grand High-Level Route. The most direct way is to climb the main Adula summit and to cross over it to the pass known as the Läntalücke: a secondary way is to go to the head of the Luzzone lake and cross the Soreda pass over into the Länta valley, and then reach the Läntalücke from that side – taking in the main summit as a diversion. I decided on the second course of action because the first would mean taking my heavy sack over the summit and crossing an extensive glacier in weather that promised to be very hot. This proved to be a sound decision. I also reckoned that by taking this direction I might be able to climb another peak as well, above the Soreda Pass.

Late that evening, after walking through a long and dripping tunnel of the hydro-electric scheme, and following a little winding path through steep forest, I came into an enclosed valley that led up to a beautiful green shelf surrounded on three sides by steep crags or slopes of snow, and with a view to the north of the beautiful Piz Medel. I say it was beautiful because it rose to a perfect snowy point; but I think that in another season, it might be a heap of loose shale. There was, I felt certain, a great deal of snow around for this time of year. It made the peaks beautiful to look at, but if the warm weather continued, it would make them difficult and possibly dangerous to cross.

I built my cairn, fed the birds, had a few words with the marmots and went to bed early. I had a strong intuition that the next two days were going to be very hard work.

From my little green shelf of alp it was not easy to tell exactly which of the several nicks in the ridge above me was the true pass; and to make matters worse, I was just one kilometre off the edge of the map. Up to this point the path had been well marked, though very narrow: but above the camp it disappeared in a field of boulders. In the dawn light I missed the way and, half asleep, had not the sense to retrace my steps. So came about my only serious route-finding error of the whole journey.

I spent the hours between five and nine climbing an immense slope that began in boulders and ended up as deep soft snow. It led out on to a crest of rocks by a final very steep section of increasingly soft and dangerous snow: the views were splendid but the descent on the other side impossible – 300 feet sheer rubbish. To my left – as the ridge ran due north – were pinnacles and a substantial rocky summit; to my right, due south, a little dome of snow. Perhaps, if I traversed this, I would descend to the pass I was seeking. And so, weighed down by my pack I laboured thigh-deep up to its crest and once again peeped over, timorously. The Soreda Pass was there, no more than a hundred yards away – but vertically beneath me. I had missed the right line by only a few steps at some point, and here I was with a morning's hard work to repeat. In trying to descend in the shortest line, instead of following my footsteps down, I found myself forced to retreat over some dangerously loose and icy slopes; in one tangle of tottering blocks and dripping icicles I cut my left hand badly on some sharp crystal, and backed all the way down the last snow-slope leading a bloody trail. At length I got round a corner and saw, 50 yards to my right, a paint-flash on the rock. The true route to the pass lay there, up a hidden gully; yet to get even that short distance I had to descend very nearly all the way back down to where I had camped and then climb up again.

The way to the pass once found was not easily lost; it was a narrow steep gully below the slanting wall of rock I had not been able to descend. It was a horrible place to be, full of loose boulders and melting snow that got deeper and steeper and altogether more dangerous as I climbed. The bandage I had put around my hand was wet with snow and blood, the sweat was running off my brow into my eyes, I was using elbows and knees on the last hundred feet. A final paint-mark showed the way and I flopped over the crest and looked down on to a sloping moor, still deep in snow but without any obvious problems. A huge deep valley lay before me, the Läntatal, and at its head the glaciers of the Adula. Thin mists drifted around me through which the sun burnt as if through a glass.

The descent of the other side was, once again, in thigh-deep snow, but it led to a line of cairns, that led to a grassy knoll that led to a path that descended a steep gully that came out into the glen below. Another two miles up the valley and I found myself at the door of the little Länta Hut.

This cheered me up immensely: it was a lovely refuge, built against and partly into a huge boulder. There was no one in residence, and I had ample space to spread myself around, to sleep on a bench, to rinse out my socks and hang my soaking breeches out to dry. My rebandaged hand was stiff, but the injury was not serious. There were even books to look at. Most pleasant of all were reproductions of the paintings of Ferdinand Hodler, who is to mountains what Cézanne is to apples.

A family came walking past; they had made the long climb up in the early morning and after lunch had gone on further to examine the source of the Rhine. The Rhine! Of course. I had crossed the watershed. This torrent below me was one of the sources of that great river . . . and so preoccupied had I been with my ups and downs and sideways movements that I had failed to notice that great geographical moment.

I had a pleasant conversation with this party and they showed me their map. Where I was now, was once again on my own sheet; but if I wanted any view of country to the north – then it would have been pure guesswork. As I supposed, there was no easy way around the Adula. In fact, it would take two days' hard walking if I didn't manage to cross the Läntalücke in the morning.

Before it got dark I strolled up the hillside to reconnoitre the path for the following day and to see what I could see. The big white curve of the Adula glacier filled the head of the valley and looked thoroughly nasty; of the slopes to the Läntalücke I could see very little. Cooking up that evening I was nervous, and took an unusually long time setting out my equipment for the morning, as if I were about to embark on a major assault. I looked incessantly at the map, to brand its details still more deeply into my brain. Thick clouds were drifting around, and desultory thunder bumped about between the spurs.

This state of mind, in which ordinary and practical anxieties are magnified by loneliness, was one which everyone who spends much time alone in mountains will experience. Thomas Traherne expresses it best when he writes of how "in a lowering and sad evening, being alone in the field, when all things were dead and quiet, a certain want and horror fell upon me, beyond imagination. The unprofitableness and silence of the place dissatisfied me; its wideness terrified me; from the utmost ends of the earth fears surrounded me. How did I know but dangers might suddenly arise from the East, and invade me from the unknown regions beyond the seas? I was a weak and little child, and had forgotten there was a man alive in the earth." In that frame of mind I went to sleep in one of the bunks.

I rose very early, to take advantage of whatever cold weather there might be, and followed the path up the valley by torchlight. The weather was insidiously warm, even close, at three in the morning without wind, but with slight and sudden shifts of air, now cool, now sultry hot. Somewhere down to the left an infant Rhine gushed out from its icy cave and somewhere up ahead, in a sort of indeterminate whiteness, were the slopes I had to find and climb. Day began to dawn as I clambered up a loose moraine and on to the level surface of the glacier.

On this morning I paid great attention to my cairn building. I walked over to a prominent flat rock lying on the ice and built one there, and then, just before beginning the climb, I made another on a smaller rock. The prospect above, in the conditions that morning, was frightening.

The direct and natural route to the pass was clearly in a dangerous condition; several small avalanches had fallen down it and fanned out on to the glacier below. A ridge of snow that rose to a rock crest and descended to a rock gable gave the obvious way upward. Keeping well to the right of the steepest snow I trekked slowly up until I came to an area where about a foot of slush was lying upon hard ice: to avoid this I crossed over on to the rocks bordering the gable end of the ridge and scrambled awkwardly up these till they became too steep and led me back to snow. This was awkward, insecure work.

The going was better for a while and then much worse. I spotted a little gully in the upper rocks with a trace of old footprints in it, and made for that. For a hundred feet or more it was very dangerous work on steep slush, and then, on the ridge, another very nasty section with plaques of melting ice lying on loose blocks. I had my axe and pick both in play, and needed both to pull and hack and sprawl my way on to better ground. It was one of those periods of high tension which every climber knows, in which concentration is at its maximum and the physical effort is lost in the surge of excitement and controlled fear. At the top of the rocks a fine curling ridge of firm snow led in a curve up to the lower summit of the Adula.

Here, on a crown of rocks I had time to look around at the main peak and at the range I had been crossing. The Adula peaks are not high or difficult, but they make a fine sight. One look over to the main summit decided me against continuing, however; several large crevasses spread over the snow-field between and in the soft conditions it was extremely uninviting. While I was sitting there I saw a party of climbers suddenly appear on the main summit, by the route I might have taken. Their bright jackets were red against the brilliant blue of the sky and the dazzling snow. Had I been there with them I should have been forced to cross that unpleasant and probably dangerous plateau that now separated me from the main peak. Once more I had contrived to make a sound decision.

I ate a few bites of food and drank a mouthful of water flavoured with lemon peel; then bandaged my hand again which had started to bleed afresh in the hurly-burly of the climb. Then began the long and weary descent into the Zapport cwm.

I met a party of six Swiss climbers, struggling upward in the snow which on this southern slope was even softer and wetter. For no good reason they were roped together and making very little progress over

very easy ground, each picking his or her own way instead of
following in and consolidating the leader's footprints. They had
made a great swathe of tracks and flounder marks all the way up the
hill. In no time I was down to the Läntalücke, and before long
descending a great sweep of easy, slabby rocks down to the glacier
and the other source of the Rhine, which most geographers reckon
to be the true source. It was certainly a larger torrent than that
which issued from the northern Adula glacier. Across from here is a
line of small peaks, on the summit of which the first supposed
ascensionists discovered the skeleton of a man in military uniform
of the early eighteenth century. He had been, it seems, a captain in a
Spanish regiment, but nothing else has ever been deduced about
him.

To honour this man I built a special cairn, in addition to my
regular marker.

The descent from here was long and wearisome – a trail across a
level wilderness of stones to the little Zapport Hut, which I visited
briefly, and then a winding narrow track through the huge gorge of
the infant Rhine, and then another immense stony wilderness. The
area is used by the Swiss Army as a training ground, and the stones
are littered with fragments of bombs and bullets; there were tanks
lined up, flagpoles, little notices and all the military paraphernalia
one expects. I dragged a weary afternoon across this Sahara of slate
and shrapnel and fainted away in some trees a mile from the village
of Hinterrhein. I brewed up several cups of tea and ate up most of
my food; and in so doing I made the one major organizational error
of the whole journey, for today was August the First.

August the First is the Swiss National Day. Now the Swiss are,
with good reason, very patriotic and they celebrate their National
Day by closing all the shops and making whoopee with flags,
fireworks, banquets and drinking bouts. There was not a soul to be
seen in Hinterrhein and the tiny village shop was locked and
shuttered: there were confused sounds of merriment coming from
within the houses, but no chance of a bite to eat. I looked at what I
had left – the makings of one meal, perhaps; then I shook my little
gas stove – the makings of three cups of tea, with luck: and I
considered myself and discovered an immense HUNGER. A hunger
of a midwinter wolf, a howling dog, a true hyena of a hunger: I sat
on a wall on the outskirts of the village of Hinterrhein and groaned.

My feet hurt, my eyes hurt from the sun, my left hand was cramped and painful; and most of all I was hungry.

From this horrible predicament I was rescued by an extremely good-natured motorist who quite spontaneously stopped his car and offered me a lift. He even took a detour off the road into the next village to see, if by chance, there was any shop open, and when there was not he took me all the way down the valley to the small town of Andeer, where he left me at the bus station.

This is a very attractive little town, and it was *en fête*, with men and women in national costume sitting in all the cafés, with garlanded children dancing in procession, with a brass band tuning its instruments in a field, with a stall of flags and bunting, with banners, with streamers and an air of a party about to begin. But no food, except (expensively) in the hotels, where special places were being laid at long tables. So, consulting my ground rules of action, I decided that this was an occasion to take a bus.

That evening I arrived at the little hamlet of Juf at the head of the Val Ferrera.

Chapter Five

MORE HARD POUNDING:
BERNINA AND ORTLER

JUF: A COLLECTION of chalets, small farms, an hotel and an old *Gasthaus* scattered in the throat of a long deep and green valley. No trees, only grassy slopes stretching up on both sides to stony ridge-tops and at the end of the valley, closing it, a cliff-skirted little mountain. The hamlet of Juf is sometimes claimed to be the highest permanent settlement in Europe.

Juf was *en fête*. The children were constructing a bonfire, flags were flying before every door, and in the *Gasthaus* some dedicated drinking had begun which I went at once to join since a menu was prominently on display. As soon as I had ascertained that there still was food to be had and not solely great foaming glasses of beer, I went into the toilet and changed out of my mountain clothes (that were showing signs of raggedness) and put on my decent trousers and a clean shirt. The carcass within still showed the signs of my travails, was still stained and scorched and barely operable from fatigue, and the brain within that carcass was more or less stunned: but the outer effect was not bad. It was the least I could do, and the most, to celebrate a national day.

Visitors do not see the Swiss in a good light, because their relation with the natives is almost always commercial; we never like someone to whom we are handing our money. They seem to be prim, inhibited and greedy. And reciprocally, our tourist consciousness is corrupted by our position as spectators; we create a kind of complicity between ourselves and what we have come to see, and this gets in the way of our ever experiencing the *real* Swiss. This is not true only of the Swiss, of course; but of any people who are visited, who are the objects of tourism and whose authentic life is turned into spectacle. It is certainly true of the Welsh and Scots who in relation to the English present themselves as self-parodies (the English in turn parodying themselves before the Americans and Germans). But in the case of the Swiss, we have a major case of a people and land that most people encounter simply as spectacle.

Here at Juf, there were holiday-makers, but they were not foreign. The atmosphere, and even the physical appearance of the place, reminded me more of the Yorkshire Dales than anywhere I had seen abroad. The evening that subsequently developed would not, in most respects, have been out of place in Upper Wharfedale.

Once again, my appearance and demeanour worked to my advantage: I was obviously not a normal tourist. I had (I guess this) an aura of hard work about me. I had hardly sat down when an immense glass of cold beer was put in front of me; and between platefuls of chips and veal steaks I put down several more glasses while the party progressed.

Most people spoke a strong dialect, like Schweizer-Deutsch, that I could barely comprehend, but since coherence and good articulation were being rapidly abandoned, this hardly mattered. A competition developed between two tables, of a sort I had heard about, but not witnessed. It was a rhyming competition, in which each contestant had to cap or to reply to the other's couplets. It concerned, in some sense I could never fully make out, the respective merits of Zurich and Berne. At one time, football was the topic, at another time the supposed table manners of the inhabitants of Berne. The two tables were, clearly, representatives of those cities, and a lot of the jokes were in and about the regional accents; and each table had a leader. The drinkers of Zurich were commanded by an energetic man with red hair and a real comedian's manner, who also doubled as a mock-waiter to the whole room, even serving the proprietor himself. The Bernese were a confederacy, who replied conjointly; their best rhymester was a middle-aged woman of rather commanding appearance and, I should guess, plenty of education. Most of the rest of us looked on, and the topics and the general rules were explained to me by a couple sitting next to me. The real winner was the one who could most often either "squash" or cap his opponent. This is a game that could be played very hard and very cruelly and take on the quality of a "flyting" in which the object is to make your opponent lose his temper.

For my part, the combination of hunger, dehydration, beer and a really solid meal began to take effect. By the time, towards midnight, that the evening drew to a close, I think I was no more sober than anyone else in Juf. Putting on my sack seemed to take an

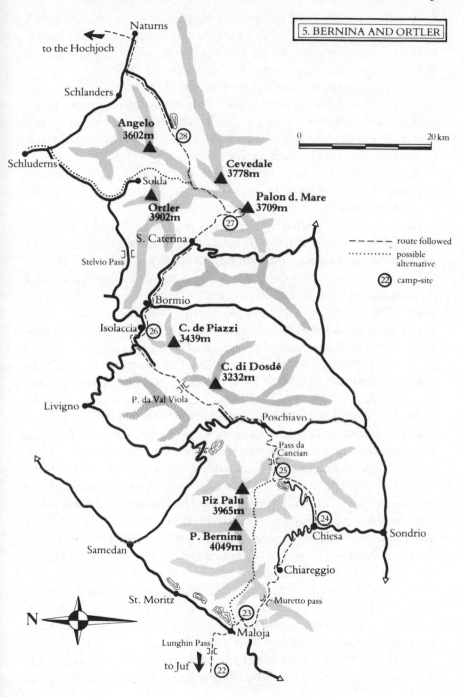

5. BERNINA AND ORTLER

Naturns

to the Hochjoch

Schlanders

Angelo
3602m

28

Schluderns

Cevedale
3778m

Solda

Palon d. Mare
3709m

Ortler
3902m

S. Caterina

27

0   20 km

Stelvio Pass

Bormio

Isolaccia

26

C. de Piazzi
3439m

—— route followed

.... possible
            alternative

22 camp-site

C. di Dosdé
3232m

Livigno

P. da Val Viola

Poschiavo

Pass da
Cancian

25

Piz Palu
3965m

24

P. Bernina
4049m

Chiesa

Sondrio

Samedan

Chiareggio

St. Moritz

Muretto pass

23

N

Maloja

Lunghin Pass

to Juf   22

unusually long time and the willing hands that were offered didn't seem too co-ordinated. Fireworks were being exploded in the street, rockets were flying in the air and catherine wheels spinning: the bonfire roared in a field, surrounded by ecstatic children.

My new acquaintances all shook my hand and clapped me on the back, and there was a general noise of cheering and hallooing in the night. More rockets went skyward. An accordion was being played and disco music came out of the hotel. Then I passed out of the circle of the fire and into the dark night.

Such was my stay in the little village of Juf. In leaving I took with me a sense of privilege; it is not every visitor that sees the Swiss in an unbuttoned mood.

I did not go very far that night, as may be imagined: and woke up in the morning, wrapped up in the tent as if in a blanket by the side of a hayfield. A heavy dew, a sky of lemon-gold, and hills of khaki and primrose. Shaking my head to see if it was in working order again, I crept out of my cocoon and discovered I was still dressed as I had been when I left the bar. But no hangover? How was that possible? I was perfectly fresh and rested. The answer to that is I think quite simple – prolonged effort, particularly of the sort I had experienced, brings about a change in the whole metabolism. One reacts very quickly to any stimulant, any intake of food or drink; and one just as quickly recovers. A single glass of beer in such circumstances can make one quite drunk, and a heavy meal can put one fast asleep in minutes. There are other effects too, such as a vividness of dreaming and a lightness of sleep. From now on, throughout the rest of my traverse, I found myself experiencing unusually lengthy, orderly and curious dreams of the sort that persist into morning. And so it seemed, on that dawn outside the village of Juf, that I had been transported into a slightly different universe that existed and exists beside the one that I knew and know – one in which the dewy grass was more sweet and long and damp and fragrant, in which the hills were more perfectly shaped and of a more variegated green, and in which the sky could change in more rapid and more varied clear tints from gold, to lemon to white, to utter blue, and in which one might as easily meet a mythical beast or a character from a painting by Breughel, as another twentieth-century positivist down on his luck.

Breakfast, however, brought me back to reality. I had none. Or little enough; and precious little for lunch and just about nothing for supper. This was an oversight, an omission, a failure; this was against the rules. Moreover, today being Sunday, I would be unlikely to find anywhere open at Maloja – which was my next objective; nor would the post office be open to collect any mail (for Maloja was one of my mailing points). And I would need to change money as well, and the *bureau de change*, the *Wechsel*, the *cambio* would be *fermé*, *geschlossen* and *chiuso*. And already my stomach was rumbling and grumbling for food. The outlook for the next 24 hours was not good.

Let this be a warning to anyone else who thinks of making a Grand High-Level Route – keep an eye on the diary and have a watch with a date on it! And learn about National Holidays.

The hills between Juf and Maloja give very good walking in a landscape something like the higher parts of the Lake District, but grander. A good path goes up the valley from Juf and over a low pass called the Forcellina, from here descending to the track that crosses the Septimer Pass. You cross this track at right angles and continue, climbing steadily to the summit of the Lunghin Pass, which is a long, low saddle in the shaly wilderness about Maloja, before descending by the beautiful Lunghin lake to the village or rather hotel settlement at which you are aiming.

I determined to forget my hunger, enjoy this walk and breathe in the beauties of the scene. My slightly light-headed, euphoric mood came back as I walked up the valley through the sweet, shining grass and along the slopes that led to the Forcellina. I had a new song too that had come into my head, remembered from schooldays:

> The hunt is up, the hunt is up
> And it is well-nigh day
> Harry our King is gone hunting
> To bring the deer to bay.
> The East is bright with morning light
> The darkness now is fled.

In between stanzas I held long conversations with the marmots.

On the way up to the Forcellina I had kept just within shadow, but at the top I was engulfed in the sunlight and in a shining burning mist that redoubled the burning power of the sun and its brilliance. Only the foreground was clear, and occasional distant rims and outlines of hills; everything else was a sway and shift of light and heat. I picked my way across the sloping moor from cairn to paint-mark to footstep and back to cairn. Now there was a path and now there was not; sometimes there were long stretches of melting snow and sometimes pools; but mostly the ground was of short turf and outcrops of rock. Once there was a brief view across the upper surface of the mist towards the steep rock summits of the Bregaglia peaks, and once or twice forward and up in the direction of Lunghin: but mostly I walked, slowly and steadily down through incandescent steam. I could feel my face and forearms and calves being steadily broiled, and the sweat ran off my bald head and into my eyes until I tied a cotton scarf across my brow.

At the Septimer track I paused and ate a very meagre second breakfast and watched the mist clear away slowly. On an outlined ridge, horned creatures were moving – the steinbock. An eagle drifted and wheeled overhead. Here, I had calculated, was a momentous location; the hydrological centre of Europe. From within a hundred yards of the shaly crest of the Lunghin saddle, streams flow south into Italy, the Po and the Adriactic Sea; they flow north and west into the sources of the Rhine and thence into the North Sea; and they flow eastward into the Inn that joins the mighty Danube that flows into the Black Sea. This landscape, which in fact was not at all beautiful in itself, looking as it did more like the slate hills of Bethesda than the mother of the rivers, had become one of the central nodes of my interior map. When I reached this place, when I passed over it, I would know by some mysterious psychic movement that, irrespective of the actual distance, I had now achieved a half-way mark, a point of fulcrum; from here on, like magnetic lines of force, like gravitational fields, like a shifting tide, the geography would be working for me, the winds would be behind me and my step would be lighter. The eastward direction I was following had by now acquired a symbolic value.

There were good practical reasons for travelling from west to east along my route, rather than in the other direction. The worst weather comes, on the whole, out from the northern and western quarters, hence, in travelling east the worst wind would be likely to be behind me (and this generally proved to be true); and a second reason was that in climbing up in the morning (since I normally slept in valleys) I would have the shady side of the hills for as long as possible, and the harder snow; furthermore, the afternoon and evening sun would not be in my eyes, whereas travelling in a westerly and southerly direction the light would have got fiercer as the day wore on. But now the easterly direction had another sort of meaning.

Perhaps the importance I attached to it was associated in my mind with an obscure desire to rewrite history, to reinvent the world by reversing the original wanderings of peoples; and in so doing to get a complete and new vision of possible futures. Only peasants can live without a future, but we can no longer be peasants even if we tried very hard. Our whole language, our whole conception of reality is predicated upon some picture of what is to be; and yet it seems that we have no picture and can form none. Thus to reverse the flow, to walk into the dawn instead of the dusk, to swing the whole perspective around to reveal new configurations of mountains or events, is to liberate the imagination from the rule of status quo and to see, just, that a future is possible and thinkable.

> The hunt is up, the hunt is up
> And it is well-nigh day

The top of the Lunghin Pass is marked with an iron post on which a board is affixed, and on that board an appropriate message to tell us that this is a place of significance: otherwise the Lunghin Pass might be mistaken for a mine-tip or a quarry spoil-heap. Down below me, however, was a shining blue lake, the Lago de Lunghin, and round its shores were green patches of grass emerging freshly from the melting snow. I descended there as quickly as I could, in a glissade down from the top almost to the water's edge.

At the further side, some hundred yards away, a variously coloured cliff of streaked granite, quartzite and shale rose up; at the far end of the lake, steep screes and snow patches went up to the skyline: and at the outflow I sat on smooth rocks and patches of scabious to admire the blue. It seemed that I had never seen such a perfectly blue lake, in which so many blues were mingled: a colour that began, at the edges, almost the colour of a purple-sheened clay, became within a yard a rich milky-green like the colour of a duck's egg, and almost as quickly turned to turquoise, then azure and then into the most intense ultramarine which, in the shade of the reddish cliff, took on a scarlet resonance.

I took out my sketch pad and spent almost two hours making different drawings of this scene, trying, with only a pen and paper, to make marks that might correspond, somehow, to the richness and clarity of the colour. There are those who can do it, who can express colours without colour; but I am not of their number. Later, back at home, I took out the drawings and made several attempts at painting what I could recall of the experience; but without the slightest success. Like a lot of people, I have the desire to paint and just enough knowledge to make success seem possible; but like a lot of people too, I completely lack the sustained and constantly renewed determination to see the matter through to a proper conclusion. When I look at my results, I see nothing but imitation and parody, and to make it worse I am sufficiently knowledgeable to see just who and what I am imitating and perverting and to know that it corresponds to nothing more or less than my weaknesses of character. And because I can't face those weaknesses, I give up painting. And that makes me even more disgusted with myself because that is a perfect example of the very weakness and paltriness I am hoping to forget. From this I ought to conclude that I should either give up trying to paint altogether, or really take it seriously and push what little talent I have as far as possible, thus overcoming the weakness, paltriness, etc. But I can't, damn it, I can't.

The activity of drawing and thinking about colour and geology was completely absorbing and helped me to forget my hunger. Several other people arrived, having walked up from the valley to visit the lake and the post with its notice.

On the walk down the steep winding path to Maloja I passed many people strolling gently up or down, all very smart and clean and in the possession of money; and when I got down to the road I found a street of hotels and cafés with many people eating and drinking. Most of all, they were eating cakes, and cream, and ices and fruits, and drinking long cool glasses of beer or Cola or cocktails: and in the fields and gardens or down by the broad blue lake amongst the pine-trees or swimming from the reeded shore were brown girls with white breasts.

I spotted a water trough off behind an old barn, and went there to wash and clean myself up and change into some decent trousers and an approximately clean shirt before joining in this bourgeois idyll.

What do all these happy people want from life, I was wondering? Have they any conception of a future, any goal at which to aim (other than simply repeating one summer holiday after another)?

What I wanted was food and drink; I walked up and down that road looking at menus and peeping over fences. The carnival of Juf was prolonging itself at Maloja, with a band, and a fair and with children dancing in a ring; but it did not have the same quality, for this settlement is essentially for travellers and consists solely of them and those who make money out of them. The commerce is done in good taste and with a certain panache, and at least one of the hotels is a splendid wooden structure of the very best Swiss style; but I found the place unsympathetic. When I went into the hotel to change money, I felt like a harijan.

These remarks are probably unfair to the hoteliers and visitors of Maloja, and arose from my quite extraordinary hunger that I could not afford to appease until late in the evening, because if I ate now in mid afternoon, I would be hungry again before bed. So I drank a single glass of tea in the cheapest café and went walking through the meadows and woods, looking for a site to pitch my tent when evening came.

The upper Engadine valley is, in truth, a very beautiful area; even to one half-dead with hunger. The beautiful lake of Segl stretches north-eastward, hemmed in by forested crags or open to wide pastures. The mountains lie back and do not bring sudden tempests, and a gentle breeze blows through it into dusty Italy below. Maloja itself stands right on the pass, and signals its strategic importance by a large stone keep upon a piney hill; the Romans came this way, and their ancient causeway can still be seen. In the early years of the century expensive villas were built to complement the hotels, and are still being built. At the end of the main and only road in Maloja the hillside slopes away and the road begins to zig and zag down towards Italy and Lake Como. I spent some time there on that side, watching the pillars of cloud form and reform around the misted outlines of the Bregaglia peaks, and then walked back through the meadows and sat for a while with my feet in the lake, watching the dinghies, the wind-surfers and the swimming girls.

As evening came on the gentle breeze that had been blowing became cold, carrying dust mixed with light rain; thunder began in the mountains, erratically. I turned back towards the road, walked through the street again and chose what seemed to be the best buy, went in and sat down and ate all I could afford – succulent schnitzel, with potatoes and a great mound of cauliflower, followed by bread and cheese and fruit. I would have repeated the meal very happily, had I had enough of a purse: but instead I had to leave, and walk off through the woods, and in the darkness find the spot I had chosen to pitch camp again. Camp 23.

The night that I spent in the woods outside Maloja was very uncomfortable because it was very hot; yet because there were so many stinging and biting insects I had to keep fastened up in my tiny tent. There were large mosquitoes that had the power and range of the Norwegian variety, and that coasted around waiting for you at every corner; the moment they got a trace, they homed in like sidewinders on your heat-trail, nose first; they would swoop down, land in a cartwheel motion and at once set down their snouts and drill as if to strike oil. These mosquitoes raised large lumps, like love-bites without the compensations. Then there was another nasty that looked like a pair of pliers, winged, and which made a noise like a 50 cc machine. These, I swear, could bite through anorak and jersey and still tear a pound of flesh; but you could hear these coming and take evasive action. It was the sound that was frightening: I have only once heard anything quite as frightening, and that was a doodlebug when I was a mere child. It was when the noise stopped that you had to be really frightened, however. But these unnecessary acts of creation were as nothing to the minute and insidious gnats which swarmed in a mist at exactly the height of the door of the tent. These gnats were of a Caledonian ferocity and more than Highland bloodthirstiness, and of subliminal size so that they could enter, it appeared, through the teeth of a zip. Once in the tent (having fought my way past the two successive waves of attack) I found my base area had been infiltrated. What is more, the tent, being too small to turn round in, was no place to hunt them down. It was enough to make a stout ox weep, to drive a grizzly bear into capitulation, blubbering. I had to burrow into my bag – and I was pursued even there – pull the drawcord above my skull and lie there, broiling and burning from myriad bites until the daylight came, when the whole process of test-to-destruction began again.

The man at the post-office looked twice at me and twice at my passport photograph before letting me have my letters; my face had quite different contours from its image, and my skull had sprung a hundred new bumps.

The sun was already hot at half-past eight in the morning, and the weather forecast, pinned to a notice board outside the tourist bureau, seemed to promise a continuing heatwave, with thunderstorms. My original plan had been to walk up the Fex valley and to cross over by the glacier pass at its head on to the Scersen snowfields, to spend my next night in the vicinity of the Marinelli hut in order to climb the Piz Bernina on the following day. But I did not want another epic on unfrozen, melting snow, on a peak of which I knew nothing and for which I had no guide notes.

Since the Piz Bernina was my main objective for this stretch of the traverse, I thought to attempt it from the south, by the normal Italian approach. In that way I could do it from a low camp, and be spared a long glacier walk with a heavy pack.

At nine I was managing to assuage my hunger with a prolonged breakfast by the beautiful Cavloc lake, before making the long climb into Italy, over the Muretto Pass. This was home ground again, for I knew this corner of the Bregaglia peaks well from years before, and in my walk up the valley I kept trying to anticipate exactly what each new corner would reveal, to test my memory. The waters of the lake were absolutely calm and perfectly mirrored the cone of Monte Forno above them.

The way led through a pleasant forested valley and then over a wooden footbridge where the path divided, left to Italy and right to the Forno glacier and hut. I took the left hand trail and began working my way up, very slowly, into the deep stony cwm below the pass. The heat and the brilliance were extreme, and the load was very heavy; there was not a breath of wind, and the light was reflected off a multitude of little rivulets and off a million million sparkling mica crystals in the rock, and higher off the burning glass of a great bed of snow. The ground shimmered with mirages and the flanks of Monte Forno threw back the heat like an open furnace door. At midday I was climbing up an immense slope of loose scree, up a barely marked path towards the frontier, scraping and slipping, with my heavy pack lurching. And the frontier, when I reached it, was every bit as stony and the descent every bit as hot and airless, though on the Italian side it was aided by a very well-built track of military appearance, that went up to what looked like an old emplacement in the rocks above the pass. From here, Italian troops would be able to look right down into the top of the Engadine valley. (Some of these military tracks, I read later, were built by Mussolini's men in order to keep them busy, well before the last war, but later towards Austria I was to encounter old trenches, wire, ammunition crates and the remnants of rifles – relics of an earlier conflict.)

The wonderful summit of Monte Disgrazia came into view, surrounded by thunder heads. I had stood there, summers earlier; but now it seemed very remote and of a Himalayan height and inaccessibility. Below, down the long and very stony track, a forested valley was coming into view. The slope I was on faced south, directly into the sun and there was still no wind or any shade of cloud. Streams splashed across my way, and I put my head under their waterfalls and drank them, copiously. A party of young people passed me, lightly loaded, laughing and joking and skipping while I trudged. My knees ached, horribly, as if I had given them some fearful internal lesion.

This uppermost section of the Val Malenco is a wonderful place if you are not burdened with a huge sack and a heatwave; there are thick pine-forests, fine, flat meadows, rocks and glaciers above. And when you get down to the roadhead at Chiareggio, there is a pleasant bar and several old houses: but my appreciation of this scene was small and lessened still further by the absence of any bus service. The road continued down on the sunny side of the valley, white and dusty: all that southern slope of the range was baking in heat and almost treeless compared with the other north-facing bank. There was shade and thick forest.

I crossed the torrent by a footbridge and continued walking down the shady side, at first on a good path but later on little discontinuous trails through thick fir undergrowth, emerging now and then into beautiful clearings only to plunge back into barely penetrable ferns and saplings. On this side all was lush and green; on the other (when I could see it through the branches) there seemed to be nothing but bare rock and brown grass. Hard work, but cool and, when you could see your way, a pretty place. My map was no use for this, at all, but it did mark another footbridge some five miles down stream, and when at last I found it I crossed over it to be sure of the last few miles down to Chiesa. It was now around five, and I reckoned it would be less hot.

Instead, it was hotter than ever, and the road wound down innumerable hairpin bends between walls of bare, glowing slate and great mounds of quarry spoil – for Chiesa, I was discovering, is a great place for stones and slates and is entirely surrounded on its upper side by huge trenches and pits and their detritus, and by ropeways and gantries and obscure rusting machinery. The heat and dust were almost past bearing, the landscape declivitous and industrial. Had I made a serious error, I was wondering?

The town of Chiesa itself, when I reached it, was an interesting mix of buildings tilted one on top of another down over and round the descending road. It had good shops, hotels, factories and cafés all mixed in together, and plenty of life. A friendly native pointed the way to a *campeggio*, right into the main street. Not far, he said, but half a kilometre. This I could not believe and so I asked another, who was equally friendly and urged me on. How was my *sacco . . . pesante*? *Alpinismo*? And yes, the *campeggio* was in *la strada*.

And so it was, right there in the middle of town, a sort of tennis court of gravel opposite a supermarket; and there was a small blue tent there already, an English tent. I sat down in the dust and suddenly began to tremble with fatigue and heat exhaustion. It had been a very long and very hard day and for the first and only time I had done too much.

The tent was occupied by two young lads from North London. How they came to be there, I never quite discovered; and they scarcely knew themselves. But they had hitched up from Milan in order to look at the mountains and the only thing they had against Chiesa was that you could not buy fish-fingers there, and fish-fingers was their principal diet. Experienced in nothing, they had got themselves there and wanted to go further. They made me a big mug of soup, to which I added extra salt, and then many cups of tea. I was really pleased to see these two. And what was more, the camp site was very cheap and had the facility of showers, hot water and clean toilets.

Out of what had seemed to be a potential error had come, with luck, the very place I needed. With my last energy I made a good meal, and to ensure a full night's sleep I downed a carafe of *rosso* in the bar across the road.

That day I had broken an essential rule for anyone making so long a traverse: I had forced the pace when I was already tired. The drive I had put into my journey through the Lepontine Alps, my storming over the Kaltwasser and up the Ofenhorn, and above all the heavy days across the Adula peaks and the long descent to Hinterrhein; and then my carousing at Juf, and the steamy crossing to Maloja, and the hunger I suffered there – all these had been the worst possible preparation for my crossing into Italy in the midst of a heatwave over what had been more or less a desert. I spent a very quiet morning in Chiesa, washing some clothes, dozing and eating.

Paul and Mick had the idea in their heads that they should visit a mountain hut, and the plan emerged that we should all three walk up that evening to the Bignami Hut. From here, I imagined, it would be convenient to set out for the Piz Bernina, if the weather held; and it was back on my original and intended line of march. The two boys had no idea whatever what might be entailed in such a walk, nor what food or equipment they might want to take to camp up there: I adopted the role of mentor.

The town of Chiesa is very low, no more than 900 m above sea level, and the only sensible way out of it was by bus up into the gorges and precipitous southern valleys of the Bernina peaks to the little settlement of Franscia. We got there in the heat of mid-afternoon by taking the postbus up an astonishingly winding, airy and be-tunnelled road that went where no road was ever meant to go. The two lads were keen to be off at one rush to the head of the valley and the hut, but I restrained them. It was going to be a heavy four hours and it would be best to have a good meal inside to fuel one to capacity, and to wait till the day got, if possible, a little cooler. We sat in the shade of some trees and ate tinned fish, peaches, bread and cheese, and drank cartons of fresh orange juice.

This was now my regular valley diet, but at Chiesa I had discovered the perfect mountain food – a dense, hard rye bread called *pane di segale*. This formidable substance required very little else except the occasional hard-boiled egg. On the first-day after reprovisioning I would set out with a loaf of it at the bottom of my sack: at the top of my sack I would have heavier and more luxurious foods (tinned ravioli was very acceptable, and fresh tomatoes, and white bread), half way down my sack there would be six eggs, two for hard-boiling and the other four for scrambling; here there would also be fish such as sardines, perhaps some cheese and, when I could buy them, porridge oats. But at the base, always from now on, *pane di segale* and a bag of coffee.

I made a mistake at Chiesa with respect to coffee – I bought a bag that turned out to be unground coffee beans. I devised a way of crushing the beans on the concave side of the adze of my axe, grinding them down with a small round pebble, but this was such a tiresome thing to do I took to eating the beans like sweets. Regular inductions of caffeine have a pleasant numbing effect which on some days was exactly what was required. But I had also acquired some mint tea, and this, drunk very strong with plenty of sugar, was my sustenance each morning and evening. (In Austria I began to supplement this drink with a tot of schnapps every morning before getting out of my sack.)

Paul and Mick had a remarkable quantity of heavy gear and heavy food with them, in spite of my advice: when we set off walking again, they started at a tearing pace.

The road above Franscia becomes narrow, almost a track, and winds back and forth up steep woods and sunburnt meadows and after a while into tunnels and cuttings again before it reaches the dam at which it ends. The best way was not to follow every winding, but to cut up steeply and slowly by connecting little paths. The heat was intense and the air was stifling on this huge hillside: our fast pace slowed to a steady plod and then almost to immobility. I noticed my companions eyeing every bit of running water with a desperate yearning. But, as I pointed out to them, there was work to be done. They were full of a willing spirit, but their flesh was not quite up to it. To our extraordinary good fortune a small bus arrived and offered us a lift – it was driven by a cheerful young man who was going up to the dam to pick up a party from a youth club who were camping there. Without him, I do not think my two companions would have made that walk in one day.

We said goodbye on the dam wall; they crossed it to set off up the trail to the Bignami hut and I saw them for the next half-hour wandering very slowly upward. Much too slowly to get there by nightfall.

Now how many British climbers can, with a clear conscience, swear they were not benighted on their first visit to the Alps, not through the difficulty of things but through underestimating the sheer size of the walks? I cheerfully admit that on my first excursion, which consisted of a walk up the Mer de Glace to the Requin Hut, I was myself benighted, and spent a chilly few hours lying out on the ice. A complete novice, with a complete novice, makes for an ignorant team. To compound that piece of gross misconception, my companion and I next day attempted to climb the Aiguille du Requin by the "voie de plaques" on the understanding that it was no more than grade three rock-climbing: we were dismayed to find it turn into a steep and deadly ice-climb and were very nearly forced to bivouac a second night running.

For my part, I had abandoned the idea of the Piz Bernina. I, too, had come up from Franscia with painful slowness, and with lowered spirits. The relentless heat and the sheer gain in vertical height necessary before I could even think of reaching summits was intimidating. A tired and intimidated climber makes a bad soloist. If the crossing of Lunghin Pass had been the geographical pivot of the traverse, this pass on which I was now embarked, the Pass da Cancian was a psychological pivot.

I walked along beside the lake of the dam and into the mouth of a lovely green valley between high stony hills. My thoughts were all about my family and how much I was missing them, and about how far I had to go. I was entertaining some vague plan to climb the Piz Scalino as a good consolation prize, but I knew this was merely a self-deception. The Bernina peaks had beaten me. Later, talking to a German climber who had been there in that same week, I learnt that the conditions high up had been very bad, without any freezing and with unpleasant stone-fall and avalanche conditions because of the heat. That reconciled me to not having done anything, and gave me a good reason in retrospect. But the true reason for my achieving nothing, in one of the best little groups of mountains in the whole Alps, was – that I was very tired and consequently suffering a crisis, not of confidence, but of loneliness.

I made a beautiful camp that night, on short turf beside a little stream, with a view back along the line I should have taken, over the Fex-Scersen saddle and below the Marinetti hut and over to Alpe Fellario, traversing at glacier height beside half a dozen decent peaks. Two hundred yards eastward was the low saddle of the pass, leading into Switzerland again. Here I made not one but several three-stone cairns, carefully selecting the best stones I could find (boulders of white quartzite), and I wrote out my wife's name in letters of pebbles across the sward. I sat and watched the sun go down, drinking my mint tea.

Much of my retrospect of the journey is of camps. It would be hard to say which was the most beautiful, but I would like to make a list of those that come first to mind.

Camp 2: on a high shelf of grass below the Col de la Ponsonnière in the Thabor group – for remoteness, stillness and mist above a deep-set lake.
Camp 8: a bivouac, in the moraine of the Morion glacier with a violet sky holding a golden moon.
Camp 15: beside the watercourse that feeds the Simplon Alm as the weather began to clear; bees, flowers and the sounds of water.
Camp 17: the cold stone bothy by the upper Vannino lake, for the sense of adventure and energy, in spite of the concrete floor.
Camp 20: on the tiny level alp below the Soreda Pass, for the view backward, for the sense of achievement, for the astonishing light reflecting off snow and rock.

And for this, my 25th camp, on the perfect level grass below the Cancian saddle, and the views of the Bernina, and the elegaic mood.

Still to come were a high camp on the Palon della Mare; a hailswept stony place on the Hochjoch, by the Austrian border; then, perhaps the most perfect of them all, a camp on a little meadow at the foot of the south ridge of the Möseler; and, finally, the one on a rock ledge 50 feet above the edge of the Venediger glaciers.

Another perfect dawn. I am high above the clouds, that fill all the valleys. The summits just touched with pink, but the sky still dark in the west. An immense descent towards Poschiavo, down scree to a little lake and then – a piece of inspired route-finding in the mist – just striking the right little path that leads down to a high pasture and down further to a chalet and a track through huge pine-trees. On down through more trees, ever on down till the knees begin to ache. Then open irrigated meadows, farms, and suddenly it is the valley and the little town of Poschiavo, venerable with churches and narrow streets, that I look down into as I come through the steep walled fields past cows grazing, men sawing logs and women hanging out their washing. And as I descend the sun disperses the clouds and another scorching day begins.

Poschiavo lies in a finger of Switzerland projecting over the watershed, facing down into Italy: I thought it an attractive little town with an architecture as mixed as the language of people that lived in it – a Gothic church with a Romanesque tower next to a neo-classical town hall. I bought a litre of apple juice and sat in the main square drinking it and wondering about taking a bus for the next four or five miles up the valley. But I seemed to be very fit and healthy and cheerful again, so, trusting to my stamina, I set out walking up the long main road that goes over to St. Moritz.

Once again, I was given a lift without raising a thumb. A young woman stopped who had just been over the border to buy cigarettes; at least I think that was what she had been doing but I found it very difficult to understand her, so dense was her accent. She dropped me off at the junction called Sfaxu, from which I proposed to cross back into Italy by the Val Viola.

Most of the Alpine valleys were obstacles to me, since I travelled across them; but the trench of the Val Viola (which on its Swiss side is called the Val de Camp), travels from south of west to east of north, and is broad and high and relatively gentle. Apart from the Val de Leisse on my sixth day, this was the only major valley I was able to use for progress.

An unmade but well-graded track ran up the valley and I followed it to the beautiful little lake at Saoseo – another field of blue milk set round with glistening conifers. Beyond that a stony track led steadily upward, not steeply but rising without interruption into a very stony, scree enclosed cwm not unlike that at the foot of the Muretto Pass. To the south of the valley is an extensive wall of rocky peaks, streaked with snow-gullies and small ice-cliffs: this line of summits builds up steadily into two impressive peaks – the Saoseo and the Dosdé. On the north side the mountains ascend in broken ridges, and their tops are hidden. Today, across all high ground, drifts of mist were floating, and veiling all but the largest features. Looking back over my shoulder I could see glimpses of the

The Adula, or Rheinwaldhorn; and below it, the infant Rhine.
To the right of the main summit is the rocky eastern summit that
I climbed over on my way from the Länta valley. A long hard day.

The green hills of Juf.

The Lagh de Cavloc, near Maloja, where I ate breakfast before trekking over the Muretto pass (*l. of centre*) back into Italy.

Peaks to the south of the Val Viola – a fairly remote area, full of surprises. There are enough good mountains in the Alps for a few lifetimes.

The Cevedale glacier; my descent took the steep snow gully on
the right of the glacier.

The soloist's friends: cairns discovered, as I descended into
the Val Martello from the snowfields of the Cevedale. Ahead
is the Cima Venezia, and other peaks. The 29th day.

The Windachscharte. An evil little pass in the Stubai Alps –
but leading to marvellous territory.

Looking westward from the summit of the Gross Möseler. With first the
Hochfeiler, and then the Stubai and then the Ötztal Alps beyond.

A pass in the Zillertal Alps; the Weisszint-scharte.

The fifth of the five Hornspitze peaks, from the Austrian side.

On the same day as the last photograph, looking
into Austria. The peaks of the Turnerkamp and Gross Möseler,
from the fourth Hornspitze.

The Hinterer Maurerkees Kopf, from the Sulzbach glacier.
This was the best and most exacting summit, which I reached
up the long right-hand skyline.

Camp 41, and a view back over the Venediger group.
In the centre is the Maurerkees Kopf and to its right the
Krimmler pass, that I had crossed that morning.

The final morning. After the storm on the Grossglockner,
I took a low walking pass, and came round, slowly and steadily,
to Heiligenblut. One must not count on good weather.

My camp below the Gross Venediger; evening sunlight.

glaciers around Piz Palü and the eastern flanks of the Bernina. Ahead, stones and more stones.

The pass I was now approaching – but which seemed never to get any nearer – was another important stage of my journey, for here the Grand High-Level Route leaves Switzerland for good. And it seemed to me, since leaving Maloja, that I had entered another region of the mountains, and moved from the central to the eastern Alps. This was a change that one felt rather than actually recognized. There may well be subtle changes that only a botanist would notice; but the climber has the sense that although the peaks are crowded and numerous, they do not have quite the same bulk as those further west. Really big summits are far apart and clearly visible. The valleys too are less inhabited, and although there are plenty of visitors such as oneself, they are less noticeable because the natural economy has adjusted to them less. The farms, too, tend to be smaller, though perhaps not poorer; the customs and appearance of the local people is less urban and more peasant. The towns – such as Chiesa, Poschiavo and Bormio (that awaited me at the further end of the Val Viola) are working towns with rather few concessions to the tourist. And then there are the languages. These upper valleys speak lingos from before the flood, miscellanies of almost unliterable mongrel-tongues bred by Roman legionaries out of Celtic backwoodsmen, a scrambling of Latinate Slavisms, Euzkadences, lockjaws and tonguesplints, real glottal blockers. It barely mattered what language I used to anyone I met, so I developed a sort of pidgin Italianate German. I believe that most of the local people had little idea of what tongue they spoke themselves, among themselves, and the jargons of these high-landers (if they have been recorded at all) will have names only in the most learned of learned papers.

My "pidgin Italianate German" was not intended for the human inhabitants of the Eastern Alps, but for the marmots, on whose company I had come to rely for all conversation. I prepared a short speech of farewell to the marmots of Switzerland, and delivered it at the crest of the pass. The gist of this message was that I had greatly appreciated their company, that I wished them well in their homes among the rocks, that I hoped they would sleep well all winter and live to see their grandchildren – and so forth. I then gave a general farewell to Switzerland and turned round to face the descent into

Italy. Do not laugh, reader, for you too may one day feel the need to
speak to dumb beasts.

This descent was down a grassy green slope, and much more
pleasant than the toil up the other side. Here the valley was very
wide and open; to the south the blunt and formidable tower of the
Cimone di Dosdè looking for all the world like a major peak, and to
the north a great wide moor rising up to easy stony ridges. Here, as
on the Muretto Pass, were the familiar military track and the
remains of an old barracks – but as usual I took an absolutely direct
line, cutting off all corners and taking advantage of the ground,
never climbing a step more than was necessary and travelling at a
steady lope.

In this way I got well down the valley and was able to spend a
long time beside a waterfall, cooking up a meal and stretching
myself on the grass. One learns quickly that good rest periods are
essential, and regular solid meals: it was the lack of these that had
worn me down in the Bernina group, and I was absolutely
determined not to let that happen again. I was also conscious of pain
in my knees, for I had already made one very long descent that day,
into Poschiavo, and the track was stony and hard on the joints. So
far, with the exception of a gashed hand, I had escaped any injury or
muscular strain, and that too I wanted to keep as my standard. In
fact, the next day my knee strain was healed and I never thereafter
had any difficulty though I always took great care on long descents,
particularly late in the day. I finished the traverse without incurring
any sprains or pulled tendons, and I put this down to taking care
about rest periods in every day, and to having a change of footwear
at regular intervals. Of full rest days I had only two, and those were
forced on me by the bad weather; I had anticipated having a day of
relaxation every tenth camp, but found I had neither the desire nor
the need for one. Instead I tried to make every third or fourth day
more gentle than the rest, and in this way I was able to develop a
very good overall rhythm that fitted in well with the terrain. It
enabled me to cover some considerable distances, vertically and
horizontally. This day, for instance, I had descended some 5,000
feet into Poschiavo, and then walked over the Viola pass, coming to
a halt outside the village of Isolaccia, a distance of about 25 miles,
carrying a 40-pound sack. And although I was thoroughly weary
when the day was done, I was fresh and relaxed the next morning

and quite capable of moving up into the mountains again, and doing an even bigger and longer trek the following day.

This rhythm depended on one essential factor: I did not have a set schedule or planned route (except in the broad sense). I never had any need to hurry or compulsion to reach any point by any special time. The corollary to this, as I have already explained, was that I had to carry rather more food than otherwise, so that I could stop whenever I wished. The speed and effectiveness of travel, which I was usually able to maintain, depended on the freedom that this approach gave me.

The Italian Val Viola gets very deep and forested, and the track which becomes a farm road clings to its northern or left bank. On the southern side of the valley is a succession of high and interesting mountains, with glaciers a good deal more extensive than the map suggested. Any one of these I would have been happy to climb, but to reach them would have meant a whole day's diversion. The best of them all is the Cima de Piazzi, which has impressive ice-cliffs and glacier terraces and from this side, no obvious route to its summit. I doubt if these peaks are climbed very often, for they all entail long, hard walks before you can even set foot on them: early in the season they would be magnificent.

I had plenty of energy left for an evening shift, and as the shadows began to lengthen I reached the road to the Foscagno Pass at a place called Arnoga. I had thought of camping here, but the pine-woods were thickly overgrown and I could find no water that I cared to use; so continued down and down, cutting off one big corner by a path, and then more road and woods and fields till I fetched up, with night coming on, at a camp site in the valley between Semogo and Isolaccia, two straggling villages that clung to the hillsides below a long rampart of limestone.

Not caring to spend money, I walked out through the site and dossed down in the woods beyond. (I was now in some financial trouble and felt I should not spend money on anything but food and the occasional bus.)

What do I remember of that spot? Disco music, caravans and frame tents seen through trees, a carpet of pine needles, and rising very early to catch the first bus into Bormio.

Bormio, too, is a fine old town, full of interesting streets and alleys in one of which I found an excellent grocery where I was able to replenish the stores of rye bread and mint tea, to buy my valley provisions, post letters and drink a cup of coffee all in the same friendly and wonderfully supplied little room. Here too I could very happily have stayed, but I had got the determination fever once more and wanted to be up there in the peaks, hammering away (my habit of pounding my right fist into my left hand had started up again). So by lunchtime I was in the little holiday village of Santa Caterina de Valfurva, and by mid-afternoon, creeping tortoisewise up the path to the Rifugio Branca.

The Ortler range, that lies between Bormio and the immense cleft of the Adige valley, offers many alternative and interesting opportunities to anyone making a high-level route. My plan was ambitious, and relied too much upon steady weather: it was to cross the range by taking in the summits of the Palon della Mare and the Cevedale. This entailed mainly high-level but easy snow ridges and plateaux, and no extensive glacier problems. It was a good plan, but as I say, it depended upon steady weather and that, it seemed, was not to be forthcoming. Grey trailers and veils were drifting in from the north, hiding the sun, or haloing it with their icy mist. There were many other easier possibilities but none of them had any aesthetic quality to them; and the harder variations all seemed to entail steep glacier work which, in the heat, I wanted to avoid. By the time I had reached the Branca hut and noticed the change in the weather I was more or less committed to my favoured plan.

The hut is built on a promontory of rock overlooking a wide open basin of moraines and meadows to one side, and above a glacier snout and looking into an immense glacier cwm on the other side. Behind it are rocky bluffs and crags and exactly opposite, two of the finest snow peaks to be seen, the Tresero and the San Matteo. From these descend and spread a crumpled eiderdown of glaciers, and a long circuit of ridges connects them with the Palon, which in turn spreads a quilt of ice to all four points of the compass, connecting with the long crest of the Cevedale (that Austrians call the Zufallspitze). A complete traverse of all four peaks and the intermediate summits is sometimes done, though there are difficult steps to negotiate. The Palon-Cevedale section looks something like the Cairngorms, capped with ice: it is essentially a linking of dissected plateaux, at a height of between 3,500 and 3,800 m. Once you have the height, you just keep on walking. But, as with plateaux everywhere, they are featureless and steep-sided, and consequently need adroit route-finding if the weather closes in. The guide book mentions these problems, and I had copied them down in my notes with great attention.

In the Branca hut I found a large-scale map which I was able to learn from, and on which a little convenient bivouac shelter was marked. This determined me to carry forward the plan to the first stage, a camp high up on the Palon. I had a conversation with some Germans in the hut, but they had no more information than I. It was agreed that the season was changeable and much too warm for comfort or safety, and they told me of their climbs on the Bernina. I did not tell them how far I meant to go, but I signed the hut book with, as before, an "Ecrins–Glockner" flourish. As evening came on I started, with a pace more of a snail than a tortoise, to climb the long ridge of moraine that led up beside the glaciers towards the Palon. I spent the night upon bare stones beside the ice, looking out over the cracked and crumpled snow-fields of the Matteo, whose summit kept vanishing into mists or being illuminated by flashes of lightning. I passed a cold and stony night there at Camp 27, with a gusting wind that spattered the tent with hail and rain, and with intermittent cracks of thunder, and with many small rocks and stones causing me to shift position much too often. I had not, of course, taken a bulky foam mattress with me, but my sack had a rigid foam pad as a liner which insulated me from ground cold quite adequately; yet it was not comfortable. So what with that and the element of apprehension I was feeling up there by myself and not trusting the weather, I was glad when three in the morning came around and it could be judged time to brew up.

These early morning cups, intricate to make, but blessed to drink. Lying there the dial of the watch is just visible and slowly, very slowly, you stretch out a hand and grope for the little gas stove (that you packed close beside you for warmth so that it will light, but not actually in the sleeping bag with you, lest it leak and suffocate you in your sleep). You lodge it somewhere safe, and feel for matches and torch. Before unzipping the porch of the tent, you pull the balaclava down over your ears and draw in your hands again, for warmth. Then, again slowly, unzip and search by torchlight. There are two small pans and one of them you fill; with great care – for a spillage could be a disaster – you set the stove up firmly on the gravel (against a small stone, if possible), light, put on the water, and shrink back into your bag to wait. All these operations can be performed one-handed, if necessary.

At this point you must be careful not to go fully back to sleep again, but a little doze is permitted. As the water approaches boiling and the tent warms up you scratch about and find the breakfast bag – in this case, porridge oats and with them the mint tea-bags. Sugar in a little canister. Most of the water is for tea but a little for the oats which are eaten warm but uncooked – this makes them much more filling, since they swell. The tea is harsh and shocks you into wakefulness and after a few sips and a few mouthfuls of mush, you pull down an outer zip and look out. Well . . . a star is visible, even two or three. You pull back the zip because that has let the cold air in. But now the stove is off, and the tent is no longer cosy; the time of decision has arrived which you try to put off by once more hiding in the bag. Your nose is extremely cold in spite of the hot tea. Slowly you dress, inside the bag and only at the last minute actually conjure yourself out of it and into your breeches. The tent is too tiny to put your boots on in its shelter so out you must go, having first of all packed all loose items into their respective nylon or plastic sacks and made perfectly sure that you know where everything lies. Then out, and for a moment the cold staggers you and you hardly have the wits to lace up your boots. Thus on all mountain mornings, when you look about at the signs of dawn and descry the weather.

On this occasion it was blowing steadily and there were many clouds dimly seen, and the light in the east was a grey diffuse light; not a sword of fire. The alternative plan was adopted – namely to leave tent and heavy gear and make a dash for the summit unencumbered, to return the same way. No traversing today. You don't have to make these decisions consciously at that hour of the day – they are pre-selected by experience.

I quickly filled my nylon sack with waterproofs, a handful of food and my pick, crampons and other little items. Gloves, torch, compass, first aid were already in my jacket. Boots re-laced, and gaiters refastened. Blow nose. Have a pee against a rock. Fasten door of tent. Look around at weather again and shrug with disgust. What the hell – forward!

The Palon is an easy mountain, but it's a long way to go and 3,000 feet to climb. After crossing a tongue of dry glacier an easy rock and boulder and gravel ridge runs up towards the summit. Visibility poor and the going underfoot bad, with a lot of half-frozen hail lying around. You try on the snowy lee of the ridge, out of the wind, but the snow is very soft and deep and wet. Bad sign. You come back to the crest or near the crest and stumble about on loose stones as the wind clouts you over the head and slaps your cheek. There is now enough light to see and this is what you see: the unmade bed of a filthy and drunken giant, all stains and creases; white mounds of ice, grey and ochre mounds of rock. Here and there are the glaciers are broken into mint-blue towers or splinters, or squeezed like sluggish toothpaste between enclosing buttresses. Racing grey clouds ahead, in the place you must go; no summits visible, or if visible, sporadically. The noise of wind, running water, and the occasional groan or crump from the ice.

I went up slowly, steadily for a long way, now on loose rock and now on deep wet snow. The wind got stronger. Views further north showed the advance of storms; the Bormio valley was hidden in a sheet of rain that was drifting my way. Still keep at it, came the message. I had a faint hope that the snow would begin to freeze around 3,500 m but it didn't. The rocks ran out and now there was nothing but a broad snowy slope, steep with cornices to the left, and further over to the right, cliffs. Ahead, somewhere, it was growing steeper and climbing up towards the plateau. Then hail and redoubled wind and sudden thick annihilating cloud. Moments of zero visibility.

I got up close to the plateau and began to be worried about where its edge might be, and how large the cornices were, and were there crevasses at the rim. The snow was abominably soft and the hail had turned from fine to very coarse; it was like being pelted by high-pressure ice-cubes. Waterproofs on, quickly; crouch down and eat chocolate. No shelter. Situation horrible. Situation probably untenable. Indication: reverse.

I had failed to climb the Palon, and the little point of 3,440 m that I had crossed over on the way up barely counted as a summit. I came down in a frustrated and irritable state of mind that was made worse as the weather began to improve, temporarily. This was not good enough; I had not come all this way for a walking holiday – I was after some mountaineering, and making a high-level traverse. Yet I had funked the Bernina and was being beaten out of the Ortler; and ages ago had been swilled off the Valais Alps. By the time I had returned to my tent, repacked and set off on my way, I was in a sort of despairing rage. It wasn't all clear what I should be doing; but whatever it was, it was not to stay still. I sped down to the hut and did not stop; a little path took me obliquely round the mountain into the main, wide Cedec Valley. Perhaps I could spend a night up there, or even, maybe at the Casati hut, high on the western side of the Cevedale. Then we'd see who was boss, in the morning! As I proclaimed to the marmots who sat outside their burrows to watch me pass — and were certainly applauding me — I would "knock the bugger dead".

I got to the Pizzini Hut at the top of the Cedec valley and ate some lunch, which began to put me in a better mood: there is a fine view of the Cevedale from here, and of the rocky hulk of the Gran Zebru (or, to Austrians, the Königspitze). A fitful sun had come out and lit up the way ahead — a high slope of scree and snow leading to the Casati Hut, just visible 2,000 feet above. But the climb up to there was frightful, for the snow was very wet and the stones very loose and the day very hot (when it wasn't hailing, it was steaming). And several, as I thought them, noisy and inconsiderate walkers were passing up and down, wrecking the trail through the snow or showering me with falling pebbles and worse. And some, to make matters worse, found something amusing in my headband. The worst of all was a small dog. What it was doing there I do not know but I wished it elsewhere because it was yapping at me and running at my ankles as I walked up the narrow, loose path. Being one of those men who dislike dogs at the best of times, I aimed a tremendous kick at it (in spite of my sack and headband) and when the first missed, a second kick. Neither connected, which was as well for its life, because I surely meant to damage it; and then when its owner, a burly but very respectable gentleman in Tyrolean shorts and a daft hat, wanted to argue with me I gave him a stream of abuse. I think my appearance was rather wild, because he stood aside, let me pass and said not a word more. Perhaps I was looking fanatical.

It has sometimes been said that mountain pursuits are character building. I reckon to have some experience of this and I know of no one whose character was actually improved by them, and quite a few who, being stubborn (myself amongst them), became more stubborn. And others, aggressive and self-centred, became yet more objectionable: ditto. A few even became vagabonds, and at that point I must have looked, as I say, wild and fanatical. I hated that slope, with its scree and its snow, and I hated those lighthearted walkers and all little dogs, and I hated the hail and the steam. And when I got to the Casati Hut, why, I hated that worst of all. It was big and shambling and surrounded by ruins and rubbish and the litter of ski-runs and drums of oil and yards of barbed wire that had been there since the great war, and old trenches, and latrines and far too many people drinking beer in a room that was far too hot. But I had to go in, for a violent icy rain was sweeping horizontally over the pass. And when I was in there was nothing I could afford and all I could do was sit and watch other well-built men in Tyrolean shorts and daft hats eating great plates of sausage with mustard, great pieces of bread, and swilling down beer. I was in truly a nasty mood that afternoon.

But I had the self-control to know that my irritability was due to hunger, so I sat down, suppressed my appetite for hot sausage and contented myself with cold sardines.

The long broad crest on which the Casati Hut stands was once a front line; the signs of trenches and emplacements are evident everywhere. I found something sinister in this, as if the mountains were not already intrinsically unfriendly places. From the crest a broad snow-field extends towards the ridge of the Cevedale east and the Königspitze group west, and wide glaciers flow north; there is normally skiing here all year round, but this summer it had been abandoned. There would, normally, be magnificent panoramas from here as well, but all that could be seen were a few yards of hail-driven mist. The idea of spending the night here was most unattractive, especially since most of my clothes were wet from sweat or the icy rain that had hit me on the last hundred metres climb. I made a second plan, to go west to the narrow little col called the Eisseejoch and to descend under the face of the Gran Zebru to the village and resort of Solda; I wanted to avoid the descent northward down the glaciers for I was certain they would be in a dangerous condition for a soloist. Four Austrians sharing my table advised me, when I asked them, that the Eisseejoch was in a bad condition with *viele Spalten*, and one of them volunteered a rather lengthy lecture on the dangers of solitary glacier travel. Now this address was something I could well have done without, since I was painfully and continually aware of such dangers and had, in fact, been acting with extreme caution for 30 days; and what was more galling was that it was patently obvious to anyone who knew one end of an axe from another that I was not a novice. One glance at my gear would have told him that, had he known how to read the signs; the concision of my movements, the Spartan diet, the self-absorption. . . .

Fortunately, the sardines had begun to take effect, and I was able to thank these gentlemen for their advice and agree that, yes, great care was necessary while crossing glaciers alone. And so I left them.

I shouldered my pack, adjusted the band, and loped off westward towards the Eisseejoch, following a well marked track in the snow; the hail whipped past and the rain lashed and the wind blew. Two large crevasses had to be jumped, but they were well marked with posts. I reached the little pass and peered over and it was just as I had been told – heavily crevassed and all crevasses open: a path wound up through these crevasses, but I did not fancy to take it. For a while I thought of camping there, on a level stretch where an old military hut had once stood but my mood had changed with the food, and I could see a way ahead. It seemed wise to sleep low that night and the head of the Val Martello was indicated. But how to reach it, since the glacier flowing north-west below me looked horribly unsafe?

Here, at a lower altitude, I was out of the worst of the weather and could see a possible way ahead. I could, if compelled, traverse the rocky crest to the next easy col, over some little summits; but a neater plan suggested itself. Half a mile away, across a concave snow slope was a small rocky boulder. The grain of the hillside suggested another slope beyond it, and other easy shoulders leading valleyward. There was no path, nor even a line of footmarks, but it was geologically obvious.

So exactly it proved: beyond the shoulder a steep, even precipit-ous snow-slope – surprisingly firm – led down in a direct way to a scree ledge on which to my delight I found a cairn, and 50 yards further on, another. Not big cairns, just three stones piled on one another, to which in thankfulness and delight I added my own. And from here on all was obvious for the terrace led down, with occasional markers, to the moraine and bare stone slopes above and beside the glacier I had hoped to avoid. And now, too, the weather was clearer and a wonderful panorama began to unfold in the evening light.

A long ridge runs north-westward from the cone of the Cevedale, comprising a line of shapely little summits, one of which I saw with satisfaction was called the Cima Marmotta. These mountains were now all visible, though veils of hail would drift across them and branches of lightning clip their crests. The Cevedale now took on a perfectly conical form of great beauty, shining with the whiteness of opaque glass against the grey and purple sky; the peaks on the ridge, all ten of them, were different shades of ochre, rust and clay and down their sides streamed white torrents below bluish glacier shelves. In one place a great stream spouted from a cave in the midst of a cliff, in another, ice-blocks had fallen the full length of the face and lay like house-sized sugar cubes on the grit-striated surface of the glacier below.

My shelf of screes became a shelf of grass, enclosing little blue lakes and ponds and flower decorated meadows; though a rain kept falling on me, still mingled with hail, I was perfectly happy. A day of defeat and misery had been turned into a day of triumph: in fourteen hours I had crammed two days of climbing, climbed the greater part of a major mountain and crossed, in bad weather, a great glacier pass by an ingenious route of my own finding, and it had brought me down on to an excellent little path that was certain to lead me to a good camp-site in the midst of wonderful countryside. And now it came to me that I had completed three-quarters of my distance and that, clearly, the traverse could be made and finished in style, and that I'd gained some sort of mastery over the problems involved.

In the upper part of the valley is the remains of a vast stone wall that appears to have been built as part of an uncompleted dam. Near this I camped, and sat for a long time under an overhanging rock, eating a leisurely meal, watching the rain teem down, and reflecting on the splendours of experience.

Reading through what I have written in the preceding two chapters I doubt if I have managed to convey how arduous the middle section of this traverse had been. Since leaving the shelter of my boulder at Täsch and crossing to the Simplon Pass in cloud and snow I had barely paused; half an afternoon at Maloja racked with hunger and a morning at Chiesa racked with indecision had been my respite. I had covered over 200 miles of hard mountain travel in weather that was either beastly cold or exhaustingly hot. My count of summits was poor, and as a result I had experienced a good deal of disappointment and some loneliness. The constantly renewed effort of each morning, and the constant need for self-reliance and decisiveness had been wearing and in complete contrast to the pure, though demanding, pleasures of the first section of my route. The difficulties, the strains, the constant call to alertness were not, in each single case, very great; but the cumulative effect had been challenging.

In writing about it, it is hard to know the best point of balance; one should not want to overemphasize the difficulty of a Grand High-Level Route; and yet to be truthful I had felt some days as if what I was doing was barely tolerable and only an extreme stubbornness had sustained me. On some days I had known more fear than I was always willing to acknowledge, and fear by oneself is difficult to overcome. But I had come through to this point and was now about to start the last long stage of my journey to the farther end of the Alps, and through all the effort, sweat, cold and tension and constantly renewed drive it had become clear that I was going to do it. That I was about to realize the absurd ambition that had crept into my mind the year before. That thought renewed my strength and confidence. There, in my 28th camp in the upper Val Martello, a willing and happy enthusiasm returned. Moreover, though I had made no careful timetable, for reasons I have explained, I now reckoned I was seven or eight days ahead of my general estimation. I could therefore look forward to the Austrian Alps with a relaxed pleasure.

Chapter Six

ÖTZTAL AND STUBAI: AND BETTER TIMES

FROM THIS CAMP in the Val Martello I had in mind a crossing of the Laaser glacier and the Angelo peaks, descending by a marked track to the village of Prad, a day and a half away. But that night passed in torrential rain and wild dreams that persisted into the morning, which was grey and windy; and since the day before had been so long and hard I was not feeling sprightly. Moreover, I had a desire to see Austria that night, or at least the night after.

I have said that the greatest and most wearing obstacles on the Grand High-Level Route are valleys; the greatest of all is the valley of the Adige. There one must descend to a mere 700 m above sea level and climb laboriously out; and the slopes by which one climbs out face into the afternoon sun and are 5,000 feet high. My next objective was the Hochjoch, a high pass into Austria; but this was at the head of a subsidiary valley beyond those high, treeless, sun-baked slopes. The direct walking way, from my present position, would have been to descend the Martello valley to the little town of Schlanders (or, in Italian, Silandro) and then to go straight up a valley north of the town called the Schlandraunertal, and this would bring me over on the second day to the track up to the Hochjoch, by some tough walking.

That way would be all on foot, very pure and very boring. Another alternative was to descend into the Adige valley and to take a bus westward to Schluderns and from there walk up steadily toward the Höller hut on the southern flanks of the Weisskugel. I had a great mind to climb the Weisskugel, and this plan seemed the best; and if the weather was bad the next day, I could walk and climb over a pass and come round to the Hochjoch by an interesting route. This was very attractive, though it depended upon reasonable weather. The third was the lazy man's way, which was to go east down the Adige valley to the town of Naturns, and take another bus or hitch up to Kurzras, whence it was a simple, steady walk up to the Hochjoch and the frontier. I decided to leave it to chance.

Perhaps the best of all combinations, which was now out of the question, would have been to continue that day over the Angelo peaks, as planned, and to continue to the Weisskugel two days later; but one is not the master of circumstances. And as it turned out, luck took me to the Hochjoch that very night.

A short walk after striking camp a little later than normal took me down the road head of the valley, and a large hotel that was, surprisingly, shut for the season. After I had walked down through a thick and lovely pine-forest, coming down towards a lake, a large car stopped and the driver offered me a lift. He was a German who owned an hotel some way on the far side of Naturns and thus was my fate decided. He was a pleasant companion, and he spoke excellent English (which compelled me to use my rapid though impressionistic German, for courtesy) and we enjoyed a general conversation about mountains as we sped down into the huge and now unfolding valley below. He knew the local mountains well, and we talked about the Cevedale and the Palon and the König-spitze, and the Ortler, which he swore was as full of character as anything in the Western Alps. Then he described the complicated history of the South Tyrol or, as it is now called, the Alto Adige, and how this vast and wonderful trench had been disputed so bitterly up to the most recent times. And no wonder, he said, pointing it out.

And there below were mile upon mile of orchards, of apple, pear, cherry, apricot and peach, and mile upon mile of vineyards; with bright farms, trim villages, old fortresses above them, and old churches within them. Dream-like fertility and sweetness smelling of meadows, resinous pine-planks and channels of swift water. If ever there was country to fight for, and if ever there was country to inspire visions in the mind of northern Europe, this was it. And to please my companion, and myself, I was able to quote, almost accurately, the most perfect utterance, the final word upon the subject:

Kennst du das Land, wo die Zitronen blühn?

The car was halted in the streets of Naturns (or Naturno) and we shook hands and parted in high spirits; and there went another helpful and friendly soul, one of the dozen or so that did much to speed me along.

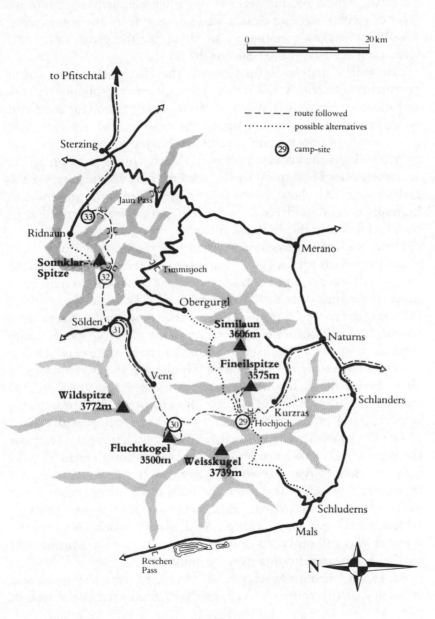

0   20 km

to Pfitschtal

– – – – route followed

·········· possible alternatives

㉙ camp-site

Sterzing

Jaun Pass

㉝ Ridnaun

Sonnklar-Spitze

㉜

Timmisjoch

Merano

Obergurgl

Sölden

㉛

Similaun 3606m

Naturns

Vent

Fineilspitze 3575m

Wildspitze 3772m

Schlanders

Kurzras

㉚

㉙ Hochjoch

Fluchtkogel 3500m

Weisskugel 3739m

Schluderns

Mals

Reschen Pass

N

In Naturns I replenished stores, drank my usual litre of fruit juice
– in this case, apricot – and ate my usual tomatoes, bread and strong
cheese, sitting on a seat in a strip of shade beside the firmly
embanked and impetuous torrent of the Adige (or the Etsch). It was
hot in the valley, but the peaks above it were invisible in a whitish
layer of swiftly moving clouds, crowding in from the south-west,
dissolving as they met the warm air above the great valley and
reforming again over the peaks to the north.

The valley that leads up towards the Hochjoch is large, but
debouches into the Adige trench through an improbably narrow
and inconspicuous cleft where there is barely room for road and
water together. A bus ran up to the roadhead at Kurzras, but
infrequently, so once again I started to hitch and once again I had
great good fortune because a pleasant elderly couple took me all the
way there after I had stood by the road for only five minutes. Such
fortune seemed to be an omen of better times to come and I was in
high spirits as I shouldered my pack to begin the long steep hill up to
the Hochjoch and the Austrian frontier.

From Naturns, as from many points on the journey, there were
always alternative routes and someone else attempting this traverse
might well want to take them. An excellent thing to do would be to
make a crossing over the Texel group of peaks directly north of
Naturns (the best path starts almost in the village main street). This
would take one through interesting country, with one or more
summits to the Eismeer just below the Austrian frontier, which one
can cross by two or three interesting high passes, with summits to
climb beside them. In that way one would descend to Obergurgl
and hence to Sölden. But for me the Hochjoch had become an
important objective, a way-mark, a point to be gained at all cost.

The Hochjoch also had the great advantage that it gave access to
the Weisskugel, which I still hoped to climb. Though I had not, as I
have written above, any information on the peak or adequate
maps, yet it was clear that from the Italian side of that pass a good
path led round towards the mountain and gave a way through
which would not entail complicated glacier work. And, if the
weather was still unsettled next morning, there were a number of
smaller and nearer mountains to be climbed.

Although I had every reason to be pleased with the speed and
efficiency of my route so far, I was very frustrated at the lack of

good summits. My whole object from now on was to crowd in as many ascents as possible, consistent with safety and forward progress.

Kurzras is yet another hotel settlement, this time one dominated by an immense and all-inclusive wooden structure – a megahostel with the appearance of a space station come to rest, but a wooden space station. Once again, it was imposssible not to be impressed by its originality and ecological usefulness. The mixture of traditional material and modern technology was intriguing and very fitting to the location. The structure had been visualized as if to stand in a snowy rather than a verdant landscape (the snowy landscape being a sort of visual "outer space"). The architecture and overall visual impact of winter-sports centres is a subject well worth thinking about; in many ways it represents what a great deal of modern architecture was always meant to be about until something or someone got their hands on it.

From Kurzras, cable cars can take you up to the high-level summer skiing on the glaciers opposite the Hochjoch, and there is a frequent coming and going of wealthy – or at least sporting and affluent – young people in fast cars, with skis attached, and with very brown faces and very bleached hair. Life at Kurzras is, it seems, one long advertisement. And then there are a large number of older people, like the couple who gave me a lift there, looking for gentle graded paths through the woods, or willing to walk up the Hochjoch, very slowly in the morning, to come down very slowly in the evening. These were the people I met; they descending leisurely, with straw hats, picnic bags and walking sticks and I ascending arduously, with headband, shorts and frequent halts. When asked I was perfectly prepared to tell them that I had come *aus Frankreich zu Fuss*. I am sorry to admit that this developed, over the next fortnight, into something of a game, watching the different expressions on the different faces pass from incredulity to amazement.

I arrived, after some two hours' hard uphill work, at the Hochjoch itself and set up camp on a broad terrace of gravel about half a mile from the large refuge that stands on the Italian edge of the saddle, a hundred yards from the edge of the ice-field that extends eastward from there, and a short distance from what I took to be the frontier itself – a large cairn and an old military hut.

No sooner was the tent in place than it started to hail and rain fiercely; and no sooner had I got inside my tent and made myself as comfortable as I could considering the stony ground, than all the water that was falling began to run in streams off the smooth, polished rocks that were all around and above me and to fill my little shelf of gravel, turning it into a pool. I hurriedly dug a drainage channel, but to no avail. I had to lever myself out of my tent, and in the howling gale and miserable cold move it over to a safer spot, doing my best to keep everything dry as I did so. Thoroughly frozen I slid into my bag and did my best to ignore the conditions.

Towards evening it became calm and I was able to sit outside to cook, well clad against the chilly breeze in my arctic underwear. Supper that night, on the banks of Austria, consisted of a soup into which large pieces of frankfurter had been chopped, followed by bread and cheese and a brew of mint tea. As the mists and hail drifted away, and as I sat on the rocks above the ice, rather as one might sit above the sea, warming my hands on the hot pan full of tea, it became quite clear what I should do next day. The clearance revealed a fine, shapely and pyramidal mountain at some distance across the ice – the Fineilspitze. That was clearly a worthwhile objective in any conditions. It was outstanding, decently high (around 3,500 m) and quickly attainable across a glacier that appeared without difficulty or danger. The actual climb itself seemed to offer interest – with a high band of rocks to overcome, a terrace of ice, and a good-looking final ridge. The Weisskugel, I concluded, was too uncertain for such unstable weather, too remote and unseen.

After the Fineilspitze it would be practical to continue over below its flanks to another hut and beyond, by a series of linked valleys and passes. That, if the weather held in its improvement, would be the next obvious step. If, on the other hand, the weather was poor I could still probably climb the peak, return to the tent and cross over the pass into Austria and work along the flanks of the northward extension of the Ötztal range towards the Wildspitze and the many peaks thereabout. The object in either case would be to arrive at Sölden on the third night, replenish, and set out for the Stubai range. The third night, too, would be my son's birthday, and I planned to ring him from there.

That night I wrote down in my little notebook the list of all my camps, passes and peaks. The camps were 29; the passes also 29, but the peaks, alas, a bare six – if I counted the Palon della Mare (which I did, cheating). I did this by the dwindling light of my torch, and then lay down to sleep with my head, as ever, on my boots and as much clothing, pack and sundry material as I could amass tucked well in between me and the very cold and stony surface. More hail passed over in the night, with cracks of thunder and prolonged flares of lightning.

Dawn was slow, grey and cheerless; but offered possibilities. With my lightest gear (leaving the tent and extra equipment behind) I trudged out across the convex plain of gritty ice, leaving the "shore" by a plank laid over a fathomless crevasse. Here the Hochjoch *Fern* is about two miles wide and almost level – an undulating sea of striated, crumbling glacier almost free of snow but seamed with little gullies running with swift, cold streams and slippery with half-frozen slush. Here and there, steeper slopes or little valleys made me pause and chip a step or two; but generally the honeycomb-and-grating surface of the ice, with its many stones and stretches of gravel, made for easy walking. A cold breeze was blowing on my right or southern side, and the usual long trails of mist and cloud were passing over the mountains. The Fineilspitze itself I could not see; and as I came closer to the far bank, a high wall of rocks would have obscured it no matter what the weather.

This wall of rocks, about 600 feet high, is called the Schwarzes Band. It is not quite a cliff, nor is it a slope: it is an intermittent and broken band of crags. I got on to it by avoiding some nasty little crevasses, by finding a sort of path up very steep scree, and then through the mist that had now begun to envelop me, sighting a large painted "target" on the side of a boulder. From here an obvious and well-scratched route led, without difficulty, up and through a succession of outcrops and blocks and loose gullies, issuing finally, after some steeper ground, on to a high balcony marked with a cairn. If the weather had been better this is where I would have left my heavy sack, since here there was a clear parting of the ways: one could go across the next stretch of glacier to a further rocky band and so over by a hidden pass to the Martin Busch hut in the next valley: a track marked the way, winding across the snow. Or, like me, you could set off uphill, following the edge of a glacier terrace.

The last few metres of the Schwarzes Band had been covered with frozen hail: here at this higher altitude it was certainly cold and windy and the snow had an unpleasant, insecure, half-frozen crust to it. I plodded up, following a line of footsteps. Now it was clear and now it was misty; to the left the summit cone of the mountain stood out, to the right the precipice of the Band fell down to the lower glacier. Easy going and no dangers, to a small dome from which I crossed the terrace, taking some care with a bergschrund and started climbing the steep ice slope up to the ridge. The ice was iron-hard here. I could have avoided the steepness by going less directly, but I felt like some technical testing after so much plod and push. Front-pointing neatly, with axe and hammer, I arrived at the crest just where it turned into rock. It was a pleasure to discover how strong my calf-muscles had become in the past month.

The final ridge gave a good scramble across icy and quite awkward rocks with a considerable drop on either side, into the mist. The summit, marked with an iron cross, had room for two or three people to sit down on, and there, in its aluminium case, was the summit book. I wrote my name with satisfaction.

There was nothing to be called a view – simply a continuing undulating and gently swirling grey-and-whiteness that parted now and again to reveal a stretch of snow, a line of rocks, a valley side. I climbed back down to the end of the rocks, put my crampons on again, and reversed the slope as directly as I had climbed it, quickly returning by the terrace and the snow hump back to the cairn and the rocks. Here I sat, eating, and wondering if the weather would lift or get worse: a very common situation. Then, rather to my surprise, I saw four other climbers approaching the summit of the Fineilspitze up the ridge opposite to that which I had climbed. Surprise, because I thought that no one else but me would be out in such patently risky weather: they moved efficiently and quickly up some steep ground, and then I saw their first man, and then the rest, gather in a group where I had been standing half an hour before. I think I envied their companionship.

Then the summit was hidden in cloud again, and this time it was a thick and determined sort of cloud with an air of permanence and threat about it: it was time to be moving. Down the rocks, fast but steadily and pell-mell down the screes. Hail began the moment I was back on the glacier; a really vicious, horizontal hail. Waterproofs on at once, crouching behind a rock. Damn, where are my waterproof trousers? To hell with them, get moving, and fast.

The two miles back across the glacier surface were trying. The hail was exceptionally violent and turned very quickly into a mixture of ice-cubes and freezing rain borne along by a knock-down wind almost straight into my face; this thrashing drench was intermingled with lightning bolts and instantaneous thunderclaps. I took several sharp electric shocks, since I was a metal-bearing prominence. Flames hissed and crackled about me. Then the myriad little streams amalgamated into a general torrent, and the stretches of slush dissolved underfoot into freezing bogs; and the larger streams became, within minutes, almost impassable torrents scouring ice runnels and washing down a slurry of gravel. I was very wet, very cold indeed and fairly well terrified by the time I made dry land.

I barely paused to take off my crampons, but ran the half-mile up to the refuge and got into a warm room as quickly as possible. I spent valuable money on a big bowl of coffee and a tot of schnapps and sat looking out at the storm, wondering a little about the party that had reached the summit behind me. They must have had a most uncomfortable couple of hours.

The suddenness and severity of the storm, and the liveliness of its electrical content re-emphasized the provisional and risky nature of even the easy style of mountaineering that I had been practising. That sort of cold drenching, conjoined with sheer fright, is a sovereign recipe for rapid cooling and incipient exposure problems: two people together would have been able to check on each other's performance and capacities, watching for the tell-tale stumbles or incoherencies. Alone, you must rely upon the unreliable business of self-observation.

The rain and wind had been sufficient to wet me even through a very good quality jacket; but my haste to cross the ice had led me to neglect putting on my overtrousers, so I was thoroughly soaked. The absolute lack of any shelter and the continuously ankle-deep water combined with all the rest into a thoroughly dangerous combination of wind, cold and wet. As for the electrical effects . . . well, in that case, two might just as well have been blasted as one, but things such as St. Elmo's fire, spurting like squibs from the point of the axe are, somehow, more alarming when one is alone.

I have had a number of unpleasant experiences with lightning in the mountains or on open moors, and this was one of them. Out on that lonely, level ice I felt extremely unprotected and vulnerable. On a peak there may well be some shelter afforded by higher ground about you, or by intervening pinnacles or ribs: and even if they afford no real protection (and "dead" ground can often become electrically "alive" because lightning tends to follow cracks or gullies down the faces of mountains), yet you can get a sort of delusion of relative safety. But out on the flat, with nothing higher than you for a mile in either direction, with a metal axe in your hand and metal all round your toes . . .

The only experience comparable to a violent electrical storm on a high mountain must be to lie out under an artillery barrage, insufficiently dug in.

As I had run up to the hut past the tent, I had dragged out some dry clothes; these I put on in the hut, and wrung out my trousers and shirt, and put them in a polythene bag. When, after half an hour, the storm passed over, I went out and down to the tent. Packed up, sorted out the wet from the dry very carefully, and (having built a celebratory cairn) continued on my way into Austria.

The path over the Hochjoch is well constructed, old and easily graded. It has had military and commercial use for centuries, I should expect. But it was still a long walk down the slopes to the glacier snout and on to green grass again. A sun had now come out, rather unsteadily, like a Monday morning drunkard. I hung the wet clothes on the outside of the sack and continued on down. A fine range of mountains appeared on my right, continuing north from the Fineilspitze which had also become visible. I was feeling tremendous satisfaction at having climbed such a good-looking peak, after so much frustration; to have snatched it through very early rising, and to have done it with speed and address, gave me a great surge of confidence. It was still before midday, and I determined to carry out the third of my possible plans by traversing round on the path known as the Seufert Weg to the Vernagt Hut. From a camp in that area I had the choice of several good peaks of moderate size, and the further possibility of a long glacier crossing to the Wildspitze and beyond, if good weather were to arrive.

The Eastern Alps are very well served by huts, and anyone with sufficient funds making a Grand High-Level Route would probably want to use them. Unlike the huts in the more westerly parts, these Austrian refuges are well placed for traversing, since many of them exist because of the access they give to skiing country; and also because such traverses are perhaps the better part of Austrian mountaineering. With some exceptions, the peaks in the Ötztal, Stubai and Zillertal ranges are all short climbs, and the local style of climbing consists in moving about from hut to another, centrifugally, rather than basing oneself in one place and climbing from there and returning, in centripetal fashion. Linking these huts are a network of high paths, some of which are good excursions in themselves. Thus from now on, most of my traverse was on acknowledged, marked and numbered trails that followed well-thought out routes that saved height when height could be saved.

The first of these huts lay somewhere, as I thought, below me; at the intersection of the gorge formed by the Hochjoch torrent and a similar ravine descending from the Weisskugel glaciers. I swung round a last turn in the path and saw the hut, not down below, but way up high on the opposite bank. Before I could get across to it I had a long descent down screes, a crossing of a swaying wire suspension bridge, and another long, hard pull up steep grass. My pack seemed to be especially heavy that midday, and my knees especially feeble; now that the sun was coming out, the valley was steaming hot one minute, and chilled with an icy breeze the next.

The Hochjoch Hospiz, when finally reached, is a solid stone building containing a warren of dark, wood-panelled rooms – dark with generations of smoke and cooking steam. It was almost deserted; two walkers in one corner of the large refectory, and a small family group up from the valley for the day and already preparing to descend. I ate a solid lunch from my sack here, stretched out my legs in front of a stove, and took forty winks of sleep. (From now on it became my custom to visit huts like this, to take in the atmosphere, drink tea or soup, eat my own food and, briefly, snooze.) I remember that at that moment I was feeling very tired indeed and was wondering if I could endure another two weeks or longer of this almost unrelenting effort, and whether or not I could face the long steep path up and round to the Vernagt hut. For a short while my system was in revolt against my determination and seemed to be winning: but that short sleep restored me.

Sleeplessness is another insidious problem, an almost unnoticed debilitation that saps your strength, concentration and health. It is very easy to find that you are not getting enough sleep on such a journey, and on this occasion I had had, in succession, a high cold bivouac on the Palon della Mare, a storm and dream disturbed night in the Val Martello, and a third stony, cold night up on my gravel shelf at the Hochjoch, wakeful with anxiety about the weather. Here at the Hospiz the accumulated weariness dropped on me, like a sandbag: and yet, once again, because of my fitness I was able to recover very quickly.

Very steadily, through the afternoon, I walked around the flanks of a great ridge until the little path I was following emerged above a side valley. From here, a vista of glaciers and peaks became visible, and the problem of the next day was solved: there was no shortage of good things to be done. Across on the other side of the main valley, the northward extension of the Fineilspitze continued in a series of high rocky summits – but on this side all was crests of snow. The Vernagt Hut itself was tucked up at the head of the side valley at the intersection of two cwms, snugly embedded in a field of boulders and outcrops of grass. Very slowly, with a tortoise gait, I reached it and, very slowly set up my tent a hundred yards away on a pleasant grassy slope.

That evening I went into the hut, and sat beside a large and jolly group of Italians. They ate gargantuan meals of pasta and wine and sausage: but I did well for myself by following the customary *Bergsteigeressen* menu that turned out to be a bucketful of sautéd potatoes and three fried eggs. Money spent on food, I reasoned, could not be money wasted. My further excuse for this quite unnecessary meal was that if the weather proved kind I might want to have a little food in hand to make sure I could take every advantage of the better conditions.

The weather, however, came in threatening again. After a clearing afternoon came another hailstorm, this time mixed with snow that settled at once on the rocks and grass around me. I slid into my sleeping bag with the thought that, once again, tomorrow would be a walking day. I slept very well, not expecting an early start.

I was woken by cold; by the cold of a very hard frost that struck about two in the morning. I knew at once what it meant. The inside of the tent hood was thick with rime, and I had to light the stove to thaw out the zips before I could open them and look out on a sky that was pulsing with star-lights.

Immediately west of the Vernagt Hut stands the Fluchtkogel and the somewhat smaller Kesselwandspitze, which is a popular and easy climb from that hut. From the narrow moraine-top path that runs up the glacier towards them, the first looks like a long white wave just breaking, and the second is a truncated pyramid of reddish broken rocks. In between them runs a mile or so of crenellated ridge with an easy col at each end. The whole is visible, at first in part and then completely, as you climb slowly up the moraine to where it merges into level glacier. The morning was perfectly clear, still and cold. A pink and then golden light picked out each summit and then began to stretch down over the grey and blue and silver of the snow.

The Fluchtkogel glacier is small but well crevassed, and needs care. This morning it was covered with perhaps eight inches of new snow that had almost completely covered the previous footprints; but there was no mistaking the way which led, by an obvious level plateau, to a steeper section and then into an upper basin. The problem was, to perceive and avoid, in all this new snow, the buried mouths of the smaller crevasses. I moved very slowly and circumspectly indeed, and wished for a long pole or a ski-stick; but the new snow was loose and powdery, and it was, in fact, quite easy to tell where the old and harder material was fractured underneath; and there were always faint traces of shadow, little trails and dimples that revealed the points of danger. In the oblique light of very early morning they showed well; but I had immediately determined not to return the same way. I could, I thought, traverse the length of the wave of the Fluchtkogel and come down the pass at the head of this glacier, thus avoiding the crevassed zone I was having to cross on my way up into the upper basin. But as I climbed up it became clear that an even better alternative might be to climb the one peak and then the other, and to return down to the tent and hut by the easy and safe slopes of the Kesselwandspitze, thus avoiding a glacier descent altogether. And that is, at length, what I did.

The upper basin was gained by a few circumventions past two or three enormous crevasses, and followed upward on a safe concave slope to the foot of the little col leading to the Fluchtkogel summit ridge. Here a small and half-hidded bergschrund required a little care, followed by a steep slope of snow; and then I stood looking over on to an undulating plain of glacier that stretched south and westward. The summit itself was reached by steadily walking up steep hard ice and *névé*, and was discovered to be a large curling cornice hanging out toward the site of my tent. I stuck my axe, my second self, in the snow and took a carefully posed photograph of the two complementary curves – of pick and of cornice, of the black, the white and the upper blue.

The view from this summit, at exactly 3,500 m was immense and of exceptional clarity and beauty of colour. To the east, peak after peak outlined in burnished pewter against the newly risen sun; that was the way I had to go. To the south-east, the main frontier range of the Ötztal Alps culminating, almost due south in my peak of the day before, now eminently clear and shining white. True south, the broad saddle of the Hochjoch and beyond that the shining outlines of the Cevedale and the Ortler rising out of brown and golden hazes; still further beyond them, the peaks of central Switzerland. Most beautiful and most clear of all, because exposed to the most perfectly slanted rays of the sun, the Weisskugel stood up in a shapely, asymmetric pyramid out of a wide plain of glaciers, in the midst of which, on a rocky headland looking something like a lighthouse facing the Atlantic, lay the remote Brandenburger refuge, well known to ski-mountaineers. And then, stretching from my feet to the northern and western horizon, a sheet of white and gently stirring cloud, grey in its depths and golden in its upper traces, across whose surface was flung the pyramidal shadow of my peak and on the peak of that shadow the moving, waving blur of my own shadow haloed in double rainbows.

There was no mistaking what this cloud sheet portended, and even as I was watching it had begun to stir a little more fitfully and to push streamers over the spine of the range; but I was not disposed to hurry away from this wonderful sight. It was all the more moving to me because it showed me, with complete clarity, how far I had come in the preceding days; and the perfection of that moment was like a blessing on all the effort and frustration.

Slowly, gently and unwillingly I retraced my steps down the steep ice back to the col; there I found four Germans who had just come up from the other side and who were making a three-day traverse of their own, from hut to hut along the range. We all ate together and drank from our water bottles, and delighted in the sun and the sky – although those streamers had now crossed the range and were pushing out their furthest tips towards us. The four Germans set out for the summit and I started to reverse the slope back into the upper basin from which I had ascended. My objective was the next easy col, about half a mile away beyond some rocky pinnacles. From there the rocks of the Kesselwandspitze might be climbed.

I must tell the truth. My grand tour nearly came to grief on that little slope; for it had now been in hot sun for nearly an hour and its consistency had changed for the worse. The edge of the bergschrund on which I had to stand, slid off abruptly as I stood on it. Well – no one pretended this was a safe way of spending the summer. I launched myself forward as one would in a racing dive off the edge of a swimming bath and landed – with pick held in outstretched arms – on my face on the far side with my toes hanging over a nasty-looking hole. Such is solo mountaineering. I did a forward roll down the slope and got to my feet and went on my way even more circumspectly than ever.

The way round to the next col was across another, safe, concave slope. This col is used as the best way between the Vernagt Hut and the Brandenburger Hut, so it was not surprising to meet a roped party of four coming down over the bergschrund in an even more heavy-footed manner than I had done. The advantage was to me, since they kicked so much of the new snow into it that it was almost filled up, and gave me no trouble at all. Now I was standing on the col, with bright sun on my left, thick mist welling up on the right, and the rocks of the peak straight ahead. These were, as I had feared they might be, covered with ice and fresh snow; the sun would not get to them till much later in the day. So my alternative plan was put into action, and the far misty side of the col descended on to the gently sloping glacier beyond. I was looking for the little passage round the back of the Kesselwandspitze, that I had noted on the map. Following a few metres below the foot of the crags, on very easy ground, led me round and down. I passed the foot of one, of two and of a third gully; the mist was dense and I could not see up them very well, but all of them looked too severe to be in regular use. The fourth, however, was wide and eminently climbable.

A few steps on very steep ice got me on to a large block, where I perched to take off my crampons: the way ahead was some 200 feet of frozen scree and rubble, with mixed harder moves. A last, rather desperate ten feet of vertical snow and I popped out of the narrows into the sun again, beside a marker pole stuck in a cairn. I had now gone anti-clockwise round my second peak from midday (north) to six (south). The south ridge went up, gently, by turrets of very loose rock. So unpleasant was this rock that I clambered round on the steep snow on their right, and so got on to the penultimate step of the ridge overlooking the normal, easy way to the summit. This lay up a gully full of loose stones, wet snow and inexpert climbers – my Italian acquaintances from the evening before, all fifteen of them. Another party of similar size was forming in a queue behind them. I thought that under these conditions I would forgo the main summit of the Kesselwandspitze, not out of snobbishness but out of prudence, since stones large and small were being discharged into the gully. It looked plainly dangerous to me, so I reversed back down the shoulder, awkwardly, and slid down the steep snow in one enormous swift glissade, then back down and round to the edge of the glacier.

Before long I had crossed back over the Fluchtkogel glacier, and had set foot on the moraine path, thus completing a circuit of the peak. In ten minutes I was back at the tent, and it still was not eleven in the morning.

I ate well and brewed a mug of tea and watched the activities around the hut; I thought myself no end of a hero.

I was not at all impressed with the local style of mountaineering, and continued to practise the severe disciplines of the Western Alps on these much smaller peaks. As a soloist, it was not only immensely safer but also much more aesthetically pleasing and pure. One has the summits to oneself by rising early, and that was the name of my game. But these large parties are very slow, and a very slow party is not a safe party unless the weather is perfect (which it rarely is); thus many days are wasted in which a small, early-rising party could still do good things. I came away from the Eastern Alps with the opinion that the local teams were overmanned, over-burdened, underpowered and under-ambitious. Some of them, of course, looked most askance at me for what must have seemed like a strange mixture of the fanatical and the casual. But of course we were approaching the same mountains from opposite mental positions; they as an extension of fell-walking, me as a smaller form of major and technical mountaineering. What they found jolly – trekking over the crevasses – I found hair-raising; what they found awe-inspiring – any technical difficulty – I took in my stride.

One learned, however, to recognize the harder local teams because their approach was more like one's own. It included some fairly prodigious walking between huts after long hours on the mountain and these parties, like me, carried rather little gear and went at a rattling pace.

By midday I was walking down towards the village of Vent, and the weather had broken again; a strong wind was swilling the morning's cloud sea right over the range and it was spilling down into the heads of the valleys. There was rain on the wind again.

I got down to Vent, an unattractive group of hotels, around two in the afternoon. At the bus stop I got talking with two German lads who, like me, were wondering how to get down the valley to Sölden without using their weary feet. They had set out from there three days before and made a traverse around the Wildspitze in the same foul weather that had afflicted me on the Hochjoch; now all they wanted was to get back to their car and a change of clothes. We sat in a café talking about mountains and weather for half an hour, and together travelled down to Sölden, a few miles of winding road away. These two were real enthusiasts, not more than twenty, but already experienced and hardy: they probably did not do difficult routes, but they followed the policy (with which I wholeheartedly agreed) of always doing something whatever the weather. I gave a short version of my traverse, and they asked some shrewd organizational questions. They could see at once that what I was doing was not really remarkable or difficult, because it was simply an extension of their regular weekend activity; I enjoyed that appraisal because it was based on a proper assessment of mountain travelling, and not on astonishment.

For the past three weeks I had been growing into a very definite pattern of existence and distinct habits of mind which every day confirmed and strengthened. What I was doing was now natural to me; and though the determination was as strong, if not stronger than ever, yet I did not have to emphasize it to myself, or drive myself on. The task I had set myself on leaving La Bérarde was now capable of completion. There was much hard work still to do, but it was not likely to present anything that I had not already encountered. There would be bad days and good days, there would be hard days and easy days, fine weather and foul, and, yes, I was going to continue in a state of permanent hunger, and some of my clothing would be in rags before long, and I was getting short of money and I could not afford a map for the next section over the Stubai Alps. But what the hell . . . I was going to do it!

That day, my 33rd, was important. I had done the best bit of mountaineering of the whole traverse, from the point of view of pure pleasure and ingenuity; I had seen, stretched out behind me, the long cordillera of my journey, peak after pass after peak into the distance; and I had described something of it on terms of equality and practicality with realistic companions. So, I was able to see both the size of what I had been doing, and the ordinariness of it, both together.

I got off the bus a short way before Sölden, shook their hands and said *Auf Wiedersehen*, walked across the road and booked myself into a well-appointed camp-site. It was four in the afternoon.

The time at Sölden was spent making an inventory of damage to clothing and equipment and to self, and repairing the same; and then in laundry–work. The camp-site there was one of those wonderfully appointed places which offer every facility for the family camper. There were power points and taps at every corner, elegantly tiled washrooms and chromium-plated showers; and a population of holiday-makers to match. It was my equipment, my minute shelter, and my frayed appearance that were ostentatious.

My breeches, old at the start, were now worn through before and behind; one shirt was torn and a pocket had been ripped off my Henri-Lloyd jacket in some encounter. These could be patched and stitched, or stuck together with "Tuf" tape (of which I carried a length). Nothing, however, could further repair my sun-glasses, which went into the rubbish skip; the spare pair were brought out of their safe place. Reduction to one pair of glasses was to have consequences later. A pair of socks had to be darned, and my cotton cricket hat (which served every purpose from hat to handkerchief, by way of dish-rag) renovated. Then everything went into the laundry and myself into the shower. And then I stretched out the rope for a clothes-line and displayed my meagre goods to the eyes of this well-appointed world.

I also turned my tent inside out, thoroughly sponged it down and cleaned it.

While these objects were drying and airing, I walked down the road to a supermarket and equipped myself with a large quantity of food. Unfortunately, while I was doing so it came on to rain fiercely, and I had to run back to gather in my drying clothes before they were soaked a second time. I put up the tent quickly and huddled in it, surrounded by the damp washing which I would have to put on the following morning.

This spring cleaning had a symbolic content, as does most housekeeping: it signified my preparation for the last stages of the Grand High-Level Route.

Opposite was a group of tents surrounded by elaborate mounds of expensive equipment: skis, canoes, scuba-diving gear and sail-boards. The four young men who owned all this hardware were travelling about in two cars, now visiting ski-resorts, now canoeing down the Inn, and now disporting themselves by the Adriatic. They looked a very competent and athletic crew, ready to try anything and probably doing it well. If any new toy had been available, I thought, they would have exploited it.

It took me some time to identify the source of my disapproval. It included, of course, some element of unattractive envy; I would like to have as much money as people like that must have. But what did "like that" mean? There was nothing wrong with them at all; absolutely nothing to take exception to in their manners. They were rather modest and serious. But between me and my activity and them and theirs there seemed to be an abyss of mutual incomprehension and latent suspicion. Am I completely alone in my fear (I wonder to myself), in my fear that my own people are about to become, and indeed, may already be, a very nasty lot? Or is this a thought born of my isolation and fatigue (though that would not make it false)? For centuries we have exported our aggression overseas: the domestic tranquillity, the horticultural genius was achieved by that release upon an outside which was unknowable, mysterious, "damn foreign". But now it flows back inward like a collapsing star and we don't know what to do with these feelings that we have, except to swallow them and their bittter taste. And as I was lying there, preparing for sleep and yet more dreams, I could imagine that slowly accumulating sourness and the sickness that it breeds.

In the morning, after a visit to Sölden in order to ring up my son for his birthday, I packed my sack very carefully and set out eastward up the valley called the Windachtal. The weather was cloudy, with intermittent rain and many low clouds.

The Windachtal runs a satisfactorily exact east for about five miles of forested gorge before opening out into a wide glen; on this rainy day much like some Highland valley. The track is closed to all but forestry vehicles, and so it is not much visited, although there is a small restaurant and a chapel on a hump of rock just at the point where the valley opens out. I walked steadily on, not trying to hurry. The sign at the valley foot said "Siegerlandhütte 6 hrs." but I decided to take the long haul gently. In spite of the clouds it was warm; and the rain turned into steam at every gleam of sun.

This corner of the Stubai Alps is at the intersection of three or even four sheets of the map and I had not been able to buy the sheet that I needed in England, or afford it in Austria. For this section, and for the subsequent day, I was working from sketches drawn hastily in the Sölden bookshop, so a deliberate and tortoise-like pace, with a great deal of second thinking, was in order. I knew the hut was at the head of this valley, but so were several other huts reached this way, by several tracks, and I wanted to be certain that I found the right one. My object was to camp near the Siegerland Hut that night and to traverse over the Sonklarspitze into the Ridnaun valley; or alternatively, to climb the peak, return to the camp and continue up and over the Windachscharte, the high pass at the head of this valley, to get into Ridnaun area by some devious and as yet undiscovered line. Here I found myself rejoining the path followed by Conway's expedition. They had come down to Sölden having climbed the Weisskugel from the north, and then, like me, set off up the Windachtal. From now on our paths continued to intersect.

After a while the drizzle turned into a steady pelting rain and I put on the tops and bottoms of my waterproofs; thick cloud rolled into the head of the valley and I trudged up into it, dripping.

This was a discouraging start to the last quarter of my journey, but there was no turning back and any other place was likely to be as wet and wretched as the next; so I persevered and arrived at the foot of the long final slope to the hut as the clouds parted a little, to show me the way, and the rain stopped. I pitched camp on one of the few patches of flat ground for several miles, just one hundred yards from the door of the hut. The hut itself was almost empty; in the dark refectory there were only four visitors: but there was a large-scale map that I studied again and from which I noted down a number of compass bearings in case of bad weather on the morrow.

That evening was still and misty, but cold; I got into my sleeping bag early and cooked in the flap of the tent.

And in the morning it was exactly the same; a dense white mist, not a breath of wind and a sharp bite of frost. The puddles of last afternoon's rain were skimmed with ice.

I spent a long time casting about in the tract of moraines behind the hut before finding a line of cairns; these I followed upward, not knowing where they might take me, until I arrived in an area of huge blocks and frozen snowdrifts; the steadily increasing light seemed to suggest, through the drifting cloud, the shapes of ridges, right and left of me, converging to form a small cwm. There I laced on my crampons, built my little three-stone cairn (which I had never neglected to do at any stop since leaving the Col de la Vanoise one month earlier) and started trudging steadily up the hard-frozen snow which shortly turned into a little ice-field and then, before long, into a long, narrow but easy gully running up between the two ridges. Here there were old footmarks, and the holes made by the shafts of axes and other obvious signs that I was on the right way to some mountain. But which? I still had not seen the Sonklarspitze. From below, I heard voices; the four people from the hut, perhaps.

The gully steepened and narrowed a while, and then opened out into another ice-sheet now visibly enclosed by the ribs of rock that converged ahead. The mist was now shining bright, almost incandescent, with gold and ruddy lights in it, but the visibility was no better. I came to a zone of freshly fallen snow that got deeper as I climbed higher.

At the intersection of the ribs, the face became a narrow ridge of corniced snow along which I walked with care; there seemed to be a substantial drop on either side and the loose new snow did not adhere well to the old icy material underneath. This ridge became a plateau that, still barely visible, became a ridge of rock that again led steadily to another plateau on which stood a cairn and metal tripod; there too the box with the summit book. No one, I noted, had been there lately; so I signed myself in with a flourish and in the "coming from" column wrote *Frankreich*.

But the true summit was yet a little further along a broad ridge, with a large cornice to the left. Standing on the snowy top the sun was strong enough to cast my shadow backward over Austria, with a fine display of rainbows, but was not strong enough to clear the cloud for anything more than fleeting moments. I saw, for five seconds, a white pyramid higher than me, some three or four miles away: the Zuckerhütl, perhaps? And I saw briefly down into a glacier basin, where, had the weather been better and clearer, I might have descended. Then later, as I turned to descend, there was a short view of a black, cliff-like summit further east: but that was all I ever saw of the Sonklarspitze and its immediate neighbours until two days later and from 50 miles' distance.

I came down the rock ridge, and at the first plateau encountered the four Austrian climbers from the hut, walking steadily up in my tracks. We exchanged a grave "good morning" and continued on our ways. The narrow snow ridge was succeeded by the left hand rocky rib which led down, by pleasant scrambling, to the first ice-field, the area of blocks and my little three-stone cairn again.

The ascent of this mountain had been a tranquil and delightful experience, but now the hard work of the day was about to begin. I ate a hurried second breakfast at the tent, packed up swiftly, and struck out across the moraines towards the Windachscharte, which the clouds now opened to view. This pass presented an unpleasant aspect; a long slope of steep snow finishing up as loose steep rocks leading to a cleft in the frontier ridge. I tried to make as fine a line as possible, gaining height by degrees as I circled round the head of the *cwm*; but the snow got softer and steeper and the sun now began to come out to make the snow still worse, and the rocks when I got to them were like a stack of broken biscuits. Three steps up, and sliding back two; holding on to whatever would not break away, I made my progress to the cleft.

From here I looked across into some wild and complicated terrain that seemed far more declivitous and confused than it had on the map in the hut or than I had managed to transcribe on to my notebook page. This face of the range was steep and rocky, with many jagged buttresses and descending ridges. There was, below, the wide bowl I had anticipated, but its floor was fissured with gorges and outcroppings of bare rock, like some corrie in Skye, and all around its rim, confused with great masses of cloud, was a complex array of peaks through which I had to thread the right needle-hole.

A descent down a gully lead to a tiny path that wandered down very steep grassy slopes between precipices; and as I descended, the geography became a little plainer. Some five miles away and almost directly east was the col I had to reach, but my route there would have to be circuitous. I took a compass bearing on a prominent mound of white rock, and found it agreed to within two degrees of the bearing I had calculated from the map. That mound now became my target.

A short clearing of the cloud revealed, on the left, a range of rocky peaks descending from a height that I assumed was the Sonklarspitze massif; these peaks had a succession of little glaciers upon them, and if I had had a map, a way might have been found through them directly to the Ridnaun valley. But I preferred to stay with a line that would lead me back, as soon as possible, on to the corner of map that I had for this region. These peaks, which were black, were succeeded by another and very striking mountain composed entirely of white marble; a brilliant, creamy white, saw-toothed crest was outlined against a dark sky. What I had taken for a mound of white rock was, in fact, the end of a dazzling white moraine falling away below a little glacier that lay, like a dirty sheet, on the steep face of this prodigy. To the right of this was my pass, and then another peak partly composed of the same shining material. Well round to the right and I found myself looking over into the valleys on the Italian side of the Ötztal Alps below the Timmis pass. An exact identification was difficult, because of the confusion of the terrain and the cloud banks that wandered round and about the ridges, like lost whales amongst an archipelago. My route now was clear, if only for a short while. A descent to a lake, a sweep round across a plain, a descent into a valley and a long climb outward and rightward to that distant col.

My narrow path came down, with many twists and turns, to the shores of the lake, by a hummock on which stood an abandoned military hut, itself surrounded by a trench and rusted wire. This and other relics I was to encounter date back to the time twenty years ago when this section of the frontier was subject to irregular violence, and was closed to mountaineers while frontier troops searched for Tyrol nationalists. Here also, arrows were carved on a flat stone and a paint-marked trail went forward to the outflow of the lake and beyond.

The path disappeared, and for the next three miles I relied on paint-flashes every hundred yards – an easy matter in clear weather, but in the shifting mist a feat requiring vigilance. I had my compass bearing and could use that for the gross calculation of my main direction, but it was little use in the undulating grassy plain I had to cross. I found myself tending too far to the right from anxiety to keep to that main bearing, while the paint marks kept leading me left until I wondered whether these *were* the right marks, and not a snare.

The first strange thing to happen was that I heard the whinnying of horses and the sound of hooves that got louder and louder; many whinnies and many hooves. Quite suddenly I saw, at some hundred yards, a herd of horses galloping together; beautiful brown and white horses galloping throught the mist. The second strange thing was that the grey mist turned creamy brown and that meant that I had covered the first stage of the crossing, for the creamy brown resolved, as I came closer, into the rampart of marble. I sat down by a stream and ate one of my tins of fish.

Tins of fish? How many tins of fish did I eat on that trip? From the noble salmon to the sturdy tuna; from the tasty mackerel to the useful herring; from the ubiquitous sardine to the humble but necessary sild. Oh admirable tins of fish and their admirable contents forked out, prised out, scooped or shaken, with knife, piton, fork, spoon, finger, bread-crust or sharp stone!

Sitting there, the cold water bathing my sore feet, I watched the clouds slowly and finally roll away. Ahead stretched a long stony slope leading to the col and back on to my map. To commemorate the morning's summit and this noon of wonderful walking I built a really fine cairn and round it scattered as many bits of bread as I thought I could afford, since, as I told the marmots in no uncertain terms, everything was now going very well indeed.

Another sustained effort followed – the long climb to my next pass that was named the Gürtelscharte. Huge blocks and slabs of grey rock abutted against the marble mass of the Schneeberg, forming a sort of terraced embankment that slanted up towards my goal and gave a good mixture of scrambling and steep walking over the next 2,000 feet. Occasional paint-marks showed the trail, but I never saw any other sign of human passing. The peak of the Gürtel stuck a prow of shattered rock out towards the pass, and on its left rose the marble cone; looking back from the crest of the pass I could see, five mile away, the Windachscharte and the gully below it, and the lake, and the outpost and the plain of horses. And then turning my face eastward there was another deep bowl flanked by the thick strata of marble passing through the peaks in a band about a thousand feet thick, like filling through a cake. The marble was white, the surrounding rock a deep blue-grey, and the narrow zone of their contact a burnt, friable red.

A faint trace of path led downward into the grassy hollow below and then left around the side of the marble mountain. I had some difficulty following it here, and went too low until my wayfarer's instinct told me to regain 300 feet and keep on going left and yet further left until I came out upon a thyme-covered balcony overlooking another immense hollow.

This one, however, included an array of buildings and huge old mine-workings, shafts, spoil heaps, runways, rusting machinery and crumbling engine sheds. Like the Coppermines valley above Coniston, this land was hollow with galleries, levels, shafts and drifts. My next objective was a third pass called the Schneeberg-scharte, and there it was, three or four miles away to the north and east, across the ravaged valley.

I was now walking with the most tortoise-like gait I had yet attained, having climbed and descended over 6,000 feet since early morning, and covered fifteen or more horizontal miles across very rough ground. And the same very slow but land-devouring tread took me into this bowl and along a series of crumbling tracks past ruined sheds and great holes in the ground, and past water-courses and rusting cableways from whose pylons long ropes of wire were still looping.

Large heaps of mineral deposits littered the ground, greenish crystalline stuffs and flaky lumps of mica; one little piece I added to the collection of such fragments that was growing, slowly, in the bottom of my sack. In the late afternoon sun I climbed even more slowly up a zig-zag path toward my third pass of the day. As always, I had counted the zigs and the zags before beginning, and as always counted them off at each corner – fifteen, sixteen, seventeen and then, at the twenty-first, the narrow crest was gained and a cold wind was blowing round about still more mine machinery, that clanked in the breeze; and I was looking down into the Ridnaun valley, with at my back the mountain of marble and at my feet another immense green basin and a huge hillside like two Skiddaws piled together. In the very far distance the band of marble could be seen glowing in the evening light, far away on an otherwise invisible range.

The path continued down to some still more ancient and dilapidated workings that looked, so vast was the masonry employed about them, like ruined Inca fortresses. And there it slowly faded out, and I was coming down a trackless green hill into a valley that was still more green, past a stone chalet and a herd of goats, to a jeep road wending heaven knows where, and down that road past yet another working, on down to the tree-line and a camp, my 33rd, on a patch of grass beside the stony way. Rest at the end of a long and magnificent day.

The morning was fresh, bright and clear. I rose in good time to enjoy its dawning and ate a good breakfast while consulting the map. I discovered that I had, once again, walked off it. But there was no good reason why I should not continue down the jeep-road beside which I had slept; it was certain to bring me down to some inhabited place and at length to the Ridnaun valley.

So I set off down, going very gently, and before long was winding through thick pine-forests with views below of green meadows and farms: and then, again without asking, I was offered a lift by a man in a Land Rover who was delivering boxes of groceries and other items. With a few halts he drove me down a broad green vale towards the Brenner Pass road and the town of Sterzing, called in Italian Vipiteno.

Clear, bright weather was spreading wonderfully out of the east.

Chapter Seven

THE BEST OF TIMES

STERZING OR VIPITENO? In this account the German, or rather
Austrian, names have always seemed more suitable because I was
using the Austrian maps which are, consistently, irredentist and
Teutonic in these matters. They argue that since most people in the
South Tyrol speak some sort of Austro-German dialect, then the
place names should reflect that reality. Occasional graffiti on the
walls and embankments reflect the same thinking. So in what
follows I shall stick to the map and write Sterzing (instead of
Vipiteno) and Ahrntal (instead of Val Aurina) and St. Jakob (instead
of St. Giacomo) etc. . . . In the case of Sterzing, however, this was
how the town seemed to me. Not Italian, not even strictly speaking
Germanic – but Habsburg, Austro-Hungarian. Now what was it
that gave me this impression? The park in which I sat? The palazzo
(I have to use the Italian word because a palazzo is what it was, not a
palast, or a palais, nor even a palace)? Or was it the towered
gateway that reminded me of Bradford Town Hall? Or eating
Bratwurst? Or the ornate stucco, or the way the trees were pruned
back? These impressions are very difficult to describe and locate.
All I can say is that the town of Sterzing was recognizable as having
some shared qualities (though, damn it, I can't pin them down with
words) with Trieste, with Zagreb (seen through train windows), or
Bekescaba, or Eger, and for all I knew with towns in Slovakia, or
distant Krakow. It bore the thumbprints, it carried the gene, it bore
the impress of the most pacific and decent of all European systems
of dominion – Kakania, the Double Monarchy. And as soon as I
recognized this – and it may have been in the taste of the sausage or
the beer, or in the swing of a peasant skirt (and the women in
Sterzing do wear a form of local costume, now and then, as do the
women in many Alpine towns), or in the combination of the
primitive with the very sophisticated (and there not being much in
between), I got an intense nostalgia for some place completely
different – a countryside level as Holland but dusty as Sicily, with

sudden thunderstorms that thrashed the willows, with a mixture of languages and creeds and an Asiatic formality of behaviour amongst everyday working people. And I started longing for and actually smelling, there in the middle of the Alps, the streets of Pest – that mixture of Glasgow and Paris – and the completely different and unrecognizable sounds of the voices.

As I have written earlier, during prolonged effort one does not think or even feel very much; but thought and feelings continue to work away unconsciously and burst out, quite suddenly, when we pause or are diverted. And some combination of taste, smell and sight, and perhaps hearing, too, triggered this release of memories and emotions which now, at this distance (and I am writing this in a room one hundred yards from Hyde Park), I recognize as belonging to my wife, rather than to distant Hungary. The last time we had been abroad together had been there, far away. By such curious roads does our memory circle back home.

I don't think that association became conscious then, but I know that when I started out, around midday, for the Pfitschertal and the village of St. Jakob, I was thinking about her continually and wanting to complete the task in hand.

It may be that this contributed to my lack of attention to the vital matters of supply: I set out from Sterzing with an empty sack in the vain hope of picking up supplies in St. Jakob. I also entertained another vain hope, that there would be a regular bus service in that direction: and when that service was discovered to be irregular and infrequent I continued the delusion by imagining that my luck would hold out. As a result, I spent the better part of that day walking up the Pfitschertal under a baking hot sun along an empty road.

It was not unpleasant; there were magnificent wooden houses to look at, bright with scarlet geraniums against whitewash and dark pine; there were sleek cows, haystacks, old women in black and high hillsides thick with silvery firs and aspens. And I did not always follow the road; at one place an old track led up beside the river through a narrow defile that the road avoided. Once there was a stretch of lane between fields full of poppies. At the very last section of the road a car drew up, and a man who had been working in Durham gave me a short ride to my destination. But what I had intended as a day of relative ease turned out to be a heavy trek; and

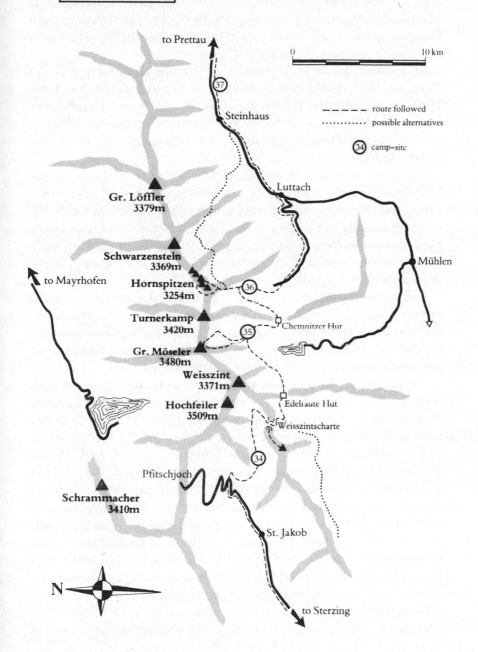

7. ZILLERTAL ALPS

to Prettau

Steinhaus

Luttach

Gr. Löffler
3379m

Schwarzenstein
3369m

Hornspitzen
3254m

to Mayrhofen

Turnerkamp
3420m

Gr. Möseler
3480m

Weisszint
3371m

Hochfeiler
3509m

Schrammacher
3410m

Pfitschjoch

St. Jakob

Mühlen

Chemnitzer Hut

Edelraute Hut

Weisszintscharte

to Sterzing

0   10 km

- - - - route followed
. . . . . . possible alternatives
(34) camp-site

N

to make matters less convenient still, the commissariat at St. Jakob, though well stocked with tins of fish and eggs and chocolate, had neither black bread nor porridge oats. I found an insubstantial loaf of whitish fluff, and took that along with me; but such bread merely occupies space. Thus, when I set out for the Hochfeiler, I had iron rations and sore feet. This, too, is "friction".

(If anyone else is daft enough to do the Grand High-Level Traverse, they would be well advised to be more purist than I, by restocking their larder at Sterzing and taking the footpath called the Pfunderer Hohenweg, which wanders scenically through the hills above the Pfitschertal and joins my lazy-man's route at the Edelraute Hut.)

The road was left at the third hairpin on the climb to the Pfitschjoch: a very narrow but purposive path dipped first into a valley and then up steeply through open pine-woods and bilberry scrub and finally out on to a steep hillside from which I could look back down the long white road to Sterzing. I climbed up very slowly indeed, resting frequently; it did not matter where I spent that night.

Just as evening came on I found a small wooden chalet by a path, not far from a tiny stream. Since streams were scarce on this slope, this was the place to stay, with just sufficient level ground to pitch the tent and a hut full of hay to sleep in if the weather came on bad. Opposite me was a great striated precipice of slates.

Supper that night was sparing, and to occupy my thoughts with something other than food I sat with my sketching pad and pencil, making what I could of the strata opposite which ran up in twists and convolutions to a spiky crest (at the back of me was a hillside like a piece of the Cairngorms, doubled). Now I look at the drawings I made they seem very facile, containing little observation and no effort; but later at home I made a stab at painting from them and that attempt, though not good, had more to it than my repeated attempts to paint the far more colourful and inspiring Lunghin tarn. My whole mood, now, was receptive and more relaxed than it had been before: I was certain that all I had to do was to proceed with caution and the route would be completed: in retrospect the last few days of my journey were like an exalted holiday.

Next morning, inevitably, I continued. The huge hillside too, continued. After a long trek I came to the upper basin of the valley where the scene suddenly changed back into high mountains – a glacier snout above me, a torrent to cross, streaks of wet snow and ridges of moraine. I was looking for a hut to halt at and to leave my sack beside whilst I climbed up the Hochfeiler. But there was no hut. Instead I found a pile of broken timbers and an even greater pile of old tins. Now every one of these old tins was of identical size and each bore the traces of an identical label, and turning them over (as a hyena might do) I discovered one tin that was unopened and had a complete label that read, in Italian, PORK AND BEANS. The mystery was dispersed; the site was that of a hut that had been occupied by troops during the Tyrol emergency; they had subsisted exclusively on pork and beans, and out of sheer boredom and culinary disgust had demolished their hut when they left it. Since a tin of pork and beans meant more to me than fine gold, I put the unopened tin in my sack, and thought about what to do next.

It was late to start off up the Hochfeiler, and it looked a very unattractive and boring mountain. I have never yet walked up the easy way on Ben Nevis and I never shall, and I shall never walk up the easy way on the Hochfeiler, either. Instead, I descended a bit and after a few hesitations found the path that leads up toward the Weisszint-scharte, across a wide but level glacier. Though the path was definite, it did not seem to be often used; and though the pass itself is often crossed by parties from the Edelraute hut going to the Hochfeiler, yet there were no tracks in the snow coming down my way. So I wandered up, and across and over, and only at the last half mile met up with a party of six who were just descending from the mountain. The snow was soft and tiresome, but there was a well-beaten track at this point, and it led me to the Weisszint-scharte very easily. From now on, all the glaciers were tracked, though this did not mean one had to throw caution to the winds.

The Weisszint-scharte was an excellent place to be at one o'clock in the afternoon, bright, airy and cooled with a steady eastern breeze. I left my sack there and climbed and scrambled up blocks and easy pitches to the sharp summit on its southern side. This enjoyable little climb, which I made more enjoyable by taking a very direct line, gave me views of the Weisszint peak itself (no giant, but well worth a visit), of the Hochfeiler (and I was glad not to have persisted on that dull whaleback) and then, far away beyond Sterzing, rising out of a blue haze, the brown hump capped with white that could only be my mountain of two mornings ago, the Sonklarspitze. Way, way off to the south and west were clouds and mountains mingled in a golden-brown confusion.

Before long I was down at the Edelraute Hut eating a plate of pasta.

The Zillertal Alps have a herring-bone pattern to them; a distinct and humpy spine that constitutes the Austro-Italian frontier, and an array of complementary ribs on each side. The Austrian side of the range, however, is more deeply cut and is quite heavily glaciated: a transverse crossing of the ribs involves much deeper descents and somewhat higher climbs. On the Italian side the glaciers are smaller and there is a natural line of passes over the ribs at around 2,500 m: a good traverse path takes advantage of six of these useful ways through, at around that altitude, beginning at the Weisszint-scharte. The two huts that serve this side of the range, the Edelraute and the Chemnitzer, are popular with walkers from the valley, and they were serving cheap and appetizing food that week. My plan was to follow this path around the range, climbing one or two peaks as opportunity arose, to descend finally into the Ahrntal.

So, in the later afternoon I walked away from the hut and continued to traverse around at much the same height, on a well cared-for and partially engineered path that led me to a point half-way between the two huts, at the foot of the Gross Möseler whose narrow and interesting south ridge came down to within a hundred yards of my way. There I found a stretch of perfect level turf, with a pool, a small waterfall, flowers and smooth rocks, and a magnificent outlook to the south; directly behind me, steep snow slopes came down to the edge of the turf and gave a natural start to any climb I chose to do from here, for they led up on to the glacier field between the Möseler and its further sister peak called the Turner-kamp.

I bathed in the pool, washed out a shirt, and set to work cooking my tin of pork and beans which, after careful inspection, proved to be in good condition. I packed my light sack with what I thought I might need for the morning, had a final brew of tea, arranged the breakfast things for ease and convenience and lay down to sleep at an early hour, having first set my organic, autonomous and totally reliable self-awakening system to the hour of half-past three. Camp 35.

I am aware now of the limitations of this story; because it threatens to be repetitious. But how else does one tell it? Every day, in the latter part of my traverse, was a magnificent day. Everything, except the last, was done as it should be done. The weather was fine whenever I needed fine weather (except, again, on that very last occasion). The climbs were all I could desire and the mornings brilliant with stars.

And then there were the dawns that came after the stars, turning the sky gold and pink and pure azure, while the valleys below were still as blue as carbon paper. One could write about rising before dawn and cooking with one hand whilst with the other you pull on your socks; or the first stiff stumbles through the boulders, scouting about by torchlight (which is superseded moments later by the sun that bursts so suddenly out of the eastern haze); or the pain of the cold in your finger tips and the stiffness at the knees as you fumble with crampon straps, and then the first steps on the snow that is hard as toffee.

My climb up the south ridge of the Gross Möseler was pure pleasure all the way: steep snow to a pinnacled gap, a long scramble over blocks of granite the colour of ginger-biscuits, a second slope of snow-ice to a dome, and beyond that more ridge, this time of grey, shattered rock. The upper half had its moments of excitement and exposure, of wondering if another way would not have been wiser; but I kept on trying it and found that whenever it looked hard there was always a way through, or a wandering by-pass on to the loose face to my right, so that just by keeping going I arrived on the summit and looked south to the Dolomites, south and east to the Carnic and Julian Alps, westward back where I had come (with a view of the formidable north wall of the Hochfeiler) and then eastward along the tangled crest of the Zillertal range to the spreading glaciers that I had to cross, and finally to a far distant ridge that culminated in a prominent and unmistakable cone; the Gross Glockner. That cone was to be my guide, my lighthouse, my meter, my mark for the next week; seen from every summit, each day nearer.

I sat on the top of the Gross Möseler for a long while, dozing. Then I built my little cairn, distributed crumbs to the choughs that were wheeling below me, and scrambled down the normal route to meet two large parties that were coming upward. Rather than descend the glacier along that normal route – that was now becoming wet and slushy – I crossed back over towards the flanks of the south ridge and followed the broad swath of *firn* that extends below the crest of the south ridge and which I had used in the first part of the day. It brought me back to my final snow slope down which I descended in a thousand foot glissade, to within 50 yards of the tent. At the time I thought that was a perfectly executed ascent; but I was yet to have better days, though none could ever have ended so neatly.

I lazed about at my camp site for a couple of hours enjoying the sun, a second breakfast and the conversation of several marmots who advised me to move on gently to the next valley where I would find a good place to camp, from which I would be able to climb two or three peaks if I wished. So I packed up in a leisurely fashion and continued round the hillsides toward the Chemnitzer hut.

After I had been walking for half an hour I met two men in walking clothes; one had a long ice axe and the other a walking stick. Where was the hut they asked me? I indicated the direction of the Chemnitzer Hut.

"Die Furtschlaglhütte?" *"Nein, das is die Chemnitzerhütte."* *"Ach so?"* (they muttered) *"Bitte . . . wo sind wir?"* An extraordinary story began to emerge as I questioned them. Now, any climber or walker who says he has never descended into the wrong valley is certainly a liar; but these two had descended into the wrong valley in the wrong country, which must be a record. What they had done – and from what depth of incompetence one must only guess – was to follow another party when they set out from the Berliner Hut (in Austria). They hoped to arrive, by travelling west, at the Furtschlagl Hut (in Austria), along a well-established track. Instead, by blind following of those who went before, they were led up and over a substantial glacier pass into Italy, due south. The party that had gone before them had probably been one of those I met on the descent of the Möseler, which is often climbed from the Austrian side in just that way. Arriving at the pass (having crossed crevasses and ice slopes to get there) they had looked southward and seen, in the valley, a lake which (to the supremely unobservant) may have looked like a lake which they would have seen looking northward if they had been where they thought they were. They had set off down towards it, and only after two hours had they begun to have

doubts. Now they were sitting on a rock trying to work out how you read a map. When I broke the news to them that not only were they a whole mountain range away from their destination, but that they were in Italy, not Austria, and that they would need to walk 30 miles round by the Pfitschjoch and that etc. . . . etc. . . . they became disconsolate, and then angry and started to blame each other vehemently. I did my best to give them a map-reading lesson, advised them against trying to cross back over the glacier in the afternoon sun, and suggested they went westward. If they kept their back to the sun, I explained, they should arrive. I did my best to impress upon them that *Die Karte ist zum Lesen*. But by then they were almost in tears of anguish. I left them and went on my way, singing.

After crossing a wide, swift and deep torrent (in cold water up to my thighs), I and the track traversed some steeper rocky slopes below the Turnerkamp peak, and then descended easily to the little pass where the Chemnitzer Hut stands. Hungry as ever, I went in and had a large plate of pasta and a litre of tea. This hut, like the Edelraute Hut the previous day, was essentially a walkers' hut, and there were many holiday-makers there who had come up for the day. I stretched myself out and slept on the grass for half an hour before continuing round along the traverse path (which had now become much narrower and on which I now met no one) into the next cwm.

This camp, though not as sublimely located as the last, was still in a memorable spot: on the moraine ridge of a huge deep corrie backed by a glacier and steep rock walls. From here I was in a position to climb the Turnerkamp, the Hornspitzen, or to carry on further yet as I wished. Again I packed my light sack for the morning and went to bed early.

Once more a perfect dawn, though intervening ridges blocked the view to the south that I had had the previous morning. A path led up towards the Hornspitzen, so I went that way; having inspected the large scale map in the hut, I had formed the plan of climbing two or three of the Hornspitzen summits, of which there are five. I trekked up to the frontier ridge by long slopes of slabs and snow and boulders. The Turnerkamp was very impressive from this side, and its long east ridge, all steps and pinnacles, came down to the col on which I was standing. The route on to the fifth

Hornspitze from this point was dismayingly steep and loose so I left that alone and peered over the edge into Austria. A clear way was visible, across an ice field, to the fourth of the five summits: if I could once get down the next 200 feet.

Every climber has something they can do particularly well: I have never had much gymnastic ability and my forays into hard technical climbing have been short and unimpressive. But loose rock and rubbishy ice is something else; it appeals to some otherwise hidden talent. The descent from this little col was a nice exercise in judgement, lowering myself from ledge to ledge by flakes of rock and flakes of crumbling ice: it required extra care because another 200 feet down was a very wide and open crevasse, into which the little stones I dislodged or the chunks of ice I chipped away, went bouncing. The ice-field when I got to it was at first very steep, and required all points and a dainty step; but it soon laid back and gave a highway up to a small summit, from which another descent and climb led on to higher things. Hornspitze number four was reached in good order, up steep blocks. The view from this summit was, needless to say, superlative. The Carnic and Dolomite peaks were very clear and distinguishable in an unnatural lucidity. Nearer to hand were the Rieserferner range and, nearer than yesterday but still distant, the cone of the Glockner.

The Hornspitzen one to three were not far away, but there was a sharp icy gap between us and I could see no obvious way of getting down into it. Moreover, though the view was magnificent, it extended across and over a valley-filling cloud sheet that was stirring about in a restless way. To the north of the range, brown and green hills went off as far as I could see, but within a few minutes, a trail of mist had got between me and the floor of the southern valleys. So I clambered back down, put on my crampons and tripped back along the ice-field.

There was some question in my mind about climbing direct to the fifth summit from here, but now my crampons were on I preferred the devil I knew and so picked daintily back to the foot of the col and, bearing the crevasse always in my mind, scampered back up the flakes of ice and the flakes of crumbling rock.

Not wanting to be put down by the fifth Hornspitze quite so easily, I walked across the snow-field to its southern ridge and scrambled up it without any difficulty, to a fine, narrow summit.

The clouds were now coming in close, and the weather was certain to change. I made the sensible decision to return to the tent and then down to the valley, instead of continuing along this high path.

The descent down into the Ahrntal was very long and very tiring indeed; an immensity of steep grass, and extendedness of stony track, through narrow valleys and gorges. There were views upward to the summits where I had passed the early hours of a long and weary day, but slowly, as the afternoon wore on, the cloud cover became complete. When complete it began to thicken; and when it was thick it began to move swiftly from the south to the north. Meanwhile the breeze that had been blowing steadily up the Ahrntal became a gale. Tarpaulins were being drawn over piles of hay, washing was being gathered in, picnickers were scattering when I fetched up in a patch of woodland between road and river, not far from the village of Steinhaus.

This was an unpleasant spot, between scraggy pines and willow scrub, with the incessant noise of the river nearby and quantities of rubbish; but I was too dog-tired to move a step further. I made a meal of everything that I had left (which was not very much) and lit a fire to burn some of the detritus and a pair of my old socks that were now beyond repair. Large drops of rain kept falling, premonitory of much worse to come. Small whirlwinds threw hay into the air across the fields, and a sort of end-of-the-world lighting effect grew steadily stronger, turning everything purple or green under a sky the colour of tarmacadam. Then it started to thunder.

My decision to come down from the Zillertal Alps ahead of planned time was very sensible, for the thunder and rain of that night was of quite remarkable violence. I barely slept a minute for the flashing and the redoubled crashing and the re-echoing of those first crashes prolonged into the second crashes which themselves prolonged into the third crashes and so into a continuous drum-rolling, an ear-splitting concatenation of bangs, booms, rumbles and roars accompanied by incessant luminous effects and torrential, wind-driven rain. Add to this the noise of the river that all night got higher and faster and noisier. There was little rest to be had, so I covered my head up in my sleeping bag and practised the yoga of absolute indifference.

When the light returned – the light of day, not the light of electrical violence – rain was still falling in intimidating quantities, but I was in such abjection, lying there in the dripping undergrowth, that I thought I might as well be wet on the move as wet stationary. Water, alas, had flooded me completely, coming not through the roof of the tent but through the door. I was lying in a puddle, very cold and tired and irritable.

In such a situation there is nothing to do but act, so I put on my arctic underwear, which was still dry, and my waterproofs and my boots; then packed the sack as well as possible under these foul conditions; then set off walking. The river, I noticed, had risen four feet in the night and was dangerously close to where I had been lying.

The road was running with water, and there were pools in every level field; every ditch ran torrents. Nevertheless, movement was preferable to stasis and there seemed to be a little less rain falling than there had been when I first awoke. I could hardly dare to hope that it might stop, but I reckoned that it was not going to get worse. In that faith I continued to trudge up the road to the village of Sankt Peter where there was a grocer's shop; I sat on the doorstep for half an hour till the door was opened. First I bought a quantity of food for instant consumption, and then made a hurried computation for the next, penultimate, effort. The lady who ran the shop, observing my very depleted condition, was extremely helpful and friendly, and gave me a bag of tomatoes, only a little bruised, to keep my spirits up. And then, a short while later, the morning bus up the valley arrived and took me some four miles up to the northernmost and final village in Italy – Prettau.

Now I began to leave Italy and the weather began, slowly, to improve. Where the clouds had hurried in thick masses, now they wandered uncertainly, pulling apart in the gusts likes old knitting: the blanket of the storm unravelled. The rain dwindled to an intermittent drizzle and finally ceased. My morale, which had been low, almost at one point to desperation, now began to revive and the long easy walk up the valley took on a ceremonious quality. Because I was now leaving Italy for the last time, the finality of my progress, the certainty of attaining my goal, became the central point of consciousness. All that I needed to do was to hold steady over the next five days. It was perhaps with this in mind that my marching songs and chants took on a sombre and serious tone –

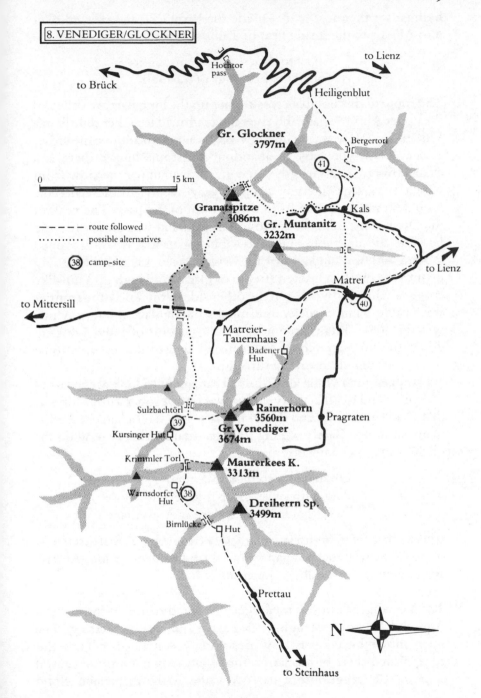

8. VENEDIGER/GLOCKNER

to Brück

Hochtor pass

to Lienz

Heiligenblut

Gr. Glockner
3797m

Bergertorl

41

0   15 km

Granatspitze
3086m

Kals

Gr. Muntanitz
3232m

– – – – route followed

· · · · · · · · possible alternatives

38   camp-site

to Mittersill

Matrei

40

to Lienz

Matreier-
Tauernhaus

Badener
Hut

Sulzbachtörl

Rainerhorn
3560m

Pragraten

39

Kursinger Hut

Gr. Venediger
3674m

Krimmler Törl

Maurerkees K.
3313m

Warnsdorfer
Hut

38

Dreiherrn Sp.
3499m

Birnlücke

Hut

Prettau

N

to Steinhaus

hymns, for the most part. I made the Birnlücke and crossed over into Austria to the steady beat of Tallis's Canon.

> Glory to thee my God this night
> For all the blessings of the night.

The route to this notable crossing lies up the long narrow valley of the upper Ahrntal; path and river are crammed together tightly in a V of ravine. Now and again the V opens a little to admit a meadow, a stone barn; you pass an abandoned customs house; there is a chapel by a rock. At length you come into an upper meadow from which 21 zigzags take you steeply, very steeply, to the venerable mountain refuge a mile from the summit of the pass. The peak of the Dreiherrnspitze stands above this hut, and was on my list as a possible and desirable objective – but today it was still wrapped around with mist and all that I saw were steep, ragged cliffs going up into the murk, a broken stretch of glacier and high up a hip-like curve of white snowcap. On the other side of the valley the frontier was visible, a line of rocky hummocks and pinnacles, one of which was the Vetta d'Italia, the northernmost point of Italy. Looking down the long stretch of the Ahrntal one could see occasional patches of sunlight breaking through.

I stopped for a while at the hut to eat again, to look at the large-scale map and to reflect; my mood was one of sober astonishment, that I had come so far and that in my last eight days I had climbed as many summits. Barely willing to begin again I laid my head on the oilcloth and slept a few moments.

> Oh may my soul on thee repose
> And with sweet sleep mine eyelids close:
> Sleep that may me more vigorous make . . .

And to that tune, an hour or so later, I came up a final stretch of snow to the well marked gap from which I could look into Austria again. Goodbye, goodbye, marmots of Italy!

The Venediger Group is the largest glaciated region in the Eastern Alps and, though not high, is extensive and very interesting. The basin into which I was now descending contained a huge and complicated sheet of glaciation funnelling down from the central spine of the range into a narrow valley – the dispersing cloud showed me glimpses of it and then, finally, the full panorama. A high wall ran from the precipitous summit of the Dreiherrnspitze, eastward to the further summit that my map informed me was called the Maurerkees Kopf: the top of the wall was composed of a succession of points, domes and rocky hummocks. There was no way up to this crest that was not a complicated glacier climb. Beyond this, invisible to me, the range continued with a second and a third glacier basin – with similar formations to the south. Whereas the Zillertal had the general form of a herring bone, the Venediger Alps was more like a flat-fish – broadly spread, but with many curious humps. During the next three days I was to cross it from end to end, first on the northern flanks, climbing over from one glacier basin to the next; and then marching right over what one might call its head. Exactly which peaks I should climb was still very uncertain, since I had no information about any of them but what I could glean from the 1:100,000 map. But I immediately picked out the furthermost of the Maurer peaks as a possibility, since it threw down a long rocky ridge to the pass I would have to cross next day.

But first, I had to descend right down into the funnel of the glaciers, down a long tiring slope of scree, moraine and grass.

I was conscious of being very tired, and of my knees hurting, and of the sack that seemed to be exceptionally heavy that afternoon. The day was growing warmer as I descended, and the moisture was steaming off the rocks. A long narrow rib of earth and rock led down, at length, to the gravel plain at the foot of the glacier.

Here the sun came out and the clouds finally cleared away, and I was able to distinguish the Warnsdorfer Hut on the opposite side of the valley, well above me. It seemed unattainably far away. Yet the wonderful sight of the shining glacier and the high wall above it kept my enthusiasm high; it was the best mountainside I had seen since leaving the Western Alps, and I believe it compares well with any in Europe.

By the time I reached the hut, around four in the afternoon, the weather was fine, bright and dry; the wind was from the north-east, and very cold.

A short reconnaissance suggested that there would be no good camp site above the hut, so I returned to a green dell just below it and set up Camp 38. The first act I performed after all necessary chores had been completed was to bring out of its folder the final map-sheet . . . "Freytag und Berndt Wanderkarten 1:100,000 sheet 12; Glockner und Venedigergruppe." For three or four months I had contemplated this sheet; this was another moment of finality when those contours, those browns and greens and blues that had imprinted themselves in the receptive material between my ears, became brute facts of ice and rocks and grass and forest. When the imagined form was comparable with the actual, as it will be when the last sheet of the world is rolled up. I felt something almost like fear as I traced out my possible routes and designated objectives. I had now been a long time by myself, with only the marmots to encourage me; had been living like a clenched fist. In the 40 days that had taken me here, through the wilderness of solitary effort, all but two had been of continuous work and every one had required the discipline, the concentration, the constantly renewed self-reliance necessary, to the full. It was the constant renewal more than any single difficulty that had been wearing me away. At that very moment, unfolding my final map-sheet, I was, not for the last time, close to tears of fatigue and fulfilment.

I drew myself together by calculating the distance between this camp and the pass of the Krimmler Törl, and from there to the summit of the Hinterer Maurerkees Kopf (height 3,313 m). Tomorrow's task was clear.

When daylight came again I was walking slowly (as ever, slowly) up the broad ridge of rocks behind the Warnsdorfer Hut towards a rocky hummock that gives access on to the upper ice-fields of the Sulzbach glaciers; as I walked I studied the north ridge of the Maurer. It was about a mile and a half long, in total, but the vertical height that it gained was only about 500 m. The first half was of snow with rocky steps; after that it became steeper and consisted of a series of rises and what appeared to be gaps. One or two of the rises looked to be high and steep – to be likely "stoppers". Nor was there any sight of an easy route of descent; I assumed one would be visible from the other side of the pass. But it was a tempting summit, in its own right and also because it entailed no extra walking. If I had to return down my route of ascent, it would bring me back exactly to where I left my load. That load I had already divided into two: the main sack and, perched on top of it, my light sack and rope.

In order to save every bit of height I did not go to the summit of the rock hump, but traversed round below it and popped out up a steep snow slope on to the very lowest point of the pass just a few minutes before the sun arrived.

A broad plain of snow extended before me, and across that plain, mountains. I spread out my yellow bivouac bag as a marker, put my red sack upon it and took a careful note of its location in case of mist (by an immaculate compass bearing); then in perfect weather but with some apprehension strolled up to the start of the ridge.

The very first twenty feet were excruciatingly hard. The first rock step had to be passed on its left-hand, sunny side; all the snow had melted off leaving a stretch of very steep glassy ice ending on a wall of cracked rock. The only way across this was by skirting along the top edge of the ice, using the flake that it made as a hold for the right hand whilst with my left hand I cut out a line of nicks until, with a horrible heave, I was able to "mantel-shelf" on the edge of the flake and get hold of a similar flake, this time of rock, and then repeat the manoeuvre again till I got to the top of the obstacle. I was not at all sure I was able to reverse what I had just done, and it did not seem possible to abseil down the step – so there I was, committed. Thence followed a short walk along a snowy crest, followed by another easier but still athletic rock step. Then another walk, and then the true crest of the ridge began.

My admiration for the great soloist rock climbers is now increased. Once again, the problems were not those of technical difficulty – apart from a few moves the climb had no technical difficulty at all; the challenge was entirely psychological. The ridge was long and contained innumerable little obstacles many of which, from below, looked far more difficult than they were when my nose was pressed against them. The lay of the strata, the grain of the rock was such that anything that jutted towards me, was, or appeared, overhanging: thus one might have been stopped at any moment by some small but insuperable step. The rock consisted almost entirely of slates and a sort of mudstone, with bands of much harder limestone in between (which gave the obstacles). Because the strata lay back into the slope, the rock was, in effect, very liberally supplied with good holds except where it was crumbling away. Such rock is very loose indeed under normal circumstances, but on this occasion it was held in a very hard frost. The torrential rain of the preceding day, that had caused me so much desperation in the Ahrntal, had set into a firm glue of ice, binding together rocks that would at other times just have fallen apart in my hands. Yet the crest was always narrow and there was very rarely any choice of way: it was up, straight, all the time or, on some short occasions, a succession of moves on the left-hand face of the ridge. This left-hand face was, to begin with, at an easy angle, but it gradually grew steeper and any excursion on to it became more problematic and much airier. I tried to make a mental note of every difficult section, and by the time I had reached the summit area, I had counted some seven "nasties". Down none of these was it feasible to abseil; each one would have to be descended by climbing. The higher I got the more formidable an undertaking it appeared to be. The last two nasties were fairly frightening and there still remained a prominent tower-like step that I had noted from far below. Would this, I asked myself, be the "stopper" I was expecting?

Progress was assisted by humming and gently whistling a range of notes – not fit to be described as a tune – and by keeping a good pace with them. I was climbing fast, but doing my best not to hurry; nearer the top, runnels of ice and patches of hail caused me to take extra care. On a few occasions I found the very faint traces of another party – a trail of wool caught on a spike, a bootprint in gravel. And what about the way off, I kept asking myself. And what the hell do I do if that tower up there is impassable?

The tower, like most of the other obstacles below it, was no tower, but a sharp overhanging step. Like the others I had passed it required a moment's pause and then a sideways wander to the left. Impossible to climb directly, it could, again like the others, be turned by a careful shuffle across creaking blocks and scree-covered ledges, followed by a loose bridging groove back on to the crest. Here there was a small gap, with a short climb into it, but thereafter the angle laid back still further and I came up on to the flat summit around nine in the morning.

The view, it need hardly be said, was superlative . . . to me the most revealing perspective was back over the Birnlücke down the length of the Zillertal Alps and beyond. That I had done. Nearer that way was the vista along the top of the Krimmler glacier basin: then in the other direction, the friendly Venediger and beyond that (nearer every day) the cone of the Glockner. South the Dolomites and north any number of mountains. But my main preoccupation was my safety. After building a three stone cairn and eating a piece of chocolate, I made a tour of my little kingdom – a few square yards of boulders, roughly triangular. A descent to the west was certainly feasible but would take me many miles out of my way; a descent to the east looked easy at first but then suddenly steepened out of sight. A descent to the north it would have to be. I felt strong and fit and as well prepared mentally as I would ever be, so having had a little more to eat and a swig at my water bottle (that was reinforced with sugar and lemon-peel and was infinitely precious), I turned round to descend. Were I a Catholic, I would have crossed myself; but being without any faith whatever said, out loud, "Remember, you have to get back home."

The descent was trying: the sun had begun to loosen the grip of frost upon the rocks, making my adventures out on to the eastward face of the ridge a great deal more precarious, and dazzling me with reflection from the ice-field below or blinding me when I chanced to look up. I was continually adjusting the peak of my cap to keep the light out of my eyes and in the midst of one of these manipulations, the sunglasses somehow parted company with my nose and fell off into the depths. The "nasties" I had memorized proved not to be as nasty as they might have been, because the lay of the rocks (to use the technical term, their "strike") made steep descents easy. One could lower oneself over an edge in confidence that feet would land on holds, and that new handholds would arrive as needed; it was the easier sections that were the more inconvenient, because more loose. Excursions on to the eastward face were all frightening. Yet I got down steadily, and as safely as the circumstances would allow. Then came one walk along snow and the short but awkward rock step: and then another walk on snow to the final step. The sun had now been shining for three or more hours directly on to the ice, and I anticipated great difficulty here. Peeping over the edge it became apparent at once that there had been many more holds available than I had, in fact, used on the ascent when, in the tension of early morning, I had been climbing with a certain ruthlessness: getting down to the ice was no problem. I crossed the remaining twenty feet of this crux by the simple expedient of thrashing the top of the upper flake and edging along slowly but quite safely. On the far side of the step I built another little cairn out of sheer thankfulness and walked swiftly down the glacier to my baggage, which I had been able to see throughout the entire climb and which had acted as my link with other realities.

As I came down, I saw two figures coming up to meet me. Our paths coincided: they were a pair of young Italians, making a tour round the range in the opposite direction to me. We sat down in the snow, they to rest and me to enjoy company. My water bottle was empty, but theirs was full of schnapps. In the midst of the snow we toasted one another, ate fish, cheese and bread and talked, in a mixture of languages, about the sort of things that one does talk about at such encounters. We advised one another about the next sections of our respective routes, compared sacks, discussed meteorology – as an excuse for sociability in the midst of this beautiful but treacherous terrain.

There were traces of a path descending the glacier in the direction I was to take, so after they parted I collected my sack, repacked it, and set off as briskly as I could in order to get clear of the glacier before the sun got high. The brilliance of reflection was causing my eyes considerable pain, and, in addition, though there were no open crevasses, yet there were many unmistakable crack marks across the rolling surface between me and the moraine.

Way ahead, on a bluff of rocks above the snout of the Sulzbach glacier, the Kursinger hut was now clearly visible.

The crossing of the Obersulzbach glacier from this side to the Kursinger Hut is a tedious business, because of the loss of height involved which then must be regained. After a long descent of moraine, with an ice-fall to one's right, the little path you have been following disappears in an area of steep slabs, and you must get down these as best you can to the glacier ice. The way is not marked and is slippery and indistinct. Once on the glacier – which is only half a mile wide here – you have to find the way off on the other side which is equally indistinct. A line of poles is eventually found, but most of the poles will have fallen over by August. Then you climb over some nasty crevassed and hollow ground before scrambling up a loose gully. All this in the heat of early afternoon. The hut itself, when you get there, is a typical stone and timber building, in the steady process of being enlarged.

I got inside out of the sun, to rest my eyes, and ordered a litre of hot water for tea and porridge; only to discover the last of my oats was already eaten. I went round the refectory scooping up crusts left by other parties, and chewed those happily. The supply situation was not good and I was still some way from my next source. There was a party of walkers there, two couples of around my own age; I asked them about the possibility of buying food at the head of the next valley. No possibility, they thought. At the Matreier Tauernhaus there was simply an hotel and no *Konditorei*. Certainly there would be no gas for camping.

After climbing my next objective, the Gross Venediger, my plan was to get to Kals at the foot of the Glockner. By far the most sporting way was to carry on at the present high level by crossing the Sulzbachtörl pass and taking a marked path called the Poltener Weg that led, by numerous passes and small summits to the head of the Kals valley. But this required at least one more full day. A second alternative was to descend into the upper Matrei valley by one of several possible routes and cross to Kals by way of a peak called the Muntanitz. The third was to traverse right over the top of the Venediger range and come down by the Badener hut to the town of Matrei, from which it was an easy walk to Kals.

The second alternative was now to be considered out. The first remained a definite possibility because I was quite happy to have a day on minimal rations if it meant a successful conclusion. Besides, I had just enough money for a *Bergsteigeressen* menu at one of the huts on the way, which would just see me through, calorie-wise. But the thought of three continuous days in the high peaks without sunglasses, much of the time above the snow-line . . . when one glance in the hut mirror showed what one day could do . . . if I took my third alternative and traversed right over the Venediger and came down to Matrei in one very long day, I could buy myself new sunglasses and spend most of the next day resting there instead of at Kals, before moving on to the Glockner. I spent a full hour squinting, with painful pupils, at the large-scale map on the wall, calculating the all important vertical heights of ascent and descent that either route would require. Either way, I would take some punishment.

Late in the afternoon I moved on my way again, hat firmly down over my eyes, and spent an hour walking up the immense wilderness of rocks to the east of the hut. My 39th camp was made on a ledge overlooking the upper Sulzbach glacier.

This was another excellent site, with a little stream beside me for water and directly opposite the buttress of the north ridge of the Gross Venediger whose summit, golden in the evening sun, rose into a perfect but slightly curvilinear pyramid. Between my camp and that mountain was a rising plain of snow. Further west was the long western ridge of the mountain, another good peak called the Geiger, and finally, as the eastern skyline, my morning excursion, the north ridge of the Maurerkees Kopf.

I was, once again, tired; and on this occasion I had a bad headache and slight ophthalmia from the glare. I sat in the twilight looking out over the glacier and up at the still glowing summit above me. All that I felt was covered over with expressionless fatigue and peace and if I had been asked any question, I could hardly have replied. At times, as I sat there lazily cooking, I was near to tears again and I think that this time they were tears of gratitude, that I could come so far and see so many wonderful and fearful places. Thought was completely beyond me.

The light on the summit faded from gold to pink and then into a luminous non-colour, remaining visible long after the rest of the mountain had become a mere silhouette.

The morning of my 42nd day, which was to be my last mountain day (though of course I was not then aware of that), was even more cold and clear than the preceding morning. Up rather later than I should have been, I found myself walking behind another party across the rolling snowfields towards the Venediger. A well-beaten little path, that skirted round all crevasses, led straight up into an upper *cwm* between the Gross and Klein summits. From this path I made a short excursion eastward to spy out the condition of the glacier that went that way, in case I chose to descend in that direction; but when I saw how crevassed it was, I made up my mind there and then to follow my third alternative and traverse the whole range to Matrei.

The path now became steeper, and there were four immense crevasses to step across. As I climbed, the north ridge was revealed, elegantly shaped and very narrow; and on both sides, the wings of the north faces of the twin summits. The path, which now became very nearly a climb, went through a series of complicated ice formations and finished up a steep wall onto the wide plateau that extends above. Here I caught up with the party in front of me, and met several other groups who had come up from the Prager Hut. There was also a party of skiers. The Gross Venediger is a very popular summit indeed, and the tours over the glaciers around it are much frequented by large Austrian guided parties who move with extreme slowness and caution and great good humour, trailing ropes and poking about with long axes and ski-sticks.

About half way along this plateau I left my sack and went up to the main summit where there was a small gathering – this being a weekend. There was even a nun in her habit (though I noticed she had ski-pants on under the long skirts). This gathering was 50 feet below the true summit, on to which few cared to venture because it is a very thin ridge of ice leading out over the north face: I strolled up on to it and edged up to the very highest point. Leaving this rather crowded region I went back to the sack and set off across the plateau to the Rainer Horn, a southern summit of the group some two miles away. At once I realized the general truth of the common observation, that you need only leave the beaten track to be thoroughly alone. Four other people climbed the Rainer Horn with me and together we sat on that elegant summit, pointing out the distant Dolomites and the Glockner (that now seemed very near at hand). For my part, however, I did my best not to stare about too much, in order to protect my eyes. It is said that this group had its name for the views it gives towards Venice (Venedig); and I would not be at all surprised to learn that on certain days the plains of the Veneto are visible from here. For me, it was enough to look back east along the Zillertal Alps, and even beyond.

From the Rainer Horn the others descended back to the plateau, but I continued southward down a short but very steep ice slope on to a lower and still more extensive plateau across which I trekked, into the blazing sun. After a little while I fetched up on the shores of the Hoher Zaun, which is a bank of shale and boulders in the midst of this icy sea: here I took a rest and built a beautiful small cairn of white quartz blocks in honour of the day, and the mountains and my family. Hanging my scarf across my hat in the form of a veil, I pushed on, gently downwards, towards the Kristallwand summit. The snow was now softening, but still gave no trouble; there were occasional footprints, but no path to be seen. Not a soul was in sight.

Avoiding the Kristallwand summit so as not to climb one step higher than necessary I came down, along the edge of the plateau, to the gentle ridge leading down to the Frossnitz Törl. Descending to this little col I took the one and only fall of my whole traverse, apart from one or two stumbles in moraines; overrelaxed, I walked out over an ice-slope that had been in the sun for too long, and promptly slid the last 30 feet into the hollow of the pass. Wet with slush and disgusted at my lack of care, I sat for a while in the shadow of a rock wall, with my burning eyes closed.

It would have been possible to prolong this traverse further south still, but that would have meant longer with my face towards the sun. From here I struck off east again, down the Frossnitz glacier, travelling fast before the snow got too soft. There was a little path here, coming over the pass, but many open crevasses and some places that required great circumspection. It was, in fact, a very awkward place to be at the end of a long day, with incipient snow-blindness and a heavy sack, by oneself. But the slide I had taken had awakened me more keenly than ever to the need for watchfulness. There was nothing that could not be dealt with so long as I made no moves in haste and looked about me carefully – though crevasses continued every bit of the way to the final step on to the moraine. The very last few hundred yards were the worst of all because of the deep slush that was forming. I was heartily glad to be on firm ground again, and built another cairn to show it.

The Badener Hut was reached a short while later, perched on a spur overlooking a wide green valley. A girl was sunbathing, a family was making a picnic on the terrace, and within, in comforting darkness, an old lady dispensed *Teewasser*. From here I also bought half a loaf of tough bread, and took out my pocket knife to cut it. This knife, a very plain one-bladed folding knife, had served me well for 43 days. Flat, it took up very little space; and I had kept the blade as sharp as a razor. I took up the crusty loaf and started, gently, to saw; there was a light click; the leaf of spring that held the blade had snapped.

Another thing too had happened that day: the buckle of the breeches had broken, on the cuff of the right leg. It seemed that my objects were wearing out at the same time as my natural born equipment. If I was going to get up that Glockner, I was going to have to take the task very seriously and even more slowly. Perhaps I would not last out? Perhaps I could now say to myself that the traverse was complete? No, I could not say that: but it is certain that after leaving the Badener Hut and beginning the long winding descent into the Matrei valley I felt that the final summit could and should be treated as incidental. There was nothing necessary about another peak, so long as I reached Heiligenblut in good order. The driving determination that had carried me along for six weeks had snapped like an overworked spring.

The descent was first down a long ridge of moraine and then down even longer slopes of grass; the path and the valley were like those in Lakeland, except that the peaks above them were higher and stonier. I came down to a bridge, a great waterfall, a level meadow and a group of chalets. From here a track led on down and down further past a further alp (with the curious name of Katalalpe) and then into thick, steep forest. It was a long way to Matrei and I began to think of an intermediate camp. I had just stopped and taken out my tent, having found a shelf of green grass within the sound of water, when a curious vehicle driven at a reckless pace came round the corner and stopped beside me.

This vehicle was a six-wheeled miniature jeep, driven by a police officer. He told me, as we rattled and swung round the very steep and loose hairpins of the track, that he was out testing radio reception in the mountain valleys. He had seen me pass by and had asked himself how far I had come. I told him. Where did I want to be next? he asked. At a camp-site in Matrei. And that was where he took me, some six or seven miles down the valley road. He off-loaded me (and I was so tired it was like unloading a sack of potatoes) by a field containing tents on the southern side of the town, shook my hand and wished me well and drove off with an immensely roaring engine.

I checked in, stumbled over to a corner of the field and pitched the tent; then, taking great time and trying to do every movement I could with my eyes closed, I cooked a good meal of my remaining food. At times of great fatigue one would often prefer not to eat, but I took pains not to give in to that impulse because the effect next day is to render one almost incapable of movement. I lay for a while in the tent unable to sleep because of the heat of my eyes and the explosions of light that were occurring spontaneously on the retina.

The next morning I felt fresh again and ready for anything – save for one circumstance. During the night some malevolent being had filled my eyes with hot and rusty iron shavings, rubbed them into every corner and behind the ball of the eye, then (having filled up my sockets with a rubbery gum) had sewn the lids together. Or something like that. My headache was pretty bad too, as if my sinuses were full of molten lead that kept slopping about. In other words, I had a medium case of snow-blindness, my first in many many years of climbing. I blundered over to the shower-block, feeling like a rabbit with myxomatosis, and bathed what was left of my visual system with warm water. Only those who have had a similar experience can know the excruciating sensations you get as light starts to return through the pupil again.

Feeling a little better, I showered and put on my "clever" trousers and what passed for a clean shirt; then felt my way into town making straight for the nearest shop that sold good-quality sunglasses. I had just enough money to buy a decent pair and, feeling some relief, sat outside the bank until it opened. While I sat there I manufactured for my glasses, out of "Tuf" tape, two side-shields or blinkers, and on the inside of the lenses (so as not to be more conspicuous than necessary), I affixed strips of tape to lessen the amount of light that penetrated. This improved the vision and greatly lessened the irritation.

Equipped with cash again I went into the nearest dark café and had a large bowl of coffee and several rolls; thus fortified I visited a supermarket and bought a sackful of food, including (oh heaven) a tin of Hungarian stuffed peppers, a very large tin. I returned to the tent and ate a huge breakfast of scrambled eggs, bread, cheese and fruit juice; then I ate a second breakfast; and then, just to be perfectly certain that I would be well fuelled for the rest of the morning, a third. (This liking for three breakfasts continued for about a month after I returned to England, and there extended itself to include lunches, teas and suppers.)

Two small French children came to watch me eat, as if to watch the lion at the zoo. Faced with a spare loaf of bread (that, after all, would be inconvenient on the mountain) I ate that, as if I were a lion, growling and gnashing my teeth. Some more children arrived, to look at my very small tent; they expected to see a midget, perhaps. Instead they saw my exhibition of voracity, and I don't expect it was an improving experience. Later, I had some conversation with the parents of the first two, and they offered me peaches, which I also ate. And so passed the morning.

Round about midday I began to get restless again, in spite of sore eyes. I determined to catch the two o'clock bus round to Kals, and to treat this day as a day of rest, but still progress.

The truth of the matter is this – I wanted to be finished. My crossing of the Eastern Alps had been taken at high speed and without a single rest, except for an afternoon at Sölden (and even there I had been busy with laundry, stitching, shopping and bathing). I felt that I had one more good climb in me, but that I wouldn't make it unless I cared for myself both physically and mentally. Mentally by pampering myself with plenty of tasty food, and physically by keeping out of the afternoon sun and caring for my eyes at all times.

There was another reason too – a change in the weather. From mid-morning on it was clear that something was happening up in the higher levels; long streamers of "mare's-tail" were unrolling from the north, which is a fair good warning of impending meteorological mayhem. It would either be a prolonged period of very unsettled weather, or a single violent storm, followed by a slow clearance. In either case I did not want to be resting in the enjoyable but expensive fleshpots of Matrei. From Kals – or rather, from a camp some way above Kals – there might be the chance of snatching the summit of the Glockner in a lull between storms.

So I packed and went into town. While waiting for the bus I posted two cards to old climbing friends that read (as a hostage to fortune): "By the time you get this card, I shall have climbed the Gross Glockner."

Kals is a group of hotels and holiday villas encrusted on what was once a tiny village; because no high mountains are visible from Kals it has the air of being unnecessary, as a seaside resort might look set down in green fields. There are steep green and forested hillsides all around, but hardly anything to be described as a mighty peak; these are hidden up side valleys. At Kals I resisted the temptation to eat again and contented myself with a strong black coffee, taken in a shady, cellar-like *Stube*.

My strategy was Himalayan, to besiege the Glockner and to climb it camp by camp; for this I had three days of mountain food and my tin of stuffed peppers (with portions for three). What I had not much of, however, was cooking gas; I had failed to buy any in Matrei, and none was stocked in Kals. So my first night would be at the tree-line where a fire could be lit. That was a pleasant two and a half hours away, with my face away from the sun. The next day I would camp as high up on the peak as seemed prudent, according to weather. There, unless it was extremely bad, I could sleep out a day or so in order to snatch the summit in an hour or two of clearance.

The mare's tails had been succeeded by a general whitish haze, very high in the sky, and a number of ragged clouds; yet the weather was fine and sunny and the breeze just occasionally gusting as I started to walk up a pleasant farm track out of Kals in the direction of the Luckner Hut, which is located half-way up the southern valley of the Glockner, called the Ködnitz Tal.

The walk up was a steady tread, past a succession of superb farmhouses stacked against the hillside, past hayfields and through stretches of thick forest. Slowly, slowly, I said to myself, and as I walked I kept my eyes half shut and went off into reminiscence. Recalled to myself each camp I had made, from Thabor, to Vanoise, to Rutor; then over the Ferret to my wanderings in the Valais, with each camp remembered, and from there to Simplon, to the Alpe Buscagna, to Vannino and on to the alp below the Soreda Pass. To the lush grasslands of Juf, to the streets of Chiesa, to the high hills above Poschiavo. The bivouac on the Palon, and over to the Val Martello where I sat under a dripping rock, to the shelf of gravel on the Hochjoch saddle. Sölden and the Windachtal to forests above Ridnaun. Then the upper Pfitschertal and the cliffs of shale, and the traverse path to that wonderful pool and meadow at the foot of the Möseler; Alpe Gogen, and a long night of rain near Steinhaus. Two high mountain camps with the glaciers of the Venediger group spread out before me and now, here I was, moving up to a 41st camp on the 43rd day of my traverse.

On the hillside above there was a road and after two or three steep miles my path coincided with it. A hairpin bend, a cutting or two and the end of the road was reached – a large hotel. Here there was a car park, picnickers, brightly dressed children climbing upon logs and much further ahead a view of glaciers and a wall of rock going up into a thin mist; this was the southern aspect of the Glockner. The cone that I had seen from so far away was now immediately present.

Though the road ended, the track continued, very old and stony, between walls of stone. I passed a little shrine and then, as I climbed very slowly and ruminatively up the track, another. At the third I discovered I was following the fourteen stations of the cross; every hundred yards, set into the rocks of the old wall or set on a stout post, was a little roofed image of Christ on his way up to Calvary. They were old hand-coloured engravings of a very poor quality, covered with cracked glass in dilapidated frames; some were missing. Yet just because they were so unpretentious, they succeeded in conveying the drama of that journey. The rhetorical gestures of the participants, borrowed from heaven knows how many altar-painters, good or bad, from centuries before, communicated just because their qualiy was not worth attention in itself. My sombre mood of two days before returned, and with it an image that had passed before my mind's eyc on more than one occasion, of the traveller with his heavy pack, fleeing from the City of Destruction. And he came to the hill called Difficulty. Conway too, at the end of his journey, came this way, and he too noted the shrines.

The track and the shrines led up, as they often do, to a small windowless chapcl. I set down the sack to rest and stepped inside. As usual, over-ornate, with many pictures and many flowers. Some of the flowers were of plastic, but some had been freshly picked from the meadows just beyond the woods. A man and his two children came in to look as well, while his wife stood by the gate. I stepped asidc, there being no room for more than two adults at once in the little cluttered space. When the man came out he asked me who I was and where I was going. *Aus Frankreich, zu Fuss. Morgen will ich auf den Grossglockner gehen. Vielleicht. Aber das wetter wird schlecht sein. Meine Ferien sind endet.* After they left, I stepped back in again for a few moments, in a half-dream; I wanted some ritual obscrvance of the place and the time. Of course there was none I could authentically make.

Outside I had taken a few steps towards my sack when I saw an old woman in the path, clad in a long embroidered peasant dress; she had a red, tasselled shawl about her shoulders and on her head a wide-brimmed, low-crowned hat held tightly under her chin by a white cloth. Her face, which was the colour of loam, was framed in iron-grey wisps of hair. She moved with difficulty on pattened feet and with the aid of a gnarled stick on which she leant with all her weight. With a halting motion she passed a few steps beside me and then seemed to disappear around the corner of the barn that stood beside the chapel. I write "seemed" because I am not totally convinced that she was there at all, and that I may not have projected, in my dreamlike state of mind, an image from some Breughel painting on to my weary retina.

From here, still in a sombre and reflective mood, I walked another mile or so up the valley until I had a clear view of the Luckner Hut and there, in the last stand of trees, found a small level spot not far from a stream; here there was an abundant supply of firewood.

The sun had gone down and as I made my hearth and kindled, with a little difficulty, a warm blaze, the cold breeze grew stronger. Above, a great wall of steep, slatey cliffs ran up to a ridge; this ridge in time became the long south ridge of my intended peak; straight up the valley the glacier way to the summit was still visible although the mist was thicker and moving faster. There were no stars. My big tin of peppers warmed slowly, but was wonderfully tasty. I ate it slowly, reheating it; and followed it with another, yet another, brew of mint tea. Looking at the sky I wondered about the morrow. I scrubbed the soot off the outside of the tins and the smoke-smells off my hand, and when I got into my sleeping bag it was already dark.

Night was disturbed by claps of thunder and the pattering of rain, but not to distraction. I awoke with the light, well rested, and could sense at once that the soreness in my eyes was healed. Yet there was a pattering, as if of rain, and the air about me was cold, unusually cold. Perhaps I stirred for a little while and went to sleep again; for when I woke I was at once aware that the tent had lost its shape, that it was weighed down. And the whispering sound outside told me of the snow.

Here, where I was camped, the snow was light, and damp; but a short way up the valley to the Luckner Hut (that was now invisible) the snow was lying thick. Deep snow, suddenly, in August, down to the 2,000 m mark, has one unmistakable cause – a mass of cold air moving in from the north of such extent and depth that it is unlikely to clear for three days. In order to digest that thought I went back to sleep again for half an hour and awoke to the realization that today would be the last day of my traverse. The "friction" had won.

Still lying in my sack I made an unhurried breakfast and while drinking my tea studied the map yet again. I kept up some pretence of an alternative plan by considering a move up to the Salm Hut on the eastern side of the mountain, from which a descent to Heiligenblut would be swifter than from this southern approach; but I knew it was a pretence. Perhaps I was feeling a sense of relief, that I would no longer have to drive myself out of a warm bed before dawn, fumble with frozen fingers, wipe down the tent with frozen hands and fold it away; that this was the last time of packing my sack with such care, of fastening my axe in just such a way, of packing rope and tent under the flap, of adjusting a headband, of checking the availability of jacket, or over-trousers, or woollen cap; that I would never again have to build a little cairn of three stones and scatter food for the birds. It may have been relief that I had come through without injury; that I had come through at all. I began my walk back down the valley with a mind that was open to any fancy, no longer tensed to meet the day. I came down by the trees and the chapel and the fourteen stations to the head of the road again, and took an eastward track up a steep hillside, following a signpost that read "Glorerhütte 2 Std. Salmhütte 3½ Std."

At this slightly lower level, a very fine rain was falling and the trees and steep meadows were wet with the spray of it; the valleys below were hidden in cloud as were the peaks above, and between the two layers of cloud there was a zone of rain and a zone of snow. The walk up to the Glorer Hut is pleasant but uneventful, you wind up through steep patches of grass and mixed woodlands, and then out on to open alp. At one place I was able to look across to the site of my last camp, the 41st; then I re-entered the zone of snow. The last stretch to the hut was up an open valley, now white across; a ropeway, used to supply the hut, ran up beside me. The hut itself became visible at the top of a pass, down the other side of which the streams and tracks all descended to Heiligenblut; this was the last of all my passes, the first of which had been the Col des Clots de Cavales, high above La Bérarde. After that, there would be no more uphill work; after that, it would be downhill all the way. I ran the last 50 yards, slipping on the snowy boulders. A cold wind was stealing over the crest, out of the north, bearing more snow. I knelt down on the slushy grass and carefully constructed a pile of three stones; then I went indoors.

Four visitors, the warden and his wife and their child were in one corner of the *Speisezimmer*, engaged in a merry conversation. I think I may have ordered a bowl of coffee, but I am not certain. I remember cutting cheese with my broken-backed knife, and looking over my map again, obsessively scouting out some further possibility. From here it would be possible to by-pass the Glockner altogether and work round to the east to join a path called the Jubiläumsweg that follows the crest of the peaks due east to the Hochtor pass and beyond. It would not be impossible, following that path, to go yet further and further. There are peaks east of the Glockner and high passes, and hills as far as Szombathely where you enter Hungary.

Though of course a true prolongation would require a southern sweep, towards the Julian Alps and down the scarps of the Dalmatian coast: in that way I might arrive in Macedonia, where we had stayed five years before, where there are also mountains of marble. Perhaps the marble beds of Prilep have an underground connection with the marble precipices of the Schneeberg and the Gürtelscharte that I had crossed how many days before? Everything connects underground; the order of things that we encounter is not the order of things as they happen, since the order is buckled and folded, faulted and slipped. Why should I not go on walking away, making tracks from the City, making tracks through the snow?

Like a solitary sailor unwilling to come to land, I was at that moment unwilling to complete my journey and could think of nothing more natural than to continue beyond the Glockner, going east for as far as may be.

Where had I come from and had I come far? the man with a white moustache was asking me. *Aus Frankreich, zu Fuss. Vierundvierzig Nächten. Im Zelt. Ich ende in Heiligenblut.* They took me out and shook my hand in the friendliest manner, and then took photographs of me with them in the group, as if it would bring them good luck. They watched me put on my sack and my headband, and shook my hand again. The snow had almost stopped and it was time to be making tracks.

A short way below the hut on its eastern side the path divided, with the left-hand fork signed to the Salm Hut; I turned away and took the right-hand side and in so doing resigned myself to completion. The path descended slopes of grass and scree and slabby rock, gently into a snow-filled valley. There were marmots in great plenty here, and they whistled and called at me, and I whistled and called back at them. I shouted my farewells to them, loudly and clearly; and they continued to whistle, watching me from their posts upon the rocks. Looking back up the hillside I saw the long trail of my footsteps coming down to where I stood, out of the mist and snow.

I came to the valley bottom where the snow gave way to grass again and the path grew more distinct; here I settled into a steady rhythm of walking once more. On either side, long steep slopes of grass became long steep slopes of snow before disappearing into mist. The grass at my feet, the rocks about me, the slopes above; this was quintessence of mountain. How fortunate I was. Teach me to live that I may dread the grave as little as my bed. Teach me to die.

Then, as I descended this long valley I looked up and saw the further slope of another range in front of me, and winding down that slope, out of the snow and mist and into visibility, the long thread of the road that crosses the Hochtor pass. That marked the end. Overcome with emotion and with tears in my eyes, I came to a halt and stood there looking up at the road and at the car that wound its way down across the slope, and at the further range, the snow and the mist. Crags, crowned with trees appeared and disappeared into the floating moisture that welled up from below.

If asked to describe the emotion that I felt I would only be able to compare it with the tearfulness of mixed relief and joy that one feels on recovery from serious injury or prolonged illness, or that we experience after a successful childbirth; of which the greatest part is awe and an astonishment at our continued existence.

The valley became narrower and the stream that filled its bed was swallowed into a concrete embankment; here workmen sheltered in a dug-out and sounds of machinery came out of the living rock. The path went down into steep dripping woods to an alp, then down through steeper and still wetter woods and glades from which were views, now and then, down into the lower valley, where there were houses.

And then, what is there more to say? One came to a well-made path that led, by way of chalets and a chapel, to a place where men were cutting logs, to a descent below a cliff, to hayfields steaming in the patches of sun that had begun to show through rifts in the cloud cover; and then one was on a track that looked down over meadows and there was a church spire and the roof of an hotel. And then quite suddenly, one came out of a patch of woodland to find oneself walking into the streets of the village-resort of Heiligenblut, and it was 12.30, exactly 44 days since the start. The Grand High-Level Route had been completed.

And what did I do? I set my sack on a seat and took out my decent clothes. Then I went into a smart café and ordered coffee and schnapps and drank them both down. Then I went into the toilet and washed my face and neck and changed out of my climbing breeches and sweat-sodden shirt. Smarter, I went back into the café and had another coffee, another schnapps, and a piece of pastry. I bought, wrote and posted two cards. Then I went out to my sack that had sat patiently for me, and repacked it. My old breeches I threw into a rubbish skip. Then I walked out to the main road, eating a *Bratwurst* that I bought from a stall. When that was eaten I stood by a suitable place at the roadside and started to raise my thumb.

APPENDIX

A SHORT GUIDE TO A LONG ROUTE; being a description of a "Grand High-Level Traverse" of the Alps from La Bérarde to Heiligenblut.

The route is described primarily in terms of objectives to be gained rather than routes to be followed, since the details of day-to-day travel and climbing will be determined by the conditions of the day. Routes between objectives are given as feasible or recommended alternatives, with the route taken by myself marked (*a*.). Some desirable summits are indicated. Huts and bivouac shelters are noted, as are some convenient camp-sites; but only when these are directly useful. Availability of supplies is also noted, where it is especially useful to know.

I am assuming throughout that any party following this route is competent to do so.

1. La Bérarde to Le Lauzet

From La Bérarde take the signposted track to the Refuge du Châtelleret, from which an obvious path leads back south down the eastern side of the valley, climbing slowly and then steeply towards the Col des Clots de Cavales (3,159 m). The path becomes indistinct and makes a rising traverse across a rocky rib before gaining the foot of a small glacier (space for a tent). The col is reached easily by a short steep couloir and rocks. Descend on steep snow to the left-hand moraine and follow a good path down to the Plan de Valfourche and the Chalets de l'Alpe du Villar d'Arène. Camping possible.

a. Go left, northward, down a gradually descending path that traverses steep and in one place precipitous slopes round to the Col du Lautaret; then take the old road and paths round to the hamlet of Le Lauzet, situated just below the N.91, about six kilometres down from the col.

b. (Probably better.) From the Chalets go right, southward, over the Col d'Arsine, climbing some 250 m, and descend towards the hamlet of Le Casset, reaching Le Lauzet by road and field paths.

Summit: the Pic N. des Cavales (3,362 m) is an outstanding rock climb, done directly from the col beside it. A. D.

2. Le Lauzet to Modane

Take the steep path up to the Alpe du Lauzet and further to where the valley opens out at the higher level; go north, traversing above a "blind" valley with an exitless lake, to the Col de la Ponsonnière. Continue north-east on a narrow path into the magnificent cirque of the Lac des Cerces. Take the narrow pass in the north-east corner of this bowl and descend to the Lac Rond. An unmade road descends eastward.

a. (In bad weather.) Continue north by an indistinct path over a low grassy pass into the upper corrie of the valley called the Combe de la Plagnette. Descend under the immense cliffs of the Aig. Noire (2,867 m) and gain an obvious path on the right, eastern slope of the valley and descend at length to Valloire. From here, road and steep forest paths lead down into the Maurienne valley, and public transport to Modane.

b. (Recommended but not done by me.) From the Lac Rond descend east down the unmade road into the head of the Névache valley (Refuge). Continue east by the path and cross the Col des Muandes (2,832 m). Descend east to a small lake and traverse across slopes to the saddle between the summit mass of Mt. Thabor and the peak of the Grand Seru. Cross the saddle and find an indistinct path south-east and then north-east into the upper Vallée Etroite (path marked on 1 : 50,000 map). Cross the Col de la Vallée Etroite on a good path (G.R. 5) and descend to Le Lavoi. (Refuge.) From here by steep roads down to Modane.

There are many fine camp-sites in the Thabor group, and several interesting small summits. There are no supplies at Le Lauzet. Modane has all supplies but no camp-site.

3. Modane to Val d'Isère

Take a very steep track that starts from a quarry entrance on the north side of the town, easily missed (G.R. 55). Follow up, taking the left hand fork to a footbridge over the left-hand torrent; continue up to the road and follow this to the Polset chalets (camping possible in woods). Follow G.R. 55 over the Col Chavière to the Refuge Péclet-Polset. Good camping. From here several peaks can be climbed, esp. the Dôme de Polset (3,531 m). Continue down the valley.

a. Descend to Pralognan (supplies) and then (still on G.R. 55) climb back up to the Col de la Vanoise. (Refuge.)

b. (Recommended.) From the chalets at La Motte take a path to the Valette bivouac hut. From here steep snow and broken rocks lead to a high shoulder overlooking the Col du Pelve. Descend to this col and cross snow-fields to the Col de la Vanoise. The Dôme de l'Arpont (3,614 m) can be climbed, and smaller summits.

From the Col de la Vanoise, the summit of the Grande Casse (3,852 m) can be reached (P.D. serious).

From the col follow G.R. 55 into the Leisse valley and up pleasantly over the Col de la Leisse, usually snowy. After a descent, traverse east and cross the Col de Fresse and descend by meadows and ski-tracks to La Daille and Val d'Isère. An attractive path follows the stream through a hidden gorge, but it is easily missed.

(There is a small hut in the Vallon de la Leisse from which the Pointe de la Sana can be climbed, but camping is discouraged. Supplies at Val d'Isère, but not at La Daille.)

4. Val d'Isère to Courmayeur, Val Ferret

Walk through a sequence of cuttings and tunnels until an inconspicuous path by a waterfall leads up steeply to meadows and a chapel. Take road and track up to the nature reserve (camping possible at entrance to reserve, at Le Saut); thence up past the dam. A narrow path leads up the northern slope of the valley, which may be hard to find in the early morning. Easy glacier leads up to extensive snow-fields, with several summits, notably the Tsantaleina (3,608 m). The north ridge is P.D., the north face A.D.

Traverse the summit of the Pointe de la Traversière (3,368 m) and descend steep snow into the basin below the Colle Bassac Déré. *Do not descend the glacier*, but traverse rightward across a terrace of moraines below subsidiary glaciers and find, at its end, an easy ridge of blocks descending into a grassy valley. In bad weather this may be tricky; occasional cairns and path later in season.

Descend to the Bezzi hut and the road-head at Surier.

(A strong team might reach here by traversing over the summit of the Grand Sassière 3,747 m P.D.). Camping possible near hut and at Surier. (Supplies at Valgrisanche; diversion). By tracks, road and paths on the north-west side of the lake reach Arp Vieille from which a very steep path climbs to the Rifugio Scavarda. Good sites for tent below hut.

From beside the hut traverse across the Morion glacier to pass between two rock humps; then strike up left by an easy couloir to the summit ridge of the Testa del Rutor (3,486 m). Visit summit easily and descend Rutor glacier. Large crevasses; care required; route according to conditions. Gain the right-hand moraine and descend to the Rif. S. Margherita. (Several moderate summits possible from here.) Descend to La Thuile. (Supplies.)

a. Walk down the road to Pré St. Didier and take a pleasant path on the west side of the valley to Dolonne and thence Courmayeur. Large equipped camp-site, without supplies, at Pra Sec in the Val Ferret. Supplies at Planpincieux, Entrèves etc.

b. (Suggested.) From La Thuile walk up the road and take the track leading westward up the Vallone di Chavannes over a pass into the upper Val Veni. Climbing from the Val Veni and Val Ferret will depend on the skill and ambition of the party. The normal route on the Grandes Jorasses (4,208 m, P.D.) is big and convenient. The normal route on Mont Dolent (3,823 m) is very good and adjacent to the Col Ferret, with a bivouac hut to stay in. (The normal route on Mont Blanc is sometimes very crevassed.)

5. *Val Ferret to Zermatt*
Cross the Col Ferret and descend to the chalets of les Ars dessus: here you are on the original High-Level Route between Chamonix and Zermatt.

For details of the High-Level Route see *Selected Climbs in the Pennine Alps*, ed. J. Neill, Alpine Club.

Many variations are possible; the following is recommended on this occasion, on the basis of my previous excursions. It avoids the heavily crevassed areas around the Col de Valpelline. Viz: cross the Col des Planards to Bourg St. Pierre (supplies). Take the track to the Cab. de Valsorey; do not stay there but bivouac high on the Plateau du Couloir. In descent it is vitally important to keep close to the right-hand bank of the Mont Durand Glacier after you have passed below the seracs. Camp on the Chanrion Alp. Cross to the Dix Hut by way of the upper Gietro glacier; easy; and descend to Arolla. (Supplies.) In good weather, go by way of the Bertol Hut and the Mont Miné snow-fields to the Rossier Hut on the Dent Blanche: in unsettled weather get there by way of Les Haudères and Bricola. From the Rossier Hut climb over the flanks of the Dent Blanche and descend to Schönbiel and thence to Zermatt.

In sustained bad weather there is no safe way between Arolla and Zermatt except by a long trek over the Col de Torrent, the Meid Pass and the Augstbord Pass.

It should nearly always be possible to cross from Chanrion to the Dix Hut, except in extreme conditions. The area around the Col de l'Evêque and the upper Ottemma glacier is very trying in misty conditions. The Grand Combin should be avoided in anything but good to very good conditions. There is a high-level crossing between Zinal and Täsch by way of the Tracuit Hut that is worth some study.

This whole section should be carefully researched and advice sought.

Many summits are possible, but especially recommended are Mont Blanc de Cheilon (3,870 m) P.D. from the Dix Hut, and the Dent Blanche (4,357 m) from the Rossier Hut. P.D./A.D.

6. Zermatt to Simplon Pass

Several variations possible but the following is the most direct. Walk up to the Täsch Hut and beyond to make a high bivouac below the Allalinpass. Cross the pass easily and descend to Saas Fee by way of the Britannia Hut: a long glacier route, but straightforward. (For details see *Selected Climbs*, etc.) Then take the walking pass called the Zwischbergenpass above Saas Almagell. In descent do not go all the way down to the road, but cross on to the left-hand bank of the torrent on a good track and work a way over the col (1,871 m) and descend to the village of Simplon. From here a wearisome walk up to the pass. (Occasional bus and simple supplies.) Summits for this section include the Allalinhorn (4,027 m) and the Weissmies (4,023 m) both F.

Details of other possible crossing are available in the guide book. In bad weather, a long walk over the Simeli and Bistinen Passes brings one down directly to the Simplon Pass summit, but the route-finding can be very difficult in cloud and snow. (a.)

Good site for a tent on the meadows above the road, where the water conduit from the Kaltwasser Pass comes round the hillside.

7. Simplon Pass to Airolo

Follow the water conduit round to the first stream, then strike up across the moraine following an indistinct track to a prominent cairn. Cross waterworn slabs and follow the obvious moraine ridge to the pass. There is a small bivouac hut hidden in the rock humps that mark the top of the pass. Descend directly from this hut down easy glacier; serac danger to the right. An easy path leads to Alpe Veglia and a C.A.I. refuge. From the La Balma chalets take an indistinct path up through woods and meadows and strike off left to gain the foot of the Passo di Valtendra. Climb steeply up grass and vegetation (narrow path) to the crest: a very narrow airy path, marked with an arrow, leads across steep grass slopes and through a rock passage upward to a natural amphitheatre and a terrace leading back right. Follow paint marks carefully round to open alp. Descend to Alpe Buscagna (bothy and camping). Continue down to Alpe Devero village (simple supplies). Take the track along the eastern side of the Devero lake and walk steadily up path to the Forno chalets (bothy). Indistinct paths lead up to the Scatta Minoia and down a steep gully to the Vannino basin. Traverse round left to a hollow with a (locked) bothy and over a grassy mound to the upper Vannino dam, and another bothy. Take to steep grass again and traverse into the snow gully leading up to the Colle Nefelgiu. Descend on steep snow to an alp and a path that leads round and down to the Morasco dam.

From the north end of the dam take a tiny path steeply up and then traverse across very steep grass by sheep "trods" to gain easier slopes leading by hummocks to the Rifugio Toggia (camping possible).

a. Continue easily over the S. Giacomo Pass and descend by pleasant paths either to All'Acqua or Bedretto; thence by bus to Airolo.

b. From the Toggia Alp take the good path over the Bocchetta Valle Maggia to the Basodino Hut, thence northward by a stony valley over the Cristallino Pass descending at length to Airolo. (Probably very enjoyable, with summits to choose from.)

Along the whole of this section there are many good peaks, of which Monte Leone and the Ofenhorn are the most attractive. The south face of the Cervandone has a "via ferrata". The Ofenhorn can be climbed either from the Forno chalets or the Vannino bothy. F./

P.D. Climbs on Monte Leone are long and complicated and of all grades. No information about other summits.

8. Airolo to Maloja

From Airolo gain the head of the Lago Ritom, by Piotta (rack-railway available). *a*. Continue over the Passo Colombo or the Passo Sole to Alpe Cassaccia on the Lukmanierpass road, then by the Passo di Gana Negra to Campo Blenio (supplies available). *b*. Either direct from Airolo or from Lago Ritom reach the Cadlimo Hut; continue eastward to the summit of the Lukmanierpass and thence south of east to the P. di Gana Negra. (Easy summits can be reached.) Walk up to the Luzzone dam.

a. Cross the dam and take a tunnel beside the lake and a path as far as a small chalet. A signed path leads up to the Soreda Pass by way of an alp (camping). It is essential to follow waymarks closely, up a loose gully to the pass. Descend an alp and then a steep gully into the upper Länta valley. (Small hut.) Gain the Länta glacier by its left bank moraine and from the level lower section climb up, normally by a direct snow gully, to the Läntalücke. This alternative can be trying in bad conditions.

b. Cross the dam and take the other tunnel and path to the Adula refuge, and from there traverse the Adula (3,402 m) descending to the Läntalücke. There may be large crevasses on the descent.

Descend at tiresome length past the Zapport Hut to Hinterrhein and Splügen.

It is sensible to take a bus down from Hinterrhein to Andeer, and then back up to Juf at the head of the Val Ferrera; an arduous walking route could be devised, taking two days.

There are no supplies at Juf, but good camping beyond the last chalets.

Take the well-marked track over the Forcellina and Lunghin Passes to Maloja (supplies but no camping).

9. Maloja to Poschiavo

a. (Not recommended.) Take the path to Cavloc and Plan Canin; cross footbridge and follow a small path up towards the Muretto pass. The pass is reached by steep scree on the left hand upper slope of the *cwm*, above the snow-bed, not by the head of valley. Descend at great length to Chiareggio and Chiesa (camp-site with showers, etc., in Chiesa itself, on the Lanzada road). Take a bus to Franscia and walk up to Campo Moro (camping, and path to Marinelli Hut). Continue to upper dam and after walking along beside the lake turn east into the Valle Poschiavo. Fine camping.

b. (Slight information.) From Maloja walk round the lake to Isola and take the Val Fex. Climb easily by rocks and glacier to the Fex/Scersen col (small hut). Descend the Scersen glacier (no information) and climb up towards the Marinelli Hut. From here the Colle di Musella is easily crossed to Alpe Fellario, from which a path leads round the head of the lake to the Valle Poschiavo. Several summits, notably Piz Tremoggia (3,441 m) and Piz Bernina (4,049 m).

From the Cancian Pass at the head of the valley descend easily but lengthily to Poschiavo by steep forest paths. It is important to keep to the left-hand slope as you come over the pass, following a tiny path.

10. Poschiavo to Bormio

Take a short bus ride to Sfaxu. (N. of Poschiavo on the Pontresina road). A long walk up the tracks of the Val da Camp leads to the Passo Viola. A long walk down the tracks of the Val Viola leads to the road at Arnoga; descend at length to Isolaccia (camp-site in valley below upper village). Bus to Bormio.

There are excellent camping sites in the upper Val da Camp, beyond the Saoseo lake, but few in the Val Viola. Occasional buses run down the road from Arnoga to Bormio. It is advisable to camp in the upper Val Viola.

11. Bormio to the Hochjoch

Many variations possible; consult appropriate guide books for details and act according to conditions and fitness. The following is suggested.

a. Reach Santa Caterina by bus. Take the track to the Albergo Buzzi and then to the Rifugio Branca. Camp or bivouac above the hut. From here in good weather a traverse from the Palon della Mare (3,704 m) to the Cevedale summit (3,778 m) can be made without difficulty, with short descent to the Casati Hut. If weather uncertain, the Palon or Monte Pasquale (3,559 m) can be climbed easily from there. A Pasquale-Cevedale traverse can also be made.

From the Casati Hut, descend north-east to the Eisseepass. If the conditions permit, descend to Sulden (Solda) by a crevassed glacier;

if conditions poor, continue north-east over a small shoulder and descend steep snow and scree to a terrace on the north, left-hand bank of the Langenferner. Descend pleasantly into the Val Martello (good camping). Continue down the valley (no supplies, infrequent bus) to Goldrau. Walk along the main road to Schlanders and take the path up the Schlandraunertal and over the Tascheljoch to Kurzras; thence easily uphill to the Hochjoch. Or reach Kurzras by road (buses).

b. If you have descended to Sulden, continue by road (bus) to Schluderns. Walk lengthily up to the Höllerhütte on the south side of the Weisskugel (3,739 m). The Hochjoch can be reached by a high pass, or by the Weisskugel summit (no information).

c. The peaks around the Laaser glacier basin can be traversed either from Sulden or the Val Martello, with good descents to Schlanders or the road to Schluderns.

12. Hochjoch to Sölden

Many opportunities exist, but the simplest (*a*) is to continue down to the Hochjoch Hospiz and to use the Seufert Weg high-level pathway as a base for climbs on the Weisskamm range (Fluchtkogel 3,500 m, Hoch Vernagt Sp. 3,539 m, Wildspitze 3,772 m, etc). Descend to Vent and bus or walk to Sölden. Good camp-site with facilities.

b. In good conditions ambitious parties can make a long glacier traverse down the Weisskamm from the Vernagt Hut to the Braunschweiger Hut and descend directly to Sölden. Or traverse from the Hochjoch to the Martin Busch Hut (via Fineilspitze 3,576 m), and thence to the Schalfkogeljoch to the Hockwilde Hut, descending to Sölden via Obergurgl.

See guide book *Ötztal Alps* for details.

13. Sölden to Sterzing

From Sölden take the track and path up the Windachtal to the Siegerland Hut (some level ground for a tent nearby).

a. In poor weather the following variant is very fine.

Take the path over the moraine and climb steep snow and loose rocks to the Windachscharte. Cross over into Italy and descend scree and steep grass following a little path that leads down to a small lake. An abandoned military post is on a knoll nearby; follow the lake shore below the military post and at the outflow of the lake take a narrow path across a grassy plain, eastward. The path soon fades out, but there are way-marks. Aim for a white moraine at the foot of the Schneeberg (difficult route finding in mist). From the foot of the white moraine cross the stream and follow waymarks up huge blocks and slabs and areas of scree to the Gürtelscharte. Cross this pass and descend into a grassy *cwm*. Keep well to the left, over towards a shoulder (fence visible) and traverse round it (faint path). Descend to mine workings and follow tracks up to the Schneebergscharte. Cross this pass and descend by more workings into a large green valley. A track leads down into the Ridnaunertal, through forest, to the road.

b. Climb the Sonklarspitze (3,471 m) pleasantly, and descend to the Becher Hut above the glacier in the upper Ridnaunertal. From here continue down to the road.

c. From the grassy plain between the Windachscharte and the Gürtelscharte on route *a*, passes lead through towards the Becher hut and the upper valley.

Follow the road (buses) to Sterzing. Camp-site two miles south.

14. Sterzing to the Ahrntal
Buses up the Pfitschertal are infrequent and supplies at St. Jakob are limited (no fuel).

a. From the third hairpin on the road up to the Pfitschjoch a narrow path traverses upward towards the Weisszintscharte. The hut on the Hochfeiler S. flank no longer exists; the path traverses below it and takes the moraine before crossing the wide easy glacier. Descend to Edelraute Hut. Summit: the Hochfeiler, 3,510 m.

b. An interesting alternative might be to take the Pfunderer Hohenweg, a high-level footpath that starts near the camp-site south of Sterzing and winds up through the steep hills south of the Pfitschertal, and finishes at the Edelraute Hut.

From the Edelraute Hut a traversing path links with the Chemnitzer and Schwarzenstein Huts. Follow this. There are superb tent-sites at the foot of the S. ridge of the Gross Möseler and at the upper Gogen Alp. Many good summits to climb, too numerous to list. Descend by one of several paths, lengthily, into the Ahrntal.

Camping in the Ahrntal does not seem to be encouraged; hide in the woods! Supplies and buses.

15. Ahrntal to Matrei and the Tauerntal

This is a long and magnificent section; if the party takes route *b* and is not relying on hut supplies, it will have to carry five to six days' food. Last supplies at Prettau, the last village in the Ahrntal.

a. Take the good footpath to the Tridentina Hut. (Summit: the Dreiherrnspitze, 3,499 m.) Good camping not far from hut. Continue over the Birnlücke and descend on steep moraine paths and steep grass and finally (traversing right) down an earthy rib to the terminal moraines of the Krimmler glacier basin. Climb up by a steep path to the Warnsdorfer Hut. Room for tent in grassy hollow to left of the hut, and some terraces above and beyond the hut. Continue up to the Krimmler Törl pass. (It is not necessary to go over the hump of the Gamspitzl; a snowy terrace gives direct access to the pass and saves height.) Summit: the Hinter Maurerkees Kopf, 3,313 m by the north-east ridge, is a good climb (P.D.). Descend the glacier for about a mile and then make for the left-hand moraine where a narrow path leads down to a rocky bluff overlooking the glacier snout. The way off this bluff is smooth and slabby and not instantly obvious; bear right and take a slabby rake. Cross the glacier. Do not aim directly towards the Kürsinger Hut, but further right where the glacier comes round the corner. The way on to the further bank may be tricky, and change during the season. Usually marked, but hard to see. Gain another bluff and climb it to traverse back left on a path to the hut. Continue up the stony slopes beyond; infrequent sites for a tent. (Summit: Keeskogel, 3,291 m.)

a. There will usually be a path across the glacier towards the Gross Venediger. Easy slopes, but several large crevasses in the upper *cwm*. A final steep slope leads to the broad summit plateau. Visit the main summit (3,672 m) and continue south-east to the Rainer Horn (3,560 m). Descend steep snow eastward and then continue south-east across the level snowfields. The Badener Hut is best reached by the Kristallwand summit (3,329 m); the Frossnitz glacier is very crevassed. (The traverse may be extended still further south-east, at will.) From the Badener Hut a good path leads down into the Frossnitztal (camping possible) and at great length down to the main valley and Matrei (camping on south edge of town).

Continue to Kals by an easy grassy pass, or by bus round the foot of the range. Kals may also be reached by way of the Sudetendeutsche Hut on the Gross Muntanitz (3,232 m), but there are no supplies in the Tauerntal.

 b. From above the Kürsinger Hut, take the crevassed slopes of the Zwischen- and Unter-Sulzbach Passes, descend the Vilfragen glacier and take the St. Poltner high-level footpath along the spine of the range, past or over many small summits, to the Granatspitze (3,086 m) and descend at great length down to Kals. There are probably no supplies at the Matreier Tauernhaus, but buses run from there down to Matrei.

16. Kals to Heiligenblut

The normal route from Kals to the summit of the Grossglockner (3,797 m) goes by way of the Luckner and Stüdl Huts and the little Ködnitz glacier. A recommended route is the Stüdlgrat, the southwest ridge of the peak, which gives a long classic P.D. rock climb. The best descent would probably be by the Salm hut, and into the Leittertal. (No information.)

 a. In bad weather, cross the easy Berger Törl pass into the Leitertal and continue down enjoyable forest paths to Heiligenblut.

 b. Parties who have come along the St. Poltener path have other opportunities open to them; they may pick up supplies at Enzingerboden and continue over into the upper Pasterzen glacier basin to the Oberwalder Hut and climb the Glockner or other peaks from that side. But it is proper to finish the journey at Heiligenblut.

★   ★   ★

Time

Allow for 56 days. The time of 44 days on the first crossing was possible only because continuous bad weather in the Mont Blanc and Valais Alps made mountaineering impossible and fast walking imperative.

Size of Party

One is proper; and the route is planned with lightweight, solo travel in mind.

Aids and Supports

Mechanical assistance permitted in the larger valleys! Except in the Austrian Alps it will usually be found that climbing huts are not well placed for this type of travel; the party should consider itself as unsupported, but as availing itself of huts in extreme weather, for the occasional meal and a bit of conversation.

Maps

1:100,000 scale is sufficient for most purposes; if the party can't navigate adequately with such a map then it has no business doing the route. 1:50,000 would have been useful on only two occasions (The Mont Thabor region, and the Saastal–Simplon crossing).

The following maps were used:

Carte Touristique: Sheets 54 and 53.
Carte Nationale Suisse; Sheets 46, 42, 43 and 44 (Sheets 41, 47 and 38 useful)
Freytag and Berndt Wanderkarten: Sheets 46, 45, 25, 15 and 12 (24 was needed, also).

Guide Books

There are now English-language guide books to all the major areas visited, and these can be consulted and notes taken. I was able to use the Alpine Club library, as a member, and use the local publications. I was adequately prepared for all sections except the Bernina group, where, partly as a result, I did no climbing. Do as much study as possible in order to be aware of all possible alternatives.

For both maps and guide notes, the best system is to cut the maps up into useful sections and to stick notes on the back of them, written in a waterproof ink. To save weight, make up packages and arrange for them to be sent ahead to selected post offices: but choose the offices carefully, at points you have to go through whatever the weather (for example, Zermatt is a bad place to have to collect from if you don't happen to pass through).

All huts and many stations and information offices display large- and small-scale maps and relevant information, and these will be found useful.

Communications

You can arrange to check with family and friends at agreed times and places, only to find that you are in the wrong place at the right time or the right place at the wrong time. It is best if you are blessed with philosophical relatives, who know nothing about the dangers of solo travel in high mountains. I decided simply not to bother with any regular communication system, and just to remind myself every morning, noon and night that what I was doing was dangerous. It is worth pointing out, however, that in general the Alps are not lonely mountains, and that you are far more likely to meet people and raise help in emergency than you are in the Scottish Highlands. The exceptions to this will be obvious to a competent party.

Equipment

The secret history of mountaineering in the past two decades is that it has got easier. The advent of strong, high-quality and lightweight materials has made an immense difference and nowhere is this more the case than in minimal camping and basic survival gear. Fifteen years ago, a Grand High-Level Route would have been much more difficult than today because of the extra weight to be carried. Sacks too are lighter and better designed. But some hard decisions must still be made. I give a list and description below of all that I took and how it was carried; a lot of thought was devoted to this and it worked very well.

Tent: A Phoenix "Phoxhole" (one man, hooped construction, in "Goretex"). I got wet twice; the first time because I had not adequately sealed the seams. After drying out, I resealed, and it never leaked again in spite of very severe weather. The second time was in a general flood where nothing would have remained dry except an ark. There was some condensation on the ground sheet in cold weather.

A cheap nylon bivouac sack, with interior sprayed with aluminium paint. (A surprisingly good item, very warm.)

Polythene survival bag, for use as extra groundsheet etc.

Sleeping bag (lightweight, down).

Helly-Hensen polar underwear suit, in two pieces. (Invaluable!)

Henri-Lloyd anorak and overtrousers. (If equipping myself afresh I would now choose a 'Goretex' or similar suit.)

Climbing breeches, shorts, two shirts, lightweight jersey, underwear, socks, balaclava helmet, mittens etc. Sunhat.

Alpine jacket, lined (Serac).

Smart (!) drip-dry trousers and shirt.

Small camping-gas stove, with clips for both small and medium
cartridges.

Nest of two pans, grip (one spare grip), clasp knife, spoon, opener.
Plastic mug, two plastic boxes, polythene bags, etc.

Large first aid kit.

A repair kit for tent, clothing, etc. Boot wax.

Toiletries.

Notebook, drawing pad, writing instruments, film, set of maps,
passport, money, camera (Olympus XA2 lightweight miniature
35 mm).

A cheap nylon lightweight day sack.

Two pairs sunglasses, glacier cream, lipsalve. Compass and
whistle.

MacInnes-Peck short axe (Scorpion model).

Ice hammer and crampons.

30 m×7 mm rope.

Four pitons on a ring.

Five assorted slings and abseil loops.

Four karabiners.

Boots (Terray) and a pair of light "trainers".

All this was carried in or on a Karrimor "Cougar" (smaller model)
with two large detachable pockets; with the day sack this gave a
useful combination of three possible loads. The full load was rather
wide, but was not more than 45lbs (with three days' food included);
except when wearing shorts and "trainers" and carrying extra food.
The sack also comprised a foam pad that served as mattress.

Could this be made less? The ice hammer was not used in earnest,
but I always carried it when on glacier terrain. Neither pitons nor
rope were used in earnest, but they might have been and I was glad
to have them. The smarter clothes could be dispensed with, but I
was glad to have them on several occasions. Another time I would
send spare socks ahead, with maps, etc., to a half-way point such as
Airolo. In the Valais Alps I sent a quantity of clothes and gear round
by post to Zermatt; this was a mistake.

There are two serious omissions from this list. A large rainproof cape would have been immensely useful (I had a plastic cape that lasted a very short while). With that, the plastic survival bag could be jettisoned. The other is an old-fashioned alpenstock! The modern short axe is useless for glacier travel, and any party is strongly recommended to look about for a long stick, ski-pole or similar implement to use on any extensive crevassed ground. Something like this can usually be found and left behind after use. A long axe would be inconvenient on every other occasion.

Diet, Health etc.

It would do no harm to start the journey somewhat overweight; I lost weight rather rapidly in the last ten days and found myself getting tired. The problem is, that the best source of energy and psychological comfort is large meals, often, and that is just what it is hard to carry and cook. I did not have enough money to use the huts in the Eastern Alps for those necessary extra calories, and began to suffer for it. The failure to pick up rye-bread and porridge oats in the Pfitschertal for the Zillertal Alps crossing meant three hungry days. One day's hunger at Maloja cost me a good summit in the Bernina Alps. Remoter villages do not stock gas cylinders. Make sure you do not have to descend for supplies on a Sunday. And that you always have enough money in the right currency. And that you know about national and bank holidays. This sounds obvious, but such matters are easily forgotten in the mountains. Lack of sleep may become a problem, from persistent early rising and long days and hard camping: in my first aid kit I took four mild sleeping pills, and used them strategically. The most likely and the most frustrating injury is tendon or muscular strain; the way to avoid this is to take things easily. Descend long steep hills slowly; change footwear two or three times a day; look after your feet and your boots; try to keep dry. These are obvious matters, and can be summed up in one word – discipline. I had an extensive first aid kit, but was not called on to use it for any serious purpose.

Does one need rest days? I began with the assumption that I would need regular days off, but I found that this was not the case. The two days that I had of inactivity were due to bad weather. Instead I made sure that every fourth day was an easy day, and that I never had more than two hard days after another. (The exception to this was in the Lepontine Alps, but that was after a rest day and much bad weather, and the success of those days was of psychological importance.) While the provisioning system worked well, there was no need of full rest days.

Illness or injury aside, the largest problem will always be getting enough to eat every day.

Competence

"I am assuming throughout that any party following this route is competent to do so." What does this mean? I am damned if I know! Except to say that it is a considerable exercise in mountain craft. To complete the route, taking in summits, in safety and comfort, requires tenacity, caution and sound judgement.

A Final Comment

I think this route will be found to be a sound one, geographically and logistically. It fulfils the main intention, of making a Grand High-Level Route from one end of the Alps to the other, giving access to some 30 or so good summits, in a feasible time. Interesting variations are often possible, and minimal but useful reliance on public or other transport. No claim to originality is made, but I would like to imagine that such a route would become "classic" among the small number of people who care for such activities. For my part I am happy in the belief that somehow or other, and with much good fortune, I have been able to complete the finest mountain excursion in Europe. *

---

* Shorter accounts of this journey have been published in *The Climber and Rambler*, April, May and June 1982, and in *The Alpine Journal*, 1982.

The Grand High-Level Route

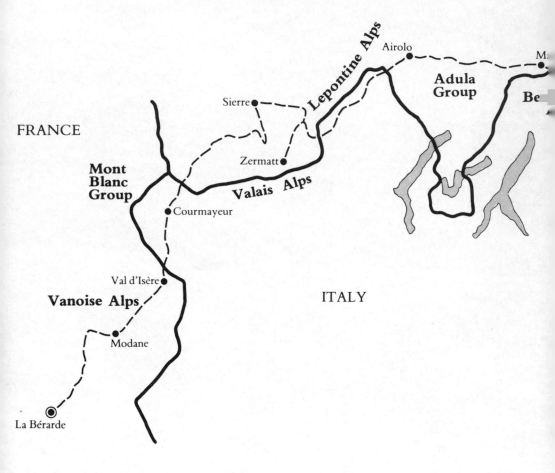

SWITZERLAND

FRANCE

Lepontine Alps

Airolo

Sierre

Adula
Group

Be

Zermatt

Mont
Blanc
Group

Valais Alps

Courmayeur

Val d'Isère

Vanoise Alps

ITALY

Modane

La Bérarde

M: